Mentors

Mentors

Making a Difference in Our Public Schools

Thomas W. Evans

Peterson's Guides
Princeton, New Jersey

To Lois
Heather, Logan, and Paige
teachers and learners
together in
the school in the home

Copyright © 1992 by Thomas W. Evans

Library of Congress Cataloging-in-Publication Data

Evans, Thomas W., 1930–
        Mentors / Thomas W. Evans.
            p.   cm.
        Includes index.
        ISBN 1-56079-152-7 : $18.95
            1. Community and school—United States.
        2. Mentors in education—United States.
        I. Title.
        LC221.E93   1992
        370.19'31'0973—dc20   92-20980
                                                                                CIP

Composition and design by Peterson's Guides

Printed in the United States of America

10 9 8 7 6 5 4 3 2 1

Contents

Foreword

Fred M. Hechinger
Former Education Editor of the *New York Times*,
Senior Adviser to Carnegie Corporation of New York

Tom Evans makes it clear throughout his book *Mentors: Making a Difference in Our Public Schools* that his important basic message is "You can make a difference." This book is both an appeal and a guide. It also spells out a fundamental idea: the institutions of a democracy can only be as good as the people are ready to make them.

The political rhetoric likes to say the public schools belong to the people. But too often the people are absentee owners. Mr. Evans wants to change that; he wants the people to exercise concerned, participating ownership. Mentoring—dealing personally with a youngster—is the most direct expression of such ownership.

Mr. Evans himself has founded MENTOR, a program in which the members of over 550 law firms in 20 states have each taken on responsibility for working directly with students, establishing a personal bond and educational inspiration and aspiration.

Citizen participation is not, of course, limited to mentoring by lawyers or even to mentoring itself. Nor does this book suggest that individual efforts alone can do the job of improving the school. Good education costs money. National, state, and local leadership must set goals and help pay to attain them. The good news of effective programs must be spread. But people, through their involvement, ultimately must make the difference.

Mr. Evans does not underestimate the demands of the job that needs to be done. He writes, "We are involved in a war. The enemies are poverty, bureaucracy, lack of personnel, and lack of funds." He warns that however well-intentioned and sound the goals for the year 2000 may be, students who are mired in poor schools cannot wait; they need help now.

Mr. Evans puts it bluntly, "Unlike proponents of some of the better-known initiatives now abroad in our country, I do not believe that educational reform can be imposed from the top down.... Both in the last century and in recent decades, the public schools have been improved only when private citizens have taken the time and the interest to become involved."

He knows that reforms imposed on the schools from above or from the outside rarely take hold, in large part because their sponsors fail to understand and respond to the problems of local classrooms and neighborhoods. He wants change to grow from the educational and community grassroots. And he wants mentoring volunteers to provide what every youngster, and especially every poor child, needs: a caring human presence.

In order to drive rather than retard school reform, however, these volunteers must themselves be reform-minded. They must not allow themselves to be used as subordinates to those who want to keep the schools running in the same old unsuccessful ways. These volunteers need to know how the best of the schools—those already deeply involved in the present school reform movement—have managed to bring about change. In their quietly effective way, these mentoring volunteers can become shock troops in the battle for better schools. Mr. Evans performs a valuable service in pointing to the many reforms that work.

His two important subthemes of this much needed book are to "start now" and to "start small." This advice applies to the immediate emergency as well as to the fact that the schools have long suffered from the consequences of bigness; youngsters, submerged in the mass, lose their identity as individuals. Some successful local school districts have addressed that basic problem by creating semiautonomous units of manageable size; but even in schools that are too big, volunteer mentors can create the essential personal feeling of trust and belonging.

Mr. Evans provides a road map for those who want to make a difference in shaping the schools our children need. He urges all who care: "Enlist Now."

The Best-Known Mentor

This book is about education, more particularly, about individuals—mainly private citizens—who have made a difference in our nation's public schools. Their roles range from working with students one-on-one to bringing about the reform of an entire school system to establishing national programs that benefit millions. Common to all is the willingness to get involved as well as the ability to work from within or to push from the outside to make a difference in local and state systems that too often are unable to help themselves.

They need to get involved because American education is in a perilous state. When compared with students in other countries, our young people's achievements generally fail to bring the U.S. within the top five—let alone the top ten—countries. American employers have learned they cannot fill jobs—even the simplest entry-level positions—with graduates of our public school system. In many cases they must first invest in expensive remedial programs to bring new employees to minimal levels of competency.

And yet there *are* successes. As you might expect, there are superb schools throughout the country, generally in the suburbs or in cities where students for magnet programs are selected based on competency testing. Some of these students compare with the best in Japan, Germany, and England.

This book deals with other successes, however, those rising from bleak situations such as impoverished inner cities and rural areas where there is little reason for hope but where individuals have come forward to make startling differences.

Immediate action is called for. Both former Secretary of Education William Bennett and American Federation of Teachers Presi-

1

dent Albert Shanker—two men not noted for frequent agreement—have said that what the schools need is not a minor change
but a revolution. This book is the handbook for that revolution. It
shows how individuals have made a difference. In some instances
their work has turned around the life of a single student or the lives
of a group of students by enhancing the methods or improving the
atmosphere by which or in which students learn; in other cases
they have invented new schools or reformed a city or state system in
ways that are truly revolutionary.

In this book these individuals are referred to as "mentors." Just
as a successful corporate executive often has a mentor in his or her
background who has been an example or has acted as a sponsor, so
too have successful students often been advised or inspired by a
mentor. The word has many definitions in the field of education—
so many that the older partner in a one-to-one relationship is now
often referred to as a "true mentor." In these pages "mentor" applies to individuals who have aided students individually or collectively. While teachers are not the primary focus of this book, they
are often mentors, bringing an extra dimension to their job. Volunteers also often act as teachers and similarly add perspectives
from their job to the classroom. In any event, if I have taken some
license in using such a broad definition, I apologize. But let's not
get bogged down in the kind of semantic debate that can become a
substitute for action. There is enough of that already.

The best-known mentor in America is undoubtedly Eugene M.
Lang. In 1981 Lang went back to the elementary school from
which he had graduated, Public School 121 in East Harlem, to deliver that year's commencement address. As he sat in the auditorium waiting his turn, he looked around and realized that the traditional pep talk he had planned to give was simply not adequate.
Instead, he delivered his now famous promise to the 61 sixth graders assembled that day: If you stay in school and graduate, I'll pay
your college tuition.

Of course, the real news story occurred five years later when 52
of those students were still attending classes. Statistics indicated
that number should have been around 30. The *New York Times* reported the story on its front page. Newspapers across the country
followed suit. Today, 34 of the students are in college, nine others
graduated from high school or received equivalency diplomas,
and of those who did not go to college, many have jobs thanks to

Lang. While not all the students were successful—one is in Sing Sing prison—the class's achievements are well above the norm.

The students at P.S. 121 benefited from a last-minute schedule change at the graduation ceremonies—the first choice for a speaker had been another former student, film star Burt Lancaster. Lancaster was scheduled to be filming out of the country the day of the ceremony, so school administrators turned to the next name on their list of distinguished alumni. Fortunately for the students, Lang himself had a mentor who changed his life, an older friend who financed his college education at Swarthmore. Before going to college, Lang was a dishwasher in a local restaurant and had little hope of going on to higher education. That long-ago mentor would be pleased with what he started.

Lang is president of REFAC Corporation, a company that develops new technologies into commercial ventures. He has made millions and given away millions—largely to education. Lang would be the first to admit that the mentor aspect of his program is important. "If you don't do your homework, I'm going to call Mr. Lang" became a household phrase among students at P.S. 121. Of even greater importance, however, were the hundreds of phone calls and meetings between Lang and the students and the help—moral and material—that he readily gave them.

But Eugene Lang couldn't stop after an isolated success. Today, under the auspices of the I Have A Dream Foundation (IHAD), Lang's program encompasses 27 classes in New York City. Thirteen hundred students are involved, almost half of whom are now juniors in high school. Nationally, 140 classes in 40 cities in 26 states participate in the IHAD program. Typically, a project has at least one full-time staff person as well as a mentor who, during the class's sixth-grade year, commits to pay college tuition for all who qualify. This generally means a commitment of $350,000 or more. Lang's ability to recruit and inspire other IHAD sponsors has led the press to call him the "Mentor of Mentors."

While the IHAD mentors have been able to bring substantial personal assets to their work, there are others who, starting with little more than a good idea, have also accomplished miracles. Over the past two decades I have had the opportunity to work with and observe many of these individuals as I performed a variety of roles. Much of my experience has occurred in New York City, which accounts for a slightly disproportionate reference to examples from

3

my hometown. But then, New York has more students—one million—than most large cities have residents, so it is a large source.

My first involvement with public schools was with projects from the New York Alliance for Public Schools. I paired five law firms with five high schools. Lawyers in each pairing worked with a social studies class, taking the students to their firm and to court and meeting with them over sandwich lunches. I called the program MENTOR because the lawyers served as friends and advisers to students. It is described in detail in "MENTOR: A Precedent" (which begins on page 182) and is now in over 500 schools throughout the country, involving some 30,000 students. As cochairman (with former Police Commissioner Ben Ward) of a commission of MENTOR lawyers, educators, and city officials, I also played a role in the establishment of The Institute for Law And Justice, a high school in Manhattan.

In 1983 I was appointed to the Presidential Advisory Board on Private Sector Initiatives (PSI); and because I had been involved with MENTOR and had written *The School in the Home*, a book on home (largely preschool) education, I was designated chair of the board's education committee. Our PSI committee established the National Symposium on Partnerships in Education in 1983 to facilitate the exchange of ideas on partnerships that were successful in various parts of the country, to encourage collaboration between the private sector and the public schools, and to reduce the amount of reinventing the wheel that inevitably takes place as volunteer efforts spring up in diverse locations.

We defined partnerships broadly to include any effort between the public and private sectors; we wanted to avoid the widespread misconception that partnerships were limited to career days or cosmetically constructed versions of adopt-a-school relationships. If handled right, we felt, a synergism might result that would encourage the proliferation of successful programs that were not widely known.

1983 was a good year to begin. On April 26 a bipartisan federal commission appointed by Department of Education (DOE) Secretary Terrell H. Bell issued a report entitled *A Nation at Risk: The Imperative for Educational Reform*. Its conclusions were not encouraging. "The educational foundations of our society are presently being eroded by a rising tide of mediocrity that threatens our very future as a nation and as a people," the report stated. "If an unfriendly foreign power had attempted to impose on America the mediocre educational performance that exists today, we might well have viewed it as an act of war. As it stands, we have allowed this to happen to ourselves."

In 36 hard-hitting pages, *A Nation at Risk* reviewed the sad state of American education and issued recommendations to address the situation. The report cited the "steady decline in science achievement scores of American seventeen-year-olds" over the preceding 15 years, pointed out that "some 23 million American adults are functionally illiterate," and quoted from a Navy Department report that "one quarter of [the Navy's] recent recruits cannot read at the ninth-grade level, the minimum needed simply to understand written safety instructions." Recommendations included extending the school day from six to seven hours; increasing the school year from 180 to 220 days; giving high school students more homework; tightening high school requirements in English, mathematics, science, social studies, and computer science; and raising teacher salaries while increasing their contracts from nine to eleven months to provide additional time for curriculum planning and helping students with special needs.

The growing national concern over the lamentable state of public education spurred on our efforts. President Reagan proclaimed 1983–84 the "National Year of Partnerships in Education." The Department of Education announced the results of a national survey that indicated over 40,000 partnerships were operating in the country. Two hundred people from all over the nation attended our first national symposium, which was held on the campus of Washington's Georgetown University and lasted one and a half days.

Over the next few years the symposium flourished and grew. In 1988, when a Department of Education survey revealed that there were 140,000 partnerships in America, the department's deputy secretary and I were selected to present the report to the president. That same year the symposium merged with the National School Volunteers organization, allowing us to hold regional meetings between symposia, conduct training institutes, and publish materials that would spread the word to those who could not attend national meetings.

National School Volunteers had been in existence for more than three decades and brought thousands of members to the new organization, which was named the National Association of Partners in Education (NAPE). The symposium is still sponsored by the White House but is now referred to as the NAPE National Symposium. It has long-since outgrown the Georgetown campus and is currently held at the Gateway Marriott in nearby Crystal City, Virginia. In 1991 more than 1,500 people from every state in the union and over 100 representatives from Great Britain attended the five-day conference.

It is fashionable these days for business executives to speak in favor of education reform or restructuring. They are fed up with half measures and believe that only fundamental change can save the public schools. But being for "reform" is a little like being for change—not every change is effective or helpful. As corporate leaders learned in the Rochester Experiment and the Boston Compact (cases reviewed later in these pages), a sweeping change may not turn out as planned. Or, as the leaders of the California Roundtable have learned, a chief executive enlisted to reform the school system can become a loose cannon who breaks ranks and tries to implement a system he or she personally favors in the face of painful consensus-building to the contrary. Each of these examples is reviewed later in these pages. We can profit from their experience.

In all fairness to the occasional critics of partnerships in education, there *are* instances in which partnerships last only a day and involve no more than giving away T-shirts or taking the kids to a ball game. These are "feel-good" undertakings that provide a morale boost in what otherwise is often a very dreary landscape, but they do not effect any serious change in the process of education. And even though partnerships have grown markedly over the past decade, results announced recently by the National Assessment of Education Progress show that students are generally not doing any better today than they were when *A Nation at Risk* was published.

This book presents programs that have worked. In the final chapters I will discuss, step by step, ways in which you can make a difference in our public schools. At that point I will also take a close look at President Bush's education program, America 2000. The president and the nation's governors unanimously adopted six education goals at the Education Summit held two years ago on the campus of the University of Virginia. The full text appears in Appendix D of this book. For now, a summary developed by educator-

by educator-author Ted Sizer will suffice:

> By the year 2000 all children will start school ready to learn... The high school graduation rate will increase to at least ninety percent... Students will leave grades IV, VIII, and XII having demonstrated competence in challenging subject matter, including English, mathematics, science, history, and geography... They will be prepared for responsible citizenship, further learning, and productive employment... U.S. students will be first in the world in science and mathematics... Every school will be free of drugs and violence and will offer a disciplined environment conducive to learning.

Although many observers believe that it may be difficult, if not impossible, to achieve all of these goals by 2000, huge strides have already been made in accomplishing them in various locations throughout the country. As educators, bureaucrats, and politicians debate cognitive theory and the niceties of implementation (discussed in "The Great Education Debate," pages 194–196), remarkable results have been achieved by individuals and groups who have chosen to act in the face of seemingly overwhelming odds.

In *Mentors* you'll read about some of these efforts—about initiatives such as a preschool program that brings children in impoverished rural areas up to the performance level of their affluent suburban peers by the time they enter school. The program was developed in Israel and costs less than Head Start. You'll read about a program in which mentors have worked with "at risk" students and reduced the dropout rate among them to 1 percent, considerably below the norm for the school and the national rate of 25 percent. You'll learn about a number of schools at which students once regarded as hopeless are now mastering a full core curriculum and going on to college. You'll visit schools in a southeastern state that has an adult illiteracy rate of 33 percent but where kindergarten students are learning to read by writing stories on personal computers. And you'll be introduced to schools in Harlem, the South Bronx, and other inner-city areas where almost all of the students graduate and 90 percent go to college or get jobs. Although other schools in those neighborhoods experience frequent outbreaks of violence, these school do not; they are drug-free, and their students are enthusiastic about learning.

Reform and restructuring of our schools will not occur in a vacuum, however. Business executives who have recently become enthralled with the notion of reform will soon learn that massive improvement of our schools will not occur without genuine community support. Initiatives, even when accompanied by "four-part strategies" or "nine-point programs," won't work without widespread citizen involvement. The real question, in the words of renowned educational innovator Deborah Meier, is: "How can we use 'top-down' reform to influence what, in the end, must be 'bottom-up' change?"

As you will read in these pages, the states and cities where real progress has been achieved are those in which the ground has been broken by individuals who have learned more about the schools by working in them. And in states such as Kentucky and South Carolina, where statewide school systems have been entirely reformed and restructured, there are even more mentors involved today than there were before reform.

Often, the most accurate pictures of American society come from observers visiting from abroad—Alexis de Toqueville and Lord Bryce from the past; from more recent times, D. W. Brogan. Interestingly, one of the most lucid reports on the partnership movement in America came from the British participants in the 1988 National Symposium on Partnerships in Education. Their report, *Education-Business Partnerships: Lessons from America*, states:

> The fact that it is possible to appeal to a national consciousness is one of America's great strengths. In the case of education it has released a tide of emotion and enterprise that has led to a staggering range of Partnership schemes. One is impressed most by the sheer scale of activity—and above all by the fact that these are genuine partnerships, involving not just education and business but entire communities. "The most serious problem," commented a representative of the Committee for Economic Development, "is to galvanize the local community.... It must be done from the ground floor up. It must be accepted at the local level or it won't stay."

As you read about individuals who have made a difference, you can decide whether you want to play a role and what it will be. Some of the individuals described in these pages are extremely wealthy, some are professional educators who have devised alternatives to the conventional system, some are celebrities, and some hold positions of leadership in major corporations or civic groups. But others—people who have no special position of wealth or prominence—are accomplishing remarkable results too. They have provided safe havens in the midst of urban chaos where young people can relax and study, tutored students with special needs, enriched courses that students previously found uninteresting or unrewarding, invented revolutionary schools and methods of teaching, and brought lawsuits that changed the educational systems of entire states.

A "full-court press" is called for if significant change is to be achieved. A single citywide or statewide cure-all that takes years to plan and that may never be implemented is not the answer. The revolution must start now. If you are concerned about educating America's children, there is an important role for you to play.

Working from
the Inside

Sooner or later, almost everyone gets upset with American public schools. Eugene Lang did when he saw the hopelessness on the faces of the sixth-grade students at P.S. 121 in the South Bronx. They looked trapped; he knew that unless he acted, these students might never have the chance that a mentor had given him decades before. On the spur of the moment he decided to do something about it.

This is a book about people who decided to "do something about it." They come from vastly different backgrounds and possess a wide spectrum of talents and interests. But each one was moved—often in a very personal way—by what he or she saw was happening to the young people in our public schools. The mentors you will meet in this chapter chose the most direct route to help out: they chose to work within the system to improve it.

Although some of the mentors in this chapter are rich in material assets, each one brings a more important wealth of personal assets to meet the crisis faced by our children. Betty Flood located some available space and took the time to turn that space into a place where Newark inner-city children could meet in safety after the schools had closed, could do their homework, and could find someone who was willing to listen to their problems. When Bill Kellogg saw first-hand the deplorable condition of the Chicago public schools, he leaped at the chance to teach children the classics as he thought they should be taught.

Almost every day we read in the newspapers that American students are falling further and further behind in math and science. Mentors with a background in these subjects have learned that they can enrich the teaching of them. Others, who feel strongly that art is the way to motivate students, have used painting and music in classrooms. Ernie Lorch recruited kids who were playing basketball in local playgrounds, put them into a program, and discovered that this was a way to motivate them to do better in school and to go on to college. When Jim Watkins was in charge of Naval personnel, he found that recruits were being discharged from boot camp because they could not read at a sixth-grade level. When he learned that 97 percent of these young illiterate seamen held high school diplomas, Watkins realized that Navy remedial programs were not enough. Something had to be done about the public schools. He set about doing it.

Not everyone who reads this book will possess the knowledge or special skills of the mentors in this chapter. In almost every case, however, these mentors were not themselves aware of the strengths they could bring to the public schools before they began to help. Certainly Tom Pilecki's knowledge of music and James Watkins's position at the top of the U.S. Navy gave these mentors special insights. But Walter Lochbaum, even with his years of experience in the school system, made a decision to help out in any way that he could and ended up simply giving the teachers and administrators working in the schools more *time* to do their jobs.

The mentors in this chapter, committed people who have chosen to work with teachers and administrators to improve public schools from the inside, have all made a difference, some to thousands of lives. They started within the system and have improved it, in some cases dramatically. Reading their stories, you will in all likelihood discover that you, too, have talents, knowledge, and experience that can be put to good use making a difference in our public schools.

Betty Flood

The Rec Center

Betty Flood begins work each weekday at 7 a.m. She is a telephone-systems assistant with Public Service Electric & Gas Company in New Jersey. At 3:30 p.m. she returns to her apartment at the Garden Spires housing complex in Newark, where, if she were anyone else, she would spend the remainder of the day watching television and enjoying a relaxed meal. But Betty Flood has other plans.

11

For years Flood was concerned about the children in her neighborhood who had no place to go after school. In 1978 she decided to do something about it and prevailed upon the owner of her 540-dwelling apartment complex to let her have space for these children. Now every Monday through Friday afternoon at 4:30, Betty Flood begins her second job; running a youth center that services approximately 250 kids from the neighborhood and provides a place where they can spend time after school. "I enjoy the kids," says Flood. "I enjoy helping. You see, I have five children of my own, and I know the struggle. My husband and I separated when our baby girl was six months old, and I raised my kids by myself."

Because the children under her supervision at the Rec Center range in age from four to eighteen, there are different times for the different age groups to have to leave or be picked up. Flood remains on the premises until the last child goes home, often 10 p.m. or later. But Flood does more than provide a safe place for the children and teens to congregate. Drawing on her experience as a mother and grandmother, as well as on more than a decade of managing the center, she provides a varied fare for her charges. "We have studies, rap sessions, game time, education—everything wrapped up in one," she explains.

Despite its name, activities at the Rec Center are not all fun and games. Flood is a firm believer in education and recognizes that for some of these children, homework presents a special challenge. "You have some children whose parents don't help them with homework," she says. "You have parents who can't help their children with homework because their education was limited. And you have some parents who work, and many, in these days and times, have two jobs!" As a result, kids know that when they enter the Rec Center they will be met by Flood's particular style of questioning: "Did you do your homework? Yeah? Well, let me see it." Flood takes her involvement in the children's education seriously and has joined most of the local Parent Teacher Associations (PTAs) because she knows that some parents aren't going to attend the meetings. "I don't care if you offered to pay them," Flood says, "[some] parents would not go." By establishing a rapport with local teachers, Flood is able to stay on top of any problems that may develop.

Flood values the Rec Center as a place where kids can let off steam in a constructive, controlled environment. Access to the Rec

Center is limited to children who live within Flood's complex. "After school they let their hair down," she says. "They tend to bring up things they know they can't ordinarily say in school. I'm a firm believer in rap sessions. We have a big togetherness with this. Even my little ones. The kids come in, put their feet up, do what they want to do, say what they want to say." Such sessions give Flood an insider's view on what's happening in her community by allowing her access to a kids' culture that traditionally is off-limits to most adults. Flood isn't able to solve all the problems related to the children at the center, but she does serve on the board of Court Appointed Special Advocates, providing valuable insight into the community in which she lives.

What makes Flood's work all the more remarkable is that the Rec Center receives no federal or state funds. "We raise funds ourselves," she says proudly. "We sell hot dogs and Cokes on the weekends." She is also a thrifty shopper and has furnished the Rec Center with items from garage sales. Though she receives no salary for her demanding second job, Flood believes she is more than adequately compensated: "I get fulfillment when I see children going in the right direction," she says. "I do this voluntarily, and I thank God I am able to do it." Flood has accepted invitations to speak to more than 600 groups. In every speech she delivers the same message: "Charity begins at home. Yet people don't realize this. They feel if they want to volunteer they have to go through United Way or a hospital or go into a big organization. No. Just give someone a call, maybe once a week. 'How's it going? What's going on?' This is a form of volunteering. Maybe it's a cousin or a great aunt or whatever. 'Do you need the paper? Okay, I'll bring it home.' It's up to us in each individual community to try to help each other."

Bill Kellogg
An Old-Fashioned Teacher

When Bill Kellogg accepted a challenge from one of the members of his running club in the mid-1980s, it involved far more than running an extra mile or clocking a faster pace. Kellogg's challenger was the superintendent of the Chicago public school system, who, having heard Kellogg profess interest in helping the system, invited him to visit the schools and assess the situation personally.

He accepted the invitation. "I couldn't believe how bad the schools were," he remembers. "I had no conception that the schools were in this physical condition or in this teaching condition. No glass in the windows. The libraries didn't have any books. Broken chairs. Broken tables. Just a total atmosphere of despondency. I decided right then and there I would offer half a day a week to teach school. It was that simple."

A short time later, W. K. Kellogg III, president of General Packaging Production, Inc., was teaching literature to seventh and eighth graders at Portage Park School on the northwest side of the city. Prior to that, his teaching experience had been limited to Sunday school classes. "I'm no scholar," he says modestly, "and I'm also no great student. I've just always loved to read, and I love the classics. I would like to see more executives and other people get into this kind of thing and really go out and tell kids that if you do good, if you study, there is a rewarding life out there. You can make something of yourself."

Kellogg's class is held at the school on Monday mornings an hour or so before the regular school day begins. He chose Mondays because, he says, if students are motivated to show up then, there's a greater chance they'll show up for the rest of the week's classes. Approximately 25 students take the class each semester, which they receive no credit for. They know, however, that since the class began, about three-quarters of the "graduates" enrolled in magnet schools and some jumped grade levels.

The class is more demanding than most of the others at Portage Park. In many ways Kellogg is an old-fashioned teacher—the emphasis is on penmanship, grammar, and sentence structure. His students write a lot of papers. They also read aloud and do some acting, exercises that help build self-confidence. Furthermore, near the end of each period the students line up and are asked questions one by one on the day's lesson and can't leave until they give a correct answer: it's Kellogg's way of reinforcing the material covered. "If their turn comes and they don't know the answer," he says, "they go to the end of the line until they do know."

Kellogg's reading lists change yearly and focus on classics such as *Romeo and Juliet*, *Jamaica Inn*, and *The Time Machine*. By introducing students to the classics early in their scholastic development, Kellogg hopes they will find out that "books can be fun and that there are alternatives to watching TV all the time." The classics, he adds, "are also great moral stories. And rightly or wrongly, I do try to teach a lot about morality, heroes, and what you have to put out in life. You can't blame society for all your problems, I tell them. You have to take the right road. I talk a lot about the road maps of life."

Kellogg does his best to put these books in a context the students can understand. By asking the students to think of the blended salts in Robert Louis Stevenson's *Dr. Jeckyll and Mr. Hyde* as cocaine, for example, he is able to transform it into a valuable contemporary lesson. In his analysis of the works of Shakespeare, he translates the stories to reflect more closely the realities of today's teen experience. "In *Romeo and Juliet*," he explains, "we talk about the gangs in the street and how being part of a gang often ends in tragedy. 'Listen,' I tell them, 'you want sex, you want killing, you want jealousy, you want hate? Read *Romeo and Juliet*. It's all there. You don't have to sit and watch all this junk on TV.'"

The students generally look forward to the section on Shakespeare—it's followed up with a trip to the theater. Watching a play they have studied in class makes it come alive for them. After the performance they get the chance to talk with the actors and learn how they prepare for their roles and what kind of education they feel is necessary to succeed as an actor. Kellogg relies on such outings to supplement the classroom experience and to give students an added incentive to maintain perfect attendance: one absence and the student forfeits his or her chance to make the trip.

Kellogg is driven by his belief that the regular high school curriculum is too light and doesn't properly prepare students for college and university course work. Advanced courses *do* prepare them, however, and Kellogg sees his class as part of that all-important preparation. "When they leave this class," he says, "they have an A-1 dictionary and about eight to ten books so that they can start a library. They're all given to them free."

In return for all the course offers, Kellogg expects students to show up. What if they don't? "I go immediately to the [school office], try to find the child, and demand to know why he or she wasn't there." Kellogg himself has missed only two days in seven years—a personal record that serves as a model. "The students must know that I'll be there every Monday morning no matter what happens. You can't tell these kids that you're going to do something and then not do it. They've been lied to so much by their parents and other people in society."

Overall, of course, Kellogg expects a lot more than good attendance, but he also realizes that for most of his students, taking the class is a major sacrifice. "In many cases," he says, "you find a student has to take care of younger siblings. There's also illness, drunkenness, and drug addiction among parents and relatives. I don't just take the top students. If I see a student who I think is willing to try but having a lot of trouble—sometimes emotional trouble—I take him or her, too."

Students sense that Kellogg cares about their lives and their futures. One former student, Lilian Acquindo, went on to become valedictorian of her high school class and received a four-year scholarship to Brown University. In a newspaper article featuring Chicago's valedictorians, Acquindo cited her mother and Kellogg as the two people she most admired. "She told me later that if it hadn't been for my encouragement, she'd probably never have had this happen," says Kellogg. "The program shows that somebody cares. We have a good time, and I really do love the kids. It's a different approach, that's all. There are no miracles here."

Geoffry Laff
A Daringly Educational Marvel of Science

When it comes to recruiting students for math and science programs, many educators feel the fight is over before it is begun. Children—natural candidates for these subjects because of their innate curiosity—are often turned off at an early age by boring math and science textbooks that have all but replaced activity-oriented programs.

Geoffrey Laff was fortunate enough to have Ronald Perkins as his senior chemistry teacher. Inspired by Perkins's "zany classroom demonstrations," Laff chose to take part in a program newly developed by Perkins in conjunction with local elementary schools. The program had students from Perkins's Advanced Placement chemistry class teaching science to younger students using a hands-on, discovery-oriented method. The hope was to preserve the natural enthusiasm of young students before uncreative teaching methods destroyed it.

After teaching a few classes, Laff became convinced that the only way to teach science was through hands-on demonstrations. "Creative problem-solving and independent discovery are at the heart of scientific research," he says, "not regurgitation of facts. Real scientists don't waste time and energy memorizing names and numbers; that's why God invented reference books."

When Laff entered Yale in 1986, he wanted to continue his involvement with children. In the spring of 1987 DEMOS (Daringly Educational Marvels of Science) became a reality. There were two teachers—Laff and another science enthusiast, Sona Abhyankar—who managed five hands-on lessons at various city elementary schools during the spring semester. By 1992 there were 75 Yale students actively involved in teaching through DEMOS. "The only prerequisites for joining," Laff says, "are a love of children, a desire to teach, and a sense of humor."

Volunteers take their self-imposed mission seriously. Witness the DEMOS credo: Science has historically been portrayed in the press and in popular fiction as boring, esoteric, and inaccessible. American high school and college students have come to view science with apathy or even fear. If we as a nation wish to reverse this disturbing trend, we must begin science education at the elementary school level.

DEMOS volunteers visit classes in teams of three at least twice a semester to put on hour-long demonstrations. These demonstrations are then integrated into the curriculum by the teachers. DEMOS also offers an after-school club in which the three-person teams (mixing men and women) meet weekly with about 50 interested students during the course of the year.

On their weekly after-school visits, the teams come armed with a strange array of equipment and supplies: chicken bones, vinegar, cornstarch, yeast, spaghetti, raisins, and cabbage juice. To the children the Yale students' demonstrations are very much "daringly educational marvels of science." Chicken bones become soft and rubbery in a bath of vinegar. Cornstarch seems solid when it is pressed together in a container but acts as a liquid when it is tipped. Sugar, when added to yeast, produces a gas that blows up a balloon. Salt is used to create invisible ink. Spaghetti and raisins are seen, separately and respectively, dancing in vinegar and Seven-Up. And cabbage juice? Under the right conditions it can produce a violent reaction or change a range of shades of color.

What has all this to do with science? The cornstarch teaches a lesson about chains of molecules. The yeast and sugar experiment demonstrates the difference between solid and gaseous substances and how they can be converted. Invisible ink becomes discernible when evaporation causes the salt molecules to be seen. The chicken bones, dancing spaghetti, and raisins show the effect of acid on solids. And the cabbage juice shows not only the interaction of an acid with a base but also introduces the children to the periodic table as well as to the symbols H, OH, and that perennial favorite, H_2O. As team members point out, the use of everyday materials brings science into a world that the students can understand.

Though their methods seem reminiscent of crowd-drawing sideshows and magical illusions, DEMOS volunteers are eager to explain the difference. "Magicians trick you," DEMOS volunteer Meira Levinson explained to a group of students, "but scientists want you to understand what they are doing. They explain how and why things happen the way they do." The experiments help DEMOS achieve three goals: first, to convince young people that science is fun; second, to show young people that they can both understand and participate in science without special training or an astronomical IQ; and third, to teach the basic principles of chemistry and physics.

The program donates do-it-yourself science activity books to eight New Haven elementary schools so that the students can continue with similar experiments out of school. (The books stress the importance of adult supervision.) Each contains a bibliography of books that are generally available in school or local libraries and enable students to follow up on experiments. Most important, the magical quality of the experiments brings students enthusiastically into science. The DEMOS team is currently developing physics and biology demonstrations to complement its chemistry program.

Since its inception DEMOS members have visited 225 classrooms and taught nearly 6,000 students in the third, fourth, and fifth grades. In the 1992–93 academic year DEMOS expects to reach another 2,500 elementary school students. Although there is no statistical way to evaluate the program, a large number of the students who have been exposed to DEMOS have entered New Haven's new science and math magnet middle school. Without question, Yale's DEMOS "magicians" are converting youngsters who were uninterested or even afraid of science into students who are enthralled by it.

Laff, now a Yale graduate student in cell biology, is confident that DEMOS is making a difference in the lives of New Haven elementary students. He feels, however, that reversing the trend of American science education will require more than biweekly volunteer intervention. "Despite the success of volunteer efforts in New Haven and other communities," says Laff, "we cannot afford to rely on volunteerism to replace a high-quality education that should be provided by federal, state, and local governments. Perhaps one day, when Americans finally begin to value education as a top priority, we can stop trying to keep children from drowning and start teaching them to swim far and fast."

The IBM Lab

As the number of students involved in science enrichment programs nationwide expands, one wonders whether there will be any lasting effect. An example from the past is encouraging. In 1940 Thomas J. Watson Sr., founder of International Business Machines, visited the Junior Hall of Science at the New York World's Fair. Henry Platt, the Hall's 23-year-old director, convinced Watson to establish an afterschool science laboratory at the IBM Building on Fifth Avenue in New York City. As Platt saw it, the lab would be a place where promising youngsters could work and expand their scientific horizons.

Some 30 to 35 high school students participated in the lab, which was established in 1940 but forced to close in 1941 when World War II intervened. Although the program operated for only 18 months, a study does exist of the students who were involved in it. Almost all went on to acquire medical degrees or PhDs. Among the participants were Dr. Joshua Lederberg, Nobel laureate and president of Rockefeller University; Dr. Barry Blumberg, Nobel laureate and master of Balliol College, Oxford, Great Britain; Dr. Pierre Rinfret, head of Rinfret Associates, a major international economic advisory firm; Dr. Robert Jastrow, founder of NASA's Goddard Institute for Space Studies and a professor at Dartmouth College; Dr. Irving Lazar, a developer of the Head Start program and a professor at Cornell University; Dr. Irwin Arias, chairman of the department of physiology at Tufts School of Medicine; and Dr. Roy Glauber, Mallinckrodt Professor of Physics at Harvard.

It may be that all of these talented individuals would have succeeded had the IBM lab not existed. Or it may be that the lab ignited a spark that led them to reach for higher ground. For what it's worth, virtually all of the participants in the project felt, looking back on the experience, that it had played an important role in their lives.

A film about the IBM lab and its graduates has been produced by Jacoby/ Storm Productions, Inc., of Westport, Connecticut.

Carol Lowery
LEGO/Logo

It's no secret that there is a shortage of engineers in America. The reason stems in part from the shortage of math and science teachers in our public schools where, as the previous profile has indicated, those courses are often taught in a manner that fails to attract student interest. With little attempt to stimulate interest in engineering in the lower grades, few students are motivated to pursue in high school the math and science necessary to qualify them for college studies in engineering. As business/school partnership coordinator for the Houston, Texas, area, Carol Lowery works hard to ensure that schools in her district present a different experience.

One of the things that differentiates classrooms at Houston's Thornwood Elementary School from many others is the profusion of Lego toys (snap-together building blocks of plastic in rectangles and other shapes) around the room. One day last year, Nicky, a fourth grader, experimented with the vibrating walker that he created. The walker had a cylinderlike body with four legs that were actually Lego axles. Lego wheels, their flat surfaces down and not used as wheels, were the walker's feet.

Nicky was seated at a computer control panel (an interface box) trying to make his invention walk a black line on a table top. At the front of the walker was a optosensor—an extension that makes the walker resemble an anteater—pointed down to keep it moving ahead on the line. The interface box used the Logo software system. When the LEGO/Logo walker moved faultlessly along the line, the group of five students with whom Nicky had been working (and each of whom has his or her own project) applauded. Lowery, the classroom teacher, and an engineer from the Bechtel Corporation who has volunteered to mentor the group, smiled with approval. Three weeks earlier, Nicky's project had failed; suggestions from his teammates and the Bechtel engineer led to its eventual success.

Originally Nicky planned to build a car. After he had completed the model and activated the computer program that started the motor, the car shook so violently that the motor fell out. Nicky was crushed; but when he discussed the failure with his teammates, his teacher, and the engineer, it occurred to him that the vibrations might be used to create a four-legged walker. Nicky thought that adding a horizontal bar to either side of the walker would provide the same balance that he achieved by using his arms when skateboarding.

Although Nicky's idea was his own, it occurred in a very well-defined environment. LEGO/Logo program involves two types of building: the first uses the familiar Lego toys, and the second uses Logo computer software. The regimen is highly flexible, can be integrated with another course, or can be shorter or longer than the model. At Thornwood the program is held during classroom hours for eight weeks and includes practical experiments with cars, turtles, elevators, and washing machines. However, students are by no means limited to these; users in classrooms across the country have built and programmed everything from roller coasters to pop-up toasters. Working on models allows students to explore engineering and design concepts such as feedback, modularity, and abstraction.

Participating in the program, Nicky learned a number of valuable lessons in what engineers refer to as "design heuristics." These include taking advantage of the unexpected, using personal experience as a guide, using materials in new ways, and collaborating with others.

While the LEGO/Logo program requires a small expenditure to purchase the equipment on which to run it, according to Lowery, it stands beautifully on its own and does not *require* volunteers from the scientific community to facilitate it. However, says Lowery, the engineers who volunteer do enhance the course, are an additional resource for the students, and allow for more individualized attention. With each engineer assigned to a small group of children, they become valuable role models; the children see them as people who are able to translate the kind of fun developed by LEGO/Logo into meaningful careers as adults. On the flip side, the engineers derive personal satisfaction from observing their fledglings working creatively and from the thought that over the long term, their efforts support the growth of the engineering profession.

As business/school partnership program director, Lowery sees an even more basic benefit of the LEGO/Logo program: fulfillment of "our dream to make this an opportunity to become excited about science, math, and technology."

Nancy Lieberman and Mary Foster
Learning through Art

Almost all of the strategic master plans and checklists for education reform ignore the arts. At best, the subject is viewed as a fringe benefit, affordable and useful only in affluent areas. But some mentors are committed to changing this mindset and promoting the enriching values of the arts.

In the early 1970s New York City faced a serious fiscal crisis. The public schools' art and music programs—not seen as integral parts of the learning process but as frills—were an obvious target for budget cuts. Nancy Lieberman disagreed. Convinced that the arts were a valuable component in a complete educational experience, in 1972 Lieberman founded Learning to Read through the Arts.

Under the aegis of the Guggenheim Museum, the program established art workshops in public schools to address the reading problems of inner-city students. "We are convinced," Lieberman says, "that helping children learn to read and write through the arts gives them a vital and important tool for the future."

Three years after it was founded, Learning to Read through the Arts was restructured as an independent, nonprofit educational organization. Today, often referred to as Learning through Art, the program continues to flourish under the guidance of Executive Director Mary Foster. "Learning through Art stands for creative thinking in the public school classroom," explains Foster. "We have found that students in our workshops are challenged by the arts, gaining knowledge not only about art but also about architecture, reading, writing, history, science, mathematics ... and the value of working together."

Put simply, Learning through Art hires artists to work with children in grades K–8 in the public schools on a yearlong basis. The artists work at the schools one or two days a week. At the beginning of the academic year, each artist meets with three classroom teachers to determine the focus of the art workshops. Customizing the curriculum for each of the various schools, the artist-in-residence uses hands-on activities and innovative teaching strategies to enhance the concepts that the classroom teachers feel are important. True to Lieberman's original goals, the programs always are linked to literacy, and they always show the children that learning can be fun.

According to Foster, the mission is to "open doors and open minds, to bring to [the children] a feeling that knowledge extends beyond the classroom." Concerned that children in poorer neighborhoods are never encouraged to look beyond their limited horizon, Foster makes sure the children in the program experience the rich cultural diversity of New York City. Students at P.S. 8 in Brooklyn, for example, work with both an artist-in-residence and the American Ballet Theatre. In keeping with the literacy theme, the children write and produce an original ballet. Professional dancers assist the children with choreography, and stage designers help the youngsters develop their set. More than just a fun diversion from textbooks, this program teaches children everything from basic cooperation skills to movement as a reflection of self.

P.S. 8 is but one of 20 schools in which Learning through Art has established yearlong programs. Another 15 schools participate in shorter workshops. In addition, a grant from Metropolitan Life enabled Arts Partners (a division of the New York City Board of Education) to select Learning through Art to develop a dropout prevention program for at-risk students attending P.S. 167 in the South Bronx. The successful after-school program, designed for seventh and eighth graders, combines art, drama, movement, and mime classes to develop the children's literacy, social, and leadership skills. "We want to excite the children while they are still young enough to be excited," says Foster about the program.

The approach seems to be paying off. According to Principal Salvatore Gulla, participating students have shown improvement in the classroom. Ninety percent of the students contend that the program has helped them academically.

Learning through Art derives much of its strength, no doubt, from the artists themselves, all of whom are convinced of the value of the arts and are eager to share their commitment with young minds. Says Jenny Holzer, an artist and Learning through Art artist-in-residence, "It's clear that children already are thinking about big topics.... They can look at what's around them and see what scares them most and what's most wonderful. After portraying the worst, maybe they can cure it, make their own utopias. Art gives you absolute freedom to tell the truth and to improve your reality. It's a good foundation for activism. Being critical, analytic, alert, and rapturous should be taught at a very early age." Another artist-in-residence, Willie Birch, reports that he feels "a special responsibility to consciously help shape the visions of present and future generations by empowering my students.... I find it important to teach students about their cultural background. These children will one day assume the responsibilities of maintaining and passing their heritage on to succeeding generations."

Learning through Art costs an estimated $18,000 per school. Of that, the school is asked to pay $3,000. The difference is made up through grants, donations, and an endowment fund that it is struggling to establish. "There are so many great programs looking for funding that we are almost forced to spend a lot of time developing innovative, attention-getting fund-raising efforts," explains Foster.

Still, the program is a success. Comments Edward W. Livingston, vice president of Consolidated Edison of New York, "Of all the contributions which elementary education can make to our young people, I believe motivation to learn to be the most precious. It is a lifelong gift.... This is the principal stuff of the Learning through Art program, and it works!"

Tom Pilecki
The Power of Music

St. Augustine School has been educating the children of the South Bronx for nearly a century. In 1984, with enrollment down to 110 from a peak of 500, the elementary school was nearly forced to close its doors. Even as St. Augustine's was threatened with closure, Augustine Fine Arts, an after-school program directed by Principal Tom Pilecki, was thriving, with more than 250 participants. Across the street from the school, in the basement of the rectory, students were receiving professional training in voice, instrumental music, drama, dance, graphic arts, and creative writing.

Pilecki, who had trained as a concert pianist, and Father Robert A. Jeffers, pastor of St. Augustine, formulated a plan to save the school by moving the thriving after-school arts program into the conventional classroom. In 1984 St. Augustine School became St. Augustine School for the Arts (SASA). Unlike similar arts-based schools, SASA does not require its applicants to audition. Pilecki believes that the child who struggles with "Chopsticks" on the piano gets just as much out of a St. Augustine education as the child who masters Mozart with ease. An education in the arts, Pilecki contends, gives these children more than a solid foundation in music theory; it reinforces skills in all academic disciplines. Music classes, for example, teach such skills as concentration, cooperation, and memorization—all keys to success in more traditional academic subjects.

SASA is a rare neighborhood elementary school: fine arts and academics are fully integrated. One-third of each school day is devoted to comprehensive arts training under the tutelage of thirteen professional artists; the remainder of the day is devoted to traditional academic course work. As the children advance from grade to grade, more art forms are incorporated into their lessons. Movement classes begin in kindergarten; voice and elementary music theory follow shortly thereafter. The fourth grade is somewhat of a benchmark for St. Augustine students; this is the year in which students begin both their study of dance (modern, ballet, and tap) and their training in piano and a second instrument of their choosing. Although proficiency is required on only two instruments, most St. Augustine students play between three and five instruments.

Pilecki approaches the academics and music at St. Augustine with equal intensity. Dissatisfied with available humanities curriculums, Pilecki developed his own, which begins at SASA in the third grade. All students in grades four through eight receive instruction in a foreign language and in computer literacy. Despite rigorous training in the arts, students are made to understand that their other studies are equally important. On standardized tests students at SASA score on average at or above grade level in mathematics, reading, and language arts. Over the past seven years all graduates have been accepted to parochial, private, or specialized arts high schools.

The artistic and academic achievements of these students are all the more remarkable given the neighborhood in which they live and learn. The Morrisania section of the Bronx is the poorest congressional district in the nation. Reflecting the demographics of the neighborhood, 95 percent of SASA's children are African American, and, with the exception of about four students, the remainder are Hispanic. Fewer than 10 percent are Catholic.

"These kids are coming from intensely underprivileged and at-risk backgrounds," notes Sebastian Herald, St. Augustine's director of public relations. "They come in here and get an incredible sense of discipline and happiness." Adds Pilecki, "There are all kind of poverties. At least our kids don't have poverty of imagination."

SASA recognizes that children growing up in the South Bronx face difficult situations. Dealing with tensions at home and in the streets can negatively impact a child's ability to reach his or her full potential. For this reason, the staff of SASA have taken steps to cultivate a positive learning environment for the children. With grants from the G.E. Foundation and the Altman Foundation, SASA has launched a family-oriented guidance program that employs a full-time guidance counselor. It incorporates workshops to train teachers in the areas of behavior and discipline and handling students' emotional problems. It also includes a training program for parents that encourages them to take an active interest in their children's education.

In September of 1991 SASA enrollment reached 410 students; more than 150 kids are currently on the waiting list. With tuition payments at $1,300 for the first child and $450 for every additional child per family, it's clear that the school demands a significant financial commitment from a family.

Still, tuition payments account for only part of the $3,100 estimated per-pupil expenditure (less than half the per capita cost of an elementary education in the NYC public schools). The difference is made up through a combination of archdiocese support and contributions from philanthropic entities and individuals. "We're a school with limited resources," says Father Jeffers. "Sometimes we cannot even pay our teachers on time. But we unite teachers, students, and their families to make it work."

Inspired by Pilecki's work, mentors like investment advisor Eldon C. Mayer Jr. and attorney Edmond Schroeder, both of whom have a deep interest in music, have assisted the school. They have also established Education Through Music, Inc., a charitable foundation with a mission to replicate the Augustine experience in other inner-city schools, public and nonpublic.

Former U.S. Secretary of Education Lauro Cavazos visited SASA in 1989. "This school is doing what all schools in the country should do," he said. "There is a sense of order, respect—a thirst for learning and an atmosphere of love." At St. Augustine the measure of success has little to do with test scores, the artistic accomplishments of its students, or even the level of national acclaim. "Our main aim," reports Pilecki, "is to turn out good people. Art enhances life, and we try to use the arts to enhance the character of our kids, to make them more interested and interesting learners, and, in general, to make them feel special."

Hillary Clinton and Miriam Westheimer
HIPPY

The Home Instruction Program for Preschool Youngsters (HIPPY) is an example of a well-established national program. In this case the nation is Israel. That the program became a reality in the United States is the result of the work of two strong-willed, effective women: Hillary Rodham Clinton and Miriam Westheimer.

HIPPY was developed in Israel by a team headed by Dr. Avima D. Lombard of the National Council of Jewish Women's Research Institute for Innovation in Education at the Hebrew University of Jerusalem. As immigrants flooded into Israel, programs were needed to bridge the educational gap between those from various underdeveloped parts of the world, immigrants who were educated or who had a family tradition of education, and residents. Designed to create a learning environment for preschool children and their parents, the program is now in place in more than 90 Israeli communities and involves about 9,000 families. Since adoption of the program is voluntary, its widespread acceptance bears testimony to its effectiveness.

Extensive research in Israel shows that the program has benefitted disadvantaged children by "improving academic achievement and adjustment to school, reducing the incidence of retention in grade, and increasing the rate of school completion."

(For a more comprehensive review of HIPPY research, see Avima Lombard, *Success Begins at Home*, Lexington, 1981.) A 1982 international workshop in Jerusalem brought HIPPY to the attention of early childhood educators outside Israel, and HIPPY now exists in Canada, Chile, the Netherlands, South Africa, Turkey, and the United States, where the major concentration of programs is in Arkansas.

Hillary Clinton, as all the world knows, is a top litigating partner in a prestigious Little Rock, Arkansas, law firm and has had a long-standing interest in education. In addition to her seat on five corporate boards, she has served as chair of the Children's Defense Fund and on the boards of numerous other community organizations. While visiting Miami in 1985, Clinton read a newspaper article about a local HIPPY program and another, the first to be established in the U.S., in Tulsa, Oklahoma.

Clinton returned from her trip to Florida with the firm conviction that HIPPY could make a difference in Arkansas. She soon convinced her husband, Governor Bill Clinton, who shares her interest in education, of the merit of the cause. The Arkansas HIPPY program was launched.

"One of the most promising aspects of HIPPY," Hillary Clinton observes, "is that preschool children and their parents have the opportunity to work together, to strengthen the bonds between them, and to develop a love and excitement for learning." In an era of single-parent homes and deteriorating family structure, this aspect of HIPPY is not to be undervalued. But it is the educational attainments of the program that have led to positive attention and to its widespread implementation in Arkansas.

Of the 58 HIPPY programs in 16 states across the U.S., Arkansas is home to 33, accounting for 4,600 participating children and families out of a nationwide total of 8,000.

The concentration in Arkansas did not come easily—Arkansas is not the richest state in the union. The Clintons have worked hard to obtain funding and services from a variety of sources. Arkansas HIPPY uses as sites local schools, a YWCA, a hospital, community colleges, educational cooperatives, and corporations. Paraprofessionals, who are essential to the success of the program, are trained in adult education, early education, and the like.

This public/private alliance has wrought great success on a national scale. In 1990 the nation's first HIPPY Regional Training and Technical Assistance Center was established at the Arkansas Children's Hospital in Little Rock.

Across the country local sponsorship of HIPPY varies. In Dallas, for instance, the public school system has a program for 30 families and uses state and federal funds allocated for bilingual studies and migrant-worker education. In Grand Rapids, Michigan, the Public Education Fund works with the Junior League to maintain 40 families in the program. In the Bedford-Stuyvesant section of Brooklyn, the Save the Children Foundation supports and administers a program for 70 families. But the engine that drives the machine is the National Council of Jewish Women (NCJW) in New York City.

The director of NCJW's HIPPY USA is Dr. Miriam Westheimer. Westheimer received a doctorate in education from Teachers College at Columbia University; the subject of her dissertation was the New York City dropout crisis. Through her studies Westheimer became convinced that the most effective way to increase interest in school and academic skills among disadvantaged children was to begin as early as possible and to engage parents actively in the process.

One of the concerns of people interested in HIPPY is whether the parents who will be involved in the program are up to the task of instructing their own children. Westheimer meets it head-on: "There are a lot of parents in this country who have not had successful school experiences, and they don't see that they themselves are able to teach their child. They've 'internalized' the societal message 'You don't know and you can't teach.' We're trying to reverse that."

HIPPY instruction is not complex, but it does demand certain minimal skills and motivation. Accordingly, the parent-instructors meet periodically, and visits from trained paraprofessionals are a mandatory component of the program. (Paraprofessionals are initially selected from the parent pool, based on their apparent educational skills, and subjected to a brief indoctrination course. Interestingly, many of the parents who are themselves barely literate when they begin their training later become paraprofessionals.) A full-time coordinator is also part of the basic program. These are professionals who come from a variety of backgrounds, including early childhood education, dropout prevention, community education, and family education. The materials for the two-year program consist of 18 storybooks, 60 activity packets for the parents, a

29

set of 16 plastic shapes (e.g., triangles, circles, and stars of different colors), and weekly instructions.

HIPPY is a national program in the United States today because of interested citizens like Hillary Clinton and skilled professionals like Miriam Westheimer. One of the most remarkable results of the program is that it increases the skills and raises the horizons of parents and children. As Westheimer observes, HIPPY breaks "the cycle of learned helplessness."

Does Early Childhood Education Really Make a Difference?

The High/Scope Foundation's Perry Preschool Study is a longitudinal study designed to answer the question "Can high-quality early education help to improve the lives of low-income children and their families and the quality of life in the community as a whole?" The project began in the early 1960s as a local initiative designed to solve a local problem: the high rate of school failure and delinquency among the poorer children in the school population.

The Perry Preschool Project is a study of 123 economically disadvantaged African-American youths in Ypsilanti, Michigan, who were at risk of failing in school. Students were drawn from a single school attendance area and randomly divided into two groups: one attended a high-quality preschool, the other (the control group) received no preschool education. Information on these young people was collected annually from ages three to 11 and again at ages 14, 15, and 19.

The preschool developed for the program was designed to be enjoyable and enriching. There was no cost to the families, and free child care was available as was an in-home instruction period. Studies of the participants at age 19 support the basic finding that early childhood education of high quality can improve the lives of low-income children and their families:

- Rates of employment and participation in college or vocational training were nearly double for those with preschool, as compared with those without preschool.
- Preschool attenders were almost half as likely to have children during their teenage years, be assigned to special education classes, or commit crimes.
- There were no indications that the control group did better than the experimental group under any circumstances.

Perhaps most important from the public viewpoint, the preschool program has payoffs for society as well in that it can enhance the quality of life for the community as a whole.

David P. Weikart, principal investigator for the project, reported in 1984 that "the Perry Preschool Project data demonstrate that preschool education of high quality can alter the lives of children living in poverty. I believe that high-quality early childhood education programs can contribute to solving the major social problems of our times; the data support this belief. Preschool programs are well worth the investment required even in times of limited resources because they have long-term, positive outcomes that make them cost effective. The challenge we face now is to develop systems of early education provision that are consistently of the highest quality so they can be widely disseminated and can guarantee delivery on their promise."

Ernest Lorch
A Full-Court Press

In 1926 John D. Rockefeller Jr. acquired a site on fashionable Morningside Heights near Columbia University on which he planned to build a Gothic cathedral. Soon thereafter, one of New York City's most splendid religious edifices, Riverside Church, was built.

As part of the architectural design, a space in the basement was left for recreational activities, and eventually that space was used for a basketball court—a challenging one in which there is virtually no out-of-bounds space. Players also have to dodge two huge pillars that support the altar on the floor of the sanctuary above.

While the space went unused for much of the 1940s and 1950s, in 1961 the trustees of Riverside Church decided to institute a basketball program. By that time, housing projects built in nearby Harlem had created an either/or situation: either the Church trustees let the kids in, or they took action to keep them out. To the trustees' credit, they chose inclusion.

Riverside Church brought in an African-American minister named Bob Polk who developed a youth department. Polk enlisted the aid of Ernest Lorch, an investment adviser who had played guard at Middlebury College in Vermont.

"He asked me to go out and see what I could do with community kids," remembers Lorch. "I decided to start a basketball program.

31

Basketball is a good lever into the community and a way to reach the kids."

Lorch began the program almost immediately. "One day I went over to the Grant Projects with 12 jerseys," he recalls. "I rounded up a dozen of the toughest kids and brought them all back to the church." That was the birth of the Riverside Hawks.

The program was not an immediate success. It took Lorch a while to learn to coach the game and to get to know the kids. As other community programs folded around him, Lorch stayed and relied on the one thing he knew—himself—to make the program successful. "If a person wants to do something like this," Lorch advises, "he needs to be himself. I don't try to be somebody out of their neighborhood. I'm me and they're they, and we just have to get comfortable with one another. That's the most important thing."

But Lorch was not the only attraction. The Riverside Hawks turned out to be winners. "Winning is important up here," Lorch says. "Not for its own sake (although some of the rival coaches don't believe that) but as a lure. Once the winning tradition was established, kids began to respect the program here and were willing to meet some of our expectations just to play for Riverside."

To date, 36 Riverside players have gone on to play for the National Basketball Association. Walter Berry, a first-round 1986 draft choice for Portland, played for the Riverside Hawks before he went to college. In 1985 three first-round NBA draft choices played for Riverside: Chris Mullin, Ed Pinckney, and Jerry Reynolds. Current NBA stars who once started for the Riverside Hawks include Mark Jackson of the New York Knicks and Kenny Anderson of the New Jersey Nets.

Lorch's expectations have always been high. Many of the players were dropouts before entering the program. In order to play at Riverside, however, they had to go back to school and pass their courses. "There's a grade requirement, or a requirement that you're doing something about [your grades]," says Lorch. "Some of the kids, when they first start, are in transition, and the requirement wouldn't be fair. But basically they can't get a grade lower than 70 and must have an average of 75."

Lorch's players have access to tutors, and older students can participate in an SAT preparation course. Because the kids have seen other players go on to higher education, they adjust to the discipline. "We provide discipline in a caring atmosphere," explains Lorch. "The kids see that the discipline is there in order to help them, not me."

Over the years the Riverside program has grown considerably. Currently there are the Biddys (ages 11–13), the Midgets (ages 13–15), the Juniors (ages 15–17), and the Seniors (ages 17–19). Usually there are enough players to field two Riverside teams at each level in the citywide club league throughout the entire winter season. Others play in the late spring and summer. Typically about 300 boys and girls play on Riverside teams each year.

As the program continues to grow, Lorch now concentrates mainly on coaching the junior and senior teams. To help he has a staff of eight volunteer coaches and assistants working during the 11 months of the program. In addition to coaching and the administrative duties of program, Lorch has, at various times, been a deacon at the church and a president of its board of trustees. In between, he has managed to fit in a successful professional life as well.

Lorch currently serves as president of the Park Avenue investment firm of Dyson-Kissner-Moran Corporation, with assets under management of more than $1 billion. He puts in a full day at the office and generally shows up at Riverside by 6:30 p.m. to work with players until at least 10 p.m. After that Lorch may phone a player at home to make sure that his schoolwork is going satisfactorily or drive players home after practice. Some of the players, having seen Lorch pick up sweaty uniforms after the game and throw them in the washing machine, are surprised to learn that he is a corporate president.

Lorch admits that he takes particular pride in the Riverside winter team. This team is made up of kids who, for whatever reason, are not playing high school basketball. They may be fifth-year seniors or kids who dropped out of school at one point. The team plays a sixteen-game college schedule, challenging the junior varsity teams of Ivy League schools. "And this year," he chuckles, "we've beaten Yale, Penn, Harvard—you know, all those real smart kids."

But Lorch's pride extends beyond the Hawks' win-loss record. Of 12 kids who were on the winter team last year, 11 are now in college.

Many of the players do well in school because they want to please the man who has done so much for them. Others try to emulate his model of hard work and humility. Clearly Lorch sees his role as much more than that of a coach. "There isn't a lot that's reliable in the players' lives, so we supply consistency above all," he says. "But if you can earn a kid's respect, make him respect himself, and at the same time show him you care, it's so easy to turn a kid around."

Lorch's players do not forget him. Berry has this to say: "I saw Mr. Lorch help guys who weren't such great ball players, like with getting them jobs and all sorts of things like that. What he did for me was unbelievable; that's why I gave him the ball I scored my one-thousandth point with at St. John's, because it meant so much to me, and without him I would never have had the chance."

"The biggest reward," says Lorch, "is not the NBA kids. It's primarily the kids we have who would not otherwise be going anywhere. We tell them that basketball is a weapon. It gets you from here to there. It's not an end. It's a means to an education, a means to get out and see the world and enlarge your perspective. Through the Riverside Church basketball program, they've basically all gone to college and done something with themselves."

===== Giving Something Back =====

On January 15, 1992, Martin Luther King Jr.'s birthday, Kevin Johnson, All-Star guard for the NBA's Phoenix Suns, established a new school, St. Hope's Academy, in South Sacramento, California.

"It didn't take a dream to realize that there are many youths who grow up with broken promises," said Johnson at the dedication ceremony. "Someone needed to disrupt this vicious cycle, and I had a dream that on this lot—once a haven for drug users and transients—it could be done."

St. Hope Academy's new building provides a homelike environment for study and recreation. A 7,000-square-foot facility, it houses six classrooms, a library, a multipurpose room, a recreation room, two bedrooms, a dining area, and an administrative office. Twenty youths, ages eight to seventeen, currently attend the academy; another 30 will be added in the 1992–93 school year.

Even with a professional sports player's stellar salary, Johnson needed help funding the $750,000 project. He turned to Converse, for whom he endorses Accelerator basketball shoes. As partners in Johnson's dream, Converse committed a percentage of shoe sales to the school.

The realization of Johnson's dream promises to help fuel the dreams of today's and tomorrow's Sacramento youth. Says Sacramento Mayor Ann Rudin: "St. Hope Academy will provide a place for kids to learn, to play, and to begin to feel better about themselves. It will also put them in touch with role models who will help them grow into productive adults."

Lyn Henderson, R.N.
A Medical Explorer

Lyn Henderson, R.N. runs the kidney dialysis unit at Clovis High Plains Hospital. She became involved with the Boy Scouts and its outdoors program in 1965 when her son, now 34, became a Cub Scout. At the time, Henderson was living on a military base in the Far East and felt a sense of obligation to set a leadership example in the community.

Back in the U.S. and settled in New Mexico, Henderson realized that her medical knowledge and occupation could be an example to young people. "It dawned on me that if you treat a child like he or she has a brain, the child will show interest in things. Children began to gravitate toward me because I was open to them," she says.

In 1971 Henderson, who holds master's degrees in counseling and social work, started the Clovis Explorer Scouts' medical program. She says, "My two sons and daughter were all interested in medicine. And so I decided to give all youngsters the opportunity to take a close look at the field. This way, they could see for themselves if it was really what they wanted, and if not, move on to different things."

Henderson's Explorer Scout's program is part of a larger program that involves students from three junior high schools in the Clovis area (population 32,000). "Our community is rural," says Henderson. "We have many of the problems of a large city, but we don't have the problems of the inner city. Generally, all the youth activities encompass the whole town and are available to everyone. We have only one high school, and there is a lot of town support. Having a military base here helps; it provides many [people] who are interested in mentoring kinds of activities."

At the beginning of each term, sheets that list interest areas are distributed to students who are instructed to check off whatever appeals to them. Their answers determine the program to which they will be assigned. For example, if a student indicates an interest in police work, he or she may be assigned the town's police detective as a mentor. Forty-five students currently are in the medical program.

One day per month student members of the medical program arrive at Clovis High Plains Hospital to learn the ins and outs of medicine. The goal is to give participants as thorough a background in medicine as possible. Within the program specialties to be observed rotate monthly and include the operating room, the intensive care unit, the X-ray and CAT scanning facilities, and the pharmacy.

"Unlike many organized groups, such as the posts dealing with law, communications, high adventure, etc.," Henderson says, "our particular [program] is loosely run, with exposure to specialized disciplines made available at the discretion and availability of the particular person in charge. In addition, we try to arrange a once-a-month tour to a nearby medical school's anatomy lab."

Henderson considers her 20 years as an Explorer adviser well spent. "I believe the program itself provides the reward," she says. "Over the 20 years I've been involved, we've had many successes, both in encouraging young people to pursue careers in health care and in assisting others to discover early on that medicine really isn't something they want to get involved in. We've had at least 10 participants who have gone on to be physicians. We've also had numerous students who became pharmacists, nurses, physical therapists, X-ray and laboratory technicians, and dieticians. My own daughter (who participated in the program) is an R.N. and a heart and kidney transplant coordinator in a large city."

But the greatest reward, Henderson says, "is when you run into a former Explorer 15 years later who is now in an internal medicine residency ... and she says, 'Your program is where it all began.' It's great to have made that kind of an impact in someone's life."

Walter Lochbaum
A Retired Volunteer

When Ethel Percy Andrus founded the American Association of Retired Persons (AARP) more than a quarter-century ago, she enunciated the mission for the organization that it follows to this day: To serve, not to be served. Dr. Andrus, a retired California educator, believed in "bringing lifetimes of experience and leadership to serve all generations."

Today, older people figure prominently among the 4 million volunteers who work with schools throughout the country. Their presence is living testimony to the fact that volunteerism is now, and has always been, an important part of American life. Anthropologist Margaret Mead, in fact, once observed that "almost anything that really matters to us depends on some form of volunteerism."

Although elected officials at every level talk about educational reform, their tendency these days is to vote for belt-tightening measures that reduce school budgets. In many cases this reflects the demographics of their constituencies; only about a quarter of U.S. households have children in public schools.

But the problem goes beyond budgets. There is also a general decline in the number of people who have time to volunteer in the public schools. Mothers who formerly ran bake sales and served as unpaid teacher aides have now joined the work force, creating a vacuum, one, however, that is slowly being filled by older people who have no direct connection with the schools aside from their interest in education and in young people. In the view of many educators and school officials, older people are particularly suited to this task.

Walter Lochbaum is a case in point. He spent 40 years as an educator in Illinois. He worked as an elementary school teacher, a curriculum coordinator, and a superintendent. As an educator, Lochbaum believed that "if you can help some child, some way, for one day, it is worthwhile." Today Lochbaum has expanded his credo to include older adults. Retired for 12 years, Lochbaum currently serves as AARP District Five Director and helps to coordinate activities for more than 2,500 members. He gets involved in a multiplicity of volunteer ventures, including student instruction and his administrative work.

Older volunteers, by dint of their patience and wisdom, are generally well suited to go one-on-one with the children. A principal reports that when older volunteers eat in the cafeteria with students, "95 percent of the discipline problems disappear." Often, students who skip classes will never miss a session with their older mentor. The withdrawn child who confides his or her hopes and fears to a calming older person might never dream of having done so with a peer or teacher. But the relationships are two-way streets. A 78-year-old widower admits, "I could not have survived the long agony of my wife's death if I didn't have my kids at school. My hours with them gave me the strength to go on because they needed me."

Some older mentors bring special skills to the task: a tutor with a foreign language expertise, for example, or an adviser to the school newspaper who had a career in the field. In the course of this work, a special relationship may develop. As one student put it: "I figured that [the volunteer] was just going to be a tutor, but she turned out to be more like a friend. Being with her was like getting practice being an adult."

Other mentors prefer to work behind the scenes. Retired lawyers, accountants, and other specialists can easily perform tasks that might take a teacher or school administrator an inordinate amount of time. Coordinating fund-raising events such as book sales, fairs, and auctions is a skill that comes easily to people who have been doing such things all their lives. And often the older volunteer has the time to provide assistance or backup where the need is simply to have another person helping out.

Many organizations help to channel volunteer activity on the part of older people. The Retired Senior Volunteer Program (RSVP), local AARP chapters, local units of retired teachers associations, the PTA, the National Association of Partners in Education (NAPE), and numerous other groups exist for just this purpose. Still, if you're interested, the advice of an Alexandria, Virginia, teacher is probably the best in most cases: "Walk into the principal's office of any school that is near where you live or work. Someone will show you what you can do that will make a difference."

HOSTS

Sometimes mentors operate in a well-structured program brought in from the outside, following a detailed plan of instruction. One such effort is HOSTS (Help One Student Succeed), which combines community mentor-tutors with electronic lesson planning to improve student achievement in language arts. Established in Vancouver, Washington, in 1972, HOSTS is not a curriculum; it's an instructional strategy. The program's reading database is composed of 4,000 learning materials from 125 publishers.

Reading proficiency is not the only measure of HOSTS's success. Lucia Gurley spent 20 years as a substitute teacher when she entered the HOSTS program in Dickinson, Texas. She spent only one day a week with seven-year-old Steven, a Hispanic. Other HOST tutors worked with him on other days. Although he had some problems with the English language, Gurley believes that Steven was innately smart and would eventually have learned to read, even without HOSTS. But, she says, without HOSTS having intervened as early as it did, "I'm not sure that he would have learned to *love* to read."

For all its vaunted database, comprehensive materials, lesson plans, and well-structured daily achievement reports, HOSTS's greatest value may well reside in the relationships that develop between the mentors and their students. As the HOSTS literature notes, "Mentors provide role models of successful people as well as insights into the world of work"; this relationship yields "both literacy *and* self-esteem."

James Watkins
The Navy in the Public Schools

James David Watkins spent 35 years in the United States Navy. By the time he retired, Admiral Watkins had held virtually every level of command that it was possible for a naval officer to hold, including commander-in-chief of the Pacific Fleet. Immediately before his retirement, Watkins held the highest commissioned position in his branch of the service: chief of naval operations. But it is not for his naval accomplishments that the admiral is included in this book; rather it is because of the role he played in the education of naval personnel and potential recruits.

In 1977, when he was chief of naval personnel, Watkins found that a surprisingly high number of recruits were dropping out of boot camp as a result of functional illiteracy. Watkins ordered a study of 23,000 files of recruits at San Diego and found that 35 percent of the boot-camp dropouts could not read at the sixth-grade level. As he continued reading the study, he was appalled to learn that 97 percent of those reading at less than sixth-grade level held high school diplomas. Although the quality of naval recruits has improved significantly since 1977, at the time of this study the all-volunteer military was at a low ebb.

The study convinced him that major remedial work was necessary, if not crucial, to the future of the Navy. For instance, the signs on aircraft carriers that read "Beware of Jet Blast" stretched the limits of sixth-grade reading competence. The modern Navy required much more. An Aegis cruiser, for example, has a crew of about 350 as well as what Watkins calls "the fanciest radar in the world," highly sophisticated systems that must be operated by sailors with a minimum of an eleventh- or twelfth-grade education. Reading technical manuals requires a twelfth-grade reading level. The Navy's challenge was to take what had emerged from America's schools and improve on it.

And improve on it they did. The Navy has been installing corrective programs at a cost of about $25 million a year since 1977. Included in them are an academic remedial program addressed largely to reading comprehension, a job-oriented basic skills program, a drug- and alcohol-abuse prevention and rehabilitation program, and a physical fitness remediation program. This last program was developed when Watkins came to the conclusion that the state of "youth fitness is even more serious than the academic situation."

Anesthetized by the high performance of professional athletes seen on television screens, most Americans are unaware of the country's general physical incompetence. Distressed by the inability of recruits to meet minimal fitness standards, in 1985 Watkins asked George Allen, coach of the Washington Redskins and then chairman of the President's Commission on Physical Fitness, to address a group of top Navy commanders on the subject of the nation's fitness. Included in Allen's distressing message was the fact that thousands of youngsters from five to twelve years of age are actually atrophying muscularly. By and large the situation is not improved by school programs. Allen pointed out, "Only 50 percent of our high schools today have any formal youth-fitness program, and of the 50 percent that do, the average program is only 20 minutes, one day a week."

In addition to what he learned about academic and physical fitness, Watkins discovered yet another factor that did not bode well for military recruiters: available demographic studies revealed that the number of 18-year-olds entering the U.S. work force over the next two decades would decline. The military would be in direct competition with private industry for qualified recruits and possibly be unable to meet its recruitment needs. The only solution was to increase the pool of such recruits before they entered the work force, which is how Watkins came to decide on a remediation program with a regime addressed to civilian 17-year-olds.

Phase two of the Navy's remediation program went far beyond the Navy and far beyond remediation. In terms of the program for naval personnel, the objective was shifted to personal excellence, raising sights to new goals of personal, mental, and physical achievement. The most striking change, however, was not in its goal but in its scope. Watkins saw the program as "a new challenge for the Navy to build on our own excellence of the past and then reach out, go the next mile, and develop a new commitment to excellence that we can share with society around us."

Who would staff this new national effort? With the confidence of a man used to command, Watkins envisioned the 4.5 million members of the military (including reserves), their spouses, and other family members as a force of 12.5 million volunteers. And although the program has not yet reached national proportions, the early efforts seem to sustain the admiral's expectation of enthusiastic volunteerism. Pilot programs, designed by a panel of experts with the help of local teachers and administrators, have attracted more than enough naval personnel to ensure their success. The programs include Saturday Scholars, in which sailors use their own weekend time to provide one-on-one tutoring for public school students in Chicago; math and science programs run by the chiefs of naval education and training in Florida, South Carolina, Virginia, and Illinois; a work-study program in Philadelphia; and an adopt-a-school program in San Diego, California.

The Navy program continues despite Watkins's retirement. When he entered civilian life, Watkins began to develop the National Coalition for Personal Excellence. He received some foundation grants, hired a small staff, and made a promising start but was sidetracked by events that he had not anticipated. In October 1987 he was appointed chairman of the Presidential Commission on the Immunodeficiency Virus Epidemic. The commission's report on AIDS, filed in June 1988, drew national praise and considerable attention to the commission chairman. President Bush appointed Watkins Secretary of Energy in 1989, a post in which he continues to serve.

It should come as no surprise to learn that Watkins's Department of Energy issued a thick report in 1990 entitled *U.S. Department of Energy: A Partner in Education.*

Adopt-A-School
Is Alive and Well

Adopt-a-school is probably the oldest model for business-school partnerships. In its earliest form it was often a transitory one- or two-day affair that entailed handing out T-shirts or sponsoring a career day. A company would move quickly in and out of the school setting, frequently benefiting from a news story about its involvement in the local community.

Today many corporate executives recall these transitory partnerships and criticize such superficial business-school relationships as a waste of time. In their current enthusiasm for reform they demand a total restructuring of the schools. Even David Kearns, now the Deputy Secretary of Education, once described school-business partnerships as "feel good enterprises." He quoted academic gadfly Ted Kolderie, who likened partnerships to "doing your daughter's homework. It's a kindness, but a misdirected kindness." Yet, before he entered the Department of Education, Kearns himself had become active in One-to-One, a national organization that encourages business mentoring.

Undoubtedly, many of the early business-school partnerships deserved criticism. But some of today's well-developed adopt-a-school and mentoring programs do provide an important enhancement to school performance. They are certainly needed—at least until we achieve significant restructuring of the schools.

This chapter introduces, among others, Barbara Russell and Wayne Carlson, leading examples of the "new professionals" who are working to enhance the public schools through skillful pairings with private industry. The two came to their present positions through entirely different routes: Barbara Russell got involved as a parent and a community leader as the issue of court-ordered desegregration threatened to cause a "white flight" from the Memphis schools. Wayne Carlson was a vocational education teacher who, as he expanded such programs, developed expertise that has led to the current Los Angeles adopt-a-school programs, which touch virtually every aspect of education.

The Memphis and Los Angeles programs have engaged the attention of thousands of kids who might otherwise have had no interest in school: pupils who have never known anyone who has gone to college are now paired with college students; corporate scientists are helping kids prepare exhibits based on laboratory experiments; a city department of water and power is promoting science achievement and career development activities; and pupils who are interested in athletics are visiting a local "sports resource center," where their interest in sports is being used to help them learn about history, geography, and social studies.

This chapter presents three other very successful adopt-a-school partnerships in action: a government office that decided to adopt a school; a more conventional relationship between a corporation and a school that matches corporate employees one-to-one with students; and a partnership between an automotive parts company and an inner-city technical school that, by venturing into vocational education, expanded the boundaries of adopt-a-school locally and eventually nationally.

Employees in these organizations learned through their company bulletin boards and their fellow workers that they could play a major role in improving education in their communities. You may find that the most effective aid that you can provide to your local schools is through the place where you report to work every morning.

Barbara Russell
Godmother of Adopt-A-School

Barbara Russell, the "Godmother of Adopt-A-School," presides over Memphis, Tennessee's adopt-a-school program. In it every one of the city's 164 schools have two or more partners. The program has become a model for the nation. Russell has received countless honors as a result of it and has presented the fundamen-

43

tals of the program to audiences at Harvard University and Georgetown University and at various national forums.

These days much of Russell's time is spent answering requests for information or accepting invitations to speak about the program. Because of the program's effectiveness and her presentation skills, most people assume that Russell is a professional educator. She is not. She first learned about the schools and began to develop her knowledge and skills in the field of educational partnerships as a parent of children in the Memphis public school system.

When Russell retired from business to raise her four sons, she became increasingly involved in school and social activities related to their education. Over the next 15 years she held a number of volunteer positions ranging from den mother to Parent Teacher Association (PTA) president to serving as a liaison between adversaries on the issue of busing.

In 1975, when her work with the PTA was drawing to a close, a former area school superintendent recruited her to help promote community involvement in 45 of the system's 164 schools. Four years later incoming superintendent Dr. W. W. Herenton invited her to coordinate volunteer services for the entire school system. It was at this time, 1979, that she initiated a partnership between the school system and the community that she called Adopt-A-School.

The U.S. Department of Labor has referred to the Memphis program as "the most energetic and illuminating program of its kind in the nation." One of the reasons for this glowing review is that the program is as deep as it is broad: it not only covers all of the schools in Memphis, but each business that works with a school is asked as it enters the program to sign a contract that acknowledges a full commitment to work with the school. According to Russell, the major focus areas are tutoring, developmental clubs, motivation, discipline, careers, shadowing experiences, jobs, special curricula, scholarships, incentive programs for academic achievement and perfect attendance, and teacher recognition.

Russell will admit that pioneering in this area wasn't easy. "In the beginning there weren't too many educators who agreed with the idea of having the business community come into the schools," she says. "They were concerned that it was going to take away from instructional time. I think that was a legitimate concern."

In time, however, teachers learned that the business partners were supportive. At the very least, the business partners could show that there was a practical career goal to education. As students "shadowed" the employees of their business partners, they got an idea of how a typical workday was spent. They also saw that the employees who were working with them found time to enjoy life and that education helped in that aspect too.

Recently Russell facilitated a partnership between Memphis's Rhodes College and Snowden Elementary School that especially excited her. Thirty to forty percent of Snowden's students had never known anyone in college. The adoption was the subject of a public ceremony. Such focus is useful, Russell says, because it signals the significant commitment that is expected from all adopters.

Despite the close monitoring to make sure adopting companies live up to their commitments, adoption has become the thing for corporations to do in Memphis, and the business partners now compete with each other to see who can do the most for their adopted school.

Memphis-based Procter & Gamble Cellulose has followed its parent company's national policy and tradition and adopted Hamilton Junior High School. As with other business partners, they emphasized their special knowledge in the course of the adoption. "Students have studied life, earth, and physical sciences, and we came up with experiments in those disciplines," says Naomi Byson, chairman of P&G's Volunteer Council and champion of its science fair project. "For each experiment there's a hypothesis—the proposed assumption—and the experiment is to prove or disprove it." There were 41 exhibits at the most recent fair, and each was accompanied by a student-written paper that included a bibliography.

Another recent adopt-a-school activity had Northwest Airlines flying a student choir of Ridgeway High School to Japan for a concert tour. Memphis's media are also prominently represented in the program.

Recently the national Committee for Economic Development evaluated the Memphis program, concluding that it had a major positive effect in increasing "white participation in the schools" after court-ordered desegregation. It also noted that the program increased support for the public school system as partners gained familiarity with it. Finally, it observed that "such programs can improve morale among students and faculty and can do the same

45

for the business employees who become involved."

Russell thrives in this environment, and as a result her program grows each year. Through her speeches across the country and the materials prepared for the program, the national partnership movement has been greatly enhanced. Interestingly, Dr. Herenton, the superintendent who invited Russell to create the citywide program, was recently elected mayor of Memphis.

═══ Preparing the Ground ═══

It's not surprising that Memphis became the first major U.S. city to join America 2000, President Bush's comprehensive plan for education. Memphis was familiar ground to Secretary of Education Lamar Alexander, a former governor of the state. The city was also fertile ground because of the extensive citizen involvement brought about by the Memphis partnership program.

A few months after Memphis 2000 was launched on July 23, 1991, the Department of Education's America 2000 newsletter reported that "at the heart of the America 2000 initiative is the President's challenge to every community to do four things: adopt specific education goals, including six national goals agreed upon by the President and all fifty governors; adopt a clear, concise local strategy to achieve those goals by the year 2000; adopt a local report card as a means of measuring the results of the community's effort; and agree to create and support the establishment of one or more New American Schools." Memphis added two of its own goals to that list: to reduce the deficit in learning among at-risk, disadvantaged children and to make it possible for parents to assume more responsibility for the education of their children.

According to the DOE, as of September 1, 1992, 44 states, one territory, and the District of Columbia had announced their own America 2000 efforts, and more than 2,500 individual communities were organizing to become America 2000 communities.

Jeffrey Graham
The Sheriff's Office and the Public School

Many people don't enjoy their meetings with Jeffrey Graham. Wearing a Stetson and starched khakis, Graham, a sergeant in the Cobb County Sheriff's Office of Marietta, Georgia, can be intimidating. In fact, it was because intimidation was so often associated with his job that Graham established a partnership between the Marietta Sheriff's Office and Bell Ferry Elementary School.

The nearly three-year-old partnership involves the pairing of officer-volunteers from the sheriff's office and a specific teacher and classroom, which allows each volunteer to become well-acquainted with between 20 and 25 students. Bell Ferry Elementary has about 700 students in kindergarten through the fifth grade. "When we go out to the school," says Graham, "we're there to see the kids. We eat with them, we talk to them, we even go to recess with them." Activities include drug awareness programs, fund-raising, sheriff's office participation in school carnivals, and field trips. (The field trips the students particularly enjoy involve child identification and fingerprinting.)

Because the sheriff's office is a tax-supported government entity and not a private business, the commitment made by its officers to Bell Ferry is personal. "We don't get any department money for this," Graham reveals, "so we organize our own fund-raisers." In 1991 the sheriff's office rented a dunking booth at the state fair. During 10 chilly fall evenings, personnel risked three dunks for every dollar they raised. The office used a portion of this money to buy a rose and a school lunch for every Bell Ferry teacher on Teacher Appreciation Day. The fact that volunteers can only make their school visits during their off-duty hours hasn't hampered the enthusiasm for the partnership. "We've put in a full-time commitment," Graham reports. "Last year we made more than 500 visits out to the school."

Graham feels that one of the biggest challenges facing the partnership is keeping things new and exciting. To maintain high interest levels, a new theme is selected each school year. With Atlanta winning the bid in 1991 for the Summer Olympics, Graham felt the obvious choice for the 1991–92 school year would be to focus on the culture that surrounds the worldwide event. During the first few weeks of school, each class adopted a country and researched its customs, clothing, and culture. At the partnership signing ceremony, each class entered carrying the flag of its chosen country and offered greetings in the native language of that country. A bulletin board in the hallway featured an Olympic torch and the words "Let the Partnership Begin!" Pictures were be added to it throughout the year to document partnership activities, and the Olympic theme was tied in to Bell Ferry's spring field days.

Through Graham's efforts Bell Ferry families have been assisted with food, clothing, and toys. Money has also been raised for hospital care for needy students. Once feared, the blinking light on Graham's police car is now considered a friendly symbol that offers transportation to medical appointments for families unable to provide their own. Recently Graham organized a mentor program that pairs officers with academically challenged students. Each officer commits to spend at least one hour a week with his or her student. These in-school help sessions are usually held in the library, where the pair concentrates on reading, writing, or simply getting to know each other. "Kids used to be hesitant about coming up and talking to officers," Graham reports, "but we've changed their view of law enforcement. These kids now see us, meet us, and get to know us as people, not just as uniforms. They trust us and respect us. There's a lot of love between us and the kids in that school"

Listen

Joan Carter trains youth motivators in Volusia County, Florida. Working with a group called Volunteers in Public Schools, Carter coordinates an effort to match at-risk students with adult and college student volunteers. Over the past two years all students have been carefully tracked. The students matched with volunteer motivators have reduced their dropout rate to 3 percent. The main objective of the training sessions, which last only two hours, is to teach the youth motivators a technique that virtually everyone can follow but is little-used and often difficult to master: how to listen.

When I ask you to listen to me and you start giving advice, you have not done what I asked.

When I ask you to listen to me and you begin to tell me why I shouldn't feel that way, you are trampling on my feelings.

When I ask you to listen to me and you have to do something to solve my problem, you have failed me, strange as that may seem.

Listen! All I asked was that you not talk.

Advice is cheap. Thirty-two cents will get you both Dear Abby and Billy Graham in the same paper.

And I can do for myself. I am not helpless. Maybe discouraged and faltering, but not helpless.

When you do something for me that I can do and need to do for myself, you contribute to my fear and weakness.

But when you accept as a simple fact that I do feel what I feel no matter how irrational, then I can quit trying to convince you and get about the business of understanding what's behind this irrational feeling.

And when that's clear, the answers are obvious and I don't need advice.

Irrational feelings make sense when we understand what's behind them.

So, please. Listen and just hear me; and if you want to talk, wait a minute for your turn, and I'll listen to you.

This formula for listening, author unknown, appears in the Volusia County School's *Youth Motivator Handbook, 1991.*

Ken Oya
A True Mentor

Cincinnati's Woodward High School has 2,000 students. Eighty-five percent belong to minority groups, and 30 percent come from low-income families. In 1987 Procter & Gamble adopted the school and established Project ASPIRE, which enlisted 95 Procter & Gamble employees to work one-to-one with students school officials considered likely to drop out. In order to create the best possible environment for the program, teachers and administrators made more counseling available, enlisted parental support, and raised their expectations for students with mentors. Tutoring was supplied where necessary.

Ken Oya was one of the P&G mentors. His student was Tirrell Larkin, who recalls being initially skeptical about the program. Oya, for his part, felt that Tirrell approached life from a confining perspective that he'd unnecessarily imposed on himself. Eventually the two established a sound relationship, and by the end of the year both reported being pleased with what had transpired.

"I made a new friend who is also my mentor," says Larkin. "He helps me out a lot. But what I like best is that I can trust him with any problem I have." Oya feels the same. "One of the pleasures I've enjoyed from being Tirrell's mentor," he says, "has been seeing him develop an interest in a broader array of activities. I hope he continues to expand his horizons in what I'm sure will be a very successful four years in college."

Of the 95 first-year pairings, all but one survived intact. Only one student with a mentor dropped out, a pretty good rate compared to the 11 percent dropout rate among the rest of the student body. Grade point averages were generally up, and over 95 percent of students with mentors were promoted to the next grade. By comparison, less than half of the Woodward students who had no mentors were promoted. Mentor relationships also helped reduce discipline referrals. Only 10 percent of the students with mentors were ever referred to the principal, as opposed to more than 77 percent of their counterparts without mentors.

The second year of the program was even more successful. One-hundred-fifty mentor/student teams were established, and students with mentors showed a significant increase across the board in grade point average.

Almost all the individuals involved in the program reported that the relationships helped to solve problems beyond school assignments. Betsy Baughman, a P&G employee who was paired with student Angela Edmons, observes that "the most valuable facet of our friendship is the trust—she knows that I will always be there to triumph in her successes and to help her bounce back from life's disappointments."

Donald Craig felt that his relationship to his mentor was similar to that of an older brother. "Many times my mentor helped me with problems outside the classroom as well as inside," he reveals. "He has been a tutor, friend, and most importantly, a counselor. I never before had a 'grown-up' with whom I could discuss my personal problems." Craig's mentor, Terry Anchrum, saw Craig as the "little kid brother" he'd always wanted while he was growing up. In his mind his friendship with Craig was one of mutual respect.

In many cases mentors discussed careers with students and helped them learn more about what certain careers entailed. Improvement in work habits, attendance, and punctuality and proper dress were encouraged. The students could see in their role models the use of business language and professional conduct.

As you might have guessed, ASPIRE is an acronym—one that incorporates the main characteristics of a mentor: Advise, Support, Prepare, Inform, Respect, Encourage.

A Retiring Executive Goes Public

As befits the man, his revolution began quietly. In 1982 the Committee for Economic Development, a group of 250 business leaders and educators, met in New York to discuss competitiveness. Speakers covered the usual: the need for investment tax credits, a higher savings rate, and better technology. At the end of the session Brad Butler, then chairman of Procter & Gamble, turned to the group in anger. "How can you talk for an hour about productivity," he asked, "and not ever mention the word 'education'?"

That question prompted two national studies by the CED that galvanized the business community and led to the Clark Kent-like transformation of Butler. The low-profile, mild-mannered chairman of a secretive company has become a trail-blazing, pulpit-pounding crusader for reform in the public schools. Since retiring from P&G in 1986, Butler, 64, has given hundreds of speeches, visited scores of students and teachers, and testified before Congress. Says BellSouth Chairman John Clendenin: "When you talk to Butler, you're talking to a pillar of the nation in terms of focusing attention on the problem."

Butler's father left school after sixth grade to help support his family; his mother quit after the ninth grade. But they made sure their son got a better chance. Indeed, Butler had such good memories of his public school education in Baltimore that when he left the Navy after World War II, he considered becoming a teacher. "I chose to become a salesman, but I felt a strong obligation to pay back what a generation of teachers had done for me. I'm finally getting around to it," he laughs, "a little late."

Fortune, November 7, 1988.

Wayne Carlson
Directing a Large City

Wayne Carlson began his career as a vocational education teacher in the Los Angeles Unified School District (LAUSD) in 1959. Working in the district, he has served as department chair, adult education instructor, consultant on industrial education, and administrative dean for regional occupation programs. He also served as part-time instructor of graduate-level courses at California State University at Los Angeles. His work in occupational education led directly into partnerships, and since 1978 he has been director of adopt-a-school partnership programs for LAUSD, which has over 800,000 students who speak more than 80 different languages.

Carlson's office produces a number of publications, including *Let's Be Partners,* a fine booklet introducing the program, the newsletter *Partnerships in Education,* and a number of detailed survey forms that enable prospective partners to gauge exactly what they can do in the time they have available. By eliciting such detailed information, Carlson, his staff, and the volunteers who work with him are able to fashion individual programs for the schools and the corporate partners.

The Adopt-A-School Council also distributes *Partnership Program Descriptions,* which details particular opportunities for new partnerships. Included in it is information about programs such as the one designed by the city's department of water and power to promote science achievement and career development. This particular program would benefit 8,000 to 10,000 students a year at nine schools and would cost the sponsoring company $100,000 annually. Another program detailed is offered by the Amateur Athletic Foundation. It would bring students in grades 3 through 6 to the Paul Ziffren Sports Resource Center, where they would learn about history, geography, and social studies with a sports twist as an incentive. It would cost the corporate partner approximately $250-$300 per year for transportation.

One of the great values of partnerships is the ability to touch particular interests that students may have. Employees are touched, too. Carlson briefly addresses this often underrated benefit: "We have no way of placing a value on the firsthand experiences that corporate people receive in our schools through the partnership programs. They are, however, referring to 'our kids' and 'our schools.'"

Carlson's participants in the Los Angeles program range in size from small companies to many of America's top 500 corporations. The alphabetical list goes from ABC Market Corporate Offices to Zsa Zsa Gabor, Inc., and also includes Mrs. Field's Cookies. L.A. Dodgers President Peter O'Malley finds that the partnership gives his personnel "the opportunity to step outside the corporate structure—whether on the player or management level—to have some input in the education process." He calls the program "exceptional."

Business Backs Education

To find out just how involved corporate America is in the effort to improve public education, *Management Review* reporter Natalie Adams surveyed 250 of America's largest companies. The results from the 156 companies that responded proved that corporate America is serious about turning around our school systems. Here is a sample:

	Yes	No
1. Is your company volunteering time and money to improve public education?	154	2
2. How would you characterize your involvement?		
Donate money or equipment	150	6
Adopt-a-school programs	110	46
Employee-student mentor programs	110	46
Job training for high school students	84	72
Dropout prevention programs	83	73
School partnerships	87	69
Teacher development/training programs	74	82
Participate in school reform	98	58
Provide management training for education leaders	57	99

3. How much money did you commit to these efforts last year? (140 respondents)

Under $100,000: 53 $1 million–$4,999,999: 22
$100,000–$499,999: 42 $5 million or more: 7
$500,000–$999,999: 16

Management Review, October 1991.

Max Miller
A Vocation for Teaching

Like Admiral Jim Watkins in the preceding chapter, Max Miller's first career was the military. After high school Miller joined the armed forces and spent the next 26 years serving in the United States Navy. When he retired in 1982, he held the highest enlisted rank in the Navy, master chief petty officer. Although the basic orientation of all career Navy personnel is military, a review of Miller's service record reveals a persistent specialty arising in virtually every assignment at every locale throughout his career: Max Miller was a teacher.

At the beginning of his career in the mid-1950s, Miller's assignments involved the usual tasks parceled out to individuals making their way up the ladder of noncommissioned posts—instructor, fire warden, and the like. By the 1970s Max had moved into the ranks of the Navy's professional trainer/teachers, and in 1977, 20 years after joining the military, he became responsible for the overall operation and administration of more than 400 training courses taught at various U.S. and overseas locations. Within the next five years Miller established indoctrination and training courses in which he moved to the next level of teaching responsibility: training the trainers.

Along the way, Miller worked on his own time to earn a college degree. After retiring from the Navy in 1982, he completed his education and earned an M.S. in curriculum and instructional design and technology from Memphis State University. In 1984, for the first time in almost three decades, Miller entered the civilian work force and became manager of training and development for AutoZone, Inc., a company in the automobile parts and repair business, with 7,000 employees in sixteen states.

A few years later, when AutoZone debated how to give something back to its communities, it considered supporting one of the many programs that help children go on to college. "But the majority of people that worked for us did not go to college," explains Miller, "and we weren't looking for them to go to college. We wanted people to come out and work in our store." At Miller's instigation, AutoZone chose instead to form a partnership in education with East Vocational Technical Center and become part of Memphis's well-developed adopt-a-school program.

In addition to his full-time position as AutoZone's executive employment officer, Miller began to travel around the country to AutoZone locations to establish partnerships and adapt the original AutoZone program to local schools. Of the 54 partnerships that he established in 18 states, close to 50 were developed over a period of only two and a half years. Miller's leadership was recognized in 1988 when he received NAPE's prestigious McKee Award as the businessperson who had contributed the most to the expansion of partnerships in education in the United States. Although Miller left AutoZone shortly thereafter, the company's national program continues to flourish today. J. R. "Pitt" Hyde, chairman and CEO of AutoZone, was Miller's enthusiastic mentor in developing this program and now presides over its continued aggressive expansion throughout the nation.

In November of 1989 Miller became senior training specialist for Federal Express, which accurately saw a need to encourage young people, particularly members of minority groups, to enter the teaching profession. Under his direction Federal Express joined the College of Education at Memphis State University and the Memphis city schools to form a three-way partnership entitled Pyramids in Education.

This year Pyramids in Education began working with chapters of Future Teachers of America (FTA) in four Memphis public schools. The goals of the program are to identify students interested in entering the teaching profession, to recruit enthusiastically to expand this number among qualified students, to develop skills and the course background needed by students to qualify for the profession, and to track and assist the students as they move forward to their goal.

Miller describes Federal Express as a resource bank, providing FTA with whatever they need to develop their programs throughout the year. "I train adults in business and industry," he says, "but I'm interested in what happens to people before they get to me. Federal Express supports FTA because we're looking toward work force 2000. What we're doing is long range. Our concern is that we will have quality educators teaching. And that will, in fact, give us a better employee."

Recently promoted, Miller is now responsible for the instructional design and development of Federal Express's worldwide customer service training. His teaching career continues.

Start Your Own Organization

The highly successful organizations profiled in this chapter often had very personal beginnings: A father discovered that his son had a vision problem that affected his learning and later came face to face with widespread illiteracy; another father, conveying moral values to his sons, wondered whether high ethical standards were being taught in his company and in his community. A mother whose son came to school age insufficiently developed to cope with conventional schools eventually helped thousands of others by first setting out to create a school for him.

Other mentors have set up organizations because they hit on a solution to a problem in their local schools: A social worker thought that handicapped children might profit from the guidance of handicapped adults. A businessman found that money available to send high school graduates to college was going untapped.

All these mentors shared a common belief that the most effective way to make a difference in our public schools is to establish an organization to deal with the problem (or opportunity) each uncovered.

Interestingly, two of them are corporate chief executives who applied their business experience in different ways. Arthur Gunther decided that pizza could be given away as an incentive to reading, so he mobilized Pizza Hut to do just that on a national scale. Sanford McDonnell began his program to teach values at McDonnell-Douglas; when he saw favorable results, he moved to establish a similar program in the St. Louis schools.

Claire Flom's success and experience in running a business and in various community activities, as well as her work in establishing a school, prepared her to deal with university officials who had much to offer the public schools but simply hadn't been asked to help. Insights gained in years as a social worker enabled Regina Snowden to work effectively with the handicapped as she fashioned her productive organization.

Mentors who start their own organizations often bring special skills to the task. You, too, may have a special background or ability that can bring unique value to our schools. The fact that no organization exists to focus your talents on the problems of the public schools should not deter you any more than it did the mentors in this chapter, who overcame big odds to make a big difference.

Milton Heimlich and Victor Bergenn
FACTS

Like Eugene Lang, Milton Heimlich was a wealthy businessman. While Heimlich did not personally pay the college tuition of high school students, his financial support and leadership managed to accomplish that very thing for thousands of youngsters. He established Financial Aid for College and Technical Schools (FACTS), an organization to provide access to the millions of dollars of financial aid—scholarships, loans, and grants—that go untapped every year.

Students and their parents often don't know about all of the government and private aid available to them, and those students who do know are sometimes at a loss as to how to apply for it. FACTS was set up to respond to the situation. Located in New Rochelle, New York, its staff was composed mainly of college students who were either paid a modest stipend or worked as volunteers. The counselors were trained to help that city's high school students locate and obtain the funds necessary to go on to higher education.

Once Heimlich's program had proved successful in New Rochelle, he set his sights on an even greater challenge: New York City's public schools, a system that provided only one guidance counselor for every 1,000 students. As he stepped up to the larger arena, Heimlich enlisted the aid of Victor Bergenn, an educational psychologist who was both willing to volunteer and anxious to help. Meeting with key people on the New York City Board of Education, Heimlich and Bergenn inched their way up the hierarchy, never missing an opportunity to put on what Bergenn refers to as their dog-and-pony show.

To ensure the program's success, the duo recognized that they needed a cadre of workers familiar with the ins and outs of financial aid and college admissions. They hit on the idea of recruiting work-study students from local colleges. Normally, work-study students work on campus for wages that are paid by both the federal government and the learning institution. Universities and colleges typically use work-study as a form of inexpensive on-campus labor. Bergenn and Heimlich successfully argued that because the intent of the federally funded work-study program is to provide students with experience that is potentially career relevant, limiting the students to on-campus jobs was not the best way to meet that goal. Local colleges and universities accepted this argument and agreed to allow a few students to accept the off-campus assignments with FACTS each year. It fell to Heimlich and Bergenn to raise additional money through private sources to complete the funding.

In New York City the greatest obstacle the two encountered was opposition from guidance counselors. Victims of serious budget cuts in the 1960s, the guidance counselors had learned—and remembered—just how vulnerable their positions within the school system could be. But Heimlich and Bergenn persisted, and the guidance counselors gradually came to realize that FACTS students were there to support them, not to replace them. Since then, says Bergenn: "We have received letters from college advisers and counselors saying they would be absolutely lost without the FACTS aides. In many instances our young people get to know the job so well that they become instrumental in running a tight ship."

The college students bring much more to the program than clerical assistance; they bring understanding. Many of the FACTS aides have been through the process of obtaining financial aid for themselves and are familiar with the problems students face emotionally and in dealing with the overwhelming paperwork. Some students, for example, face resistance from parents unwilling to reveal their income. That and other factors are all part of the challenge.

All work-study students are trained to use a computer, which enables them to access as much information as possible. Only a few years beyond high school, the FACTS aides are also able to interact with high school seniors as peers. "If a kid's parents aren't available or sophisticated enough to be able to support the financial aid effort, then it's all the more important to have the FACTS aide there. That one-on-one contact in the financial aid process is so important," says Bergenn. "Education has become such a large operation, and such a dehumanizing experience, that the more you can individualize the effort, the better."

While the FACTS aides were busy winning over the guidance counselors, Heimlich and Bergenn continued their campaign to gain support from school board officials. Because they were working from outside the system, Bergenn feels he and Heimlich were able to get to people more easily than someone who was locked into the bureaucracy. One board member, Dr. Amelia Ash, became a strong advocate of the program. Through her efforts the school board agreed to provide a paid coordinator, assistant coordinator, secretary, and clerk for FACTS. "It really was a partnership being worked out between outside groups pulling together with the Board of Education, federal monies, and universities and colleges," reports Bergenn.

The Board of Education now provides the funds that Heimlich and Bergenn once had to raise from private sources. Though the New York City program appears secure, funding is renewed on a yearly basis. "When they start talking about another round of cutbacks," says Bergenn, "you always get concerned that people who are the paid staff may be vulnerable. You're never completely comfortable with things nowadays. We've been funded each time—but sometimes it gets kind of close."

Heimlich died four years ago at the age of 81, just one week after he had traveled to Washington, D.C., to deliver a report on his successful program to the National Symposium on Partnerships in Education. In the absence of his partner and longtime friend, Bergenn is carrying on the program with the same dedication evinced by Heimlich years ago. "Milton had that kind of get-up-and-go gumption. His concern for the human condition was more of a concern to improve conditions for all," recalls Bergenn. "He felt that the minority population was not getting any support to continue their education and that opening up opportunities to minorities was only the right thing to do."

Today FACTS distributes financial aid information in English, Spanish, Chinese, Haitian Creole, Italian, and Braille. Some 85 college students are currently providing counseling to more than 50,000 high school students and their parents citywide.

Claire Flom
An Alliance for the Public Schools

Claire Flom's son, Peter, was born prematurely and not fully developed. By the time he was in kindergarten it became clear that his gross and fine deficits were preventing him from learning as other children did. His mother realized that he needed special attention. As she searched for a school equipped to deal effectively with his problems, she discovered that although there were many youngsters who reached school age with similar difficulties, there were few appropriate facilities in the New York metropolitan area. So Flom did what anyone who knows her would expect: she started a school. The Gateway School of New York, founded in 1965 by Flom and others, continues to serve children with learning disabilities. As with many mentors, Flom's interest in education rose from her role as a concerned parent.

In 1979 Flom established the New York Alliance for the Public Schools. The basic concept was to create a partnership between the New York City public schools and five of the city's schools of graduate education. Experts at the graduate schools were in a position to share in a systematic way information that would enhance the work of the public schools. This was done on a voluntary basis. In time, in addition to the deans of the schools, the Alliance's small board had on it the chancellor of the New York City Board of Education, the president of the United Federation of Teachers, the president of the Council of Supervisors and Administrators, and a few individuals who were simply interested in education (myself included). Working closely with the chancellor, the Alliance raised funds and entered into a series of activities to fulfill its mission.

The Alliance established a telephone network of 1,500 university professors who would be available to share their knowledge with high school teachers working in their respective disciplines. Another activity, the "Go Public!" campaign, was an advertising and public relations campaign designed to acquaint New York City citizens with the good work being accomplished in many of the public schools. Citywide ads, news stories, and posters were used to spread the word. Since positive news about public education was an angle rarely covered in local news reports, separate seminars and training sessions were developed to show individual schools how to enhance their own public relations in their neighborhoods as a means of increasing local support.

The Alliance also instituted an annual teacher awards luncheon, in which five teachers are honored: one from each of the city's boroughs, rotating among high school, intermediate school, elementary school, and special education teachers every four years. Although the Alliance relies on extensive voluntary assistance, funding for each of its programs is considerable. Go Public!, for example, was budgeted at $500,000 over a two-year period. In addition to her other responsibilities, Flom has been the Alliance's primary fund-raiser.

In 1982 the Alliance established a program called the Principal as a Curriculum Leader (PCL). Once again the concept was simple: Some principals, working in poor neighborhoods in which school buildings had broken windows, inadequate plumbing or air-conditioning, and otherwise rundown facilities, nevertheless accomplished significant academic achievements. PCL was designed to allow these principals to share their ideas and methods with their fellow school administrators through seminars, retreats, and printed materials. Armed with the idea and a commitment from the Board of Education to the basic premise, Flom obtained a two-year grant of $430,000 from the Chase Manhattan Bank.

The PCL project was my first exposure to the New York City Board of Education's legendary bureaucracy. I was one of seven public members of the separately constituted PCL board insisted on by the Board of Education. The remaining public members were Flom, three other representatives of the Alliance, and two officers from Chase. The eight members appointed by the Board of Education included the chancellor of the board (the city's chief education officer) and the deputy chancellor for finance. A respected school principal, Herb Balish from Staten Island, served as PCL's full-time director.

The first two meetings of the PCL board consisted of hopeful reports but no real action. Probing by the public directors soon revealed that conferences of principals were being planned but not held because the Board of Education did not have an appropriate means to pay many of the expenses required by the scheduled conferences. Only when faced with a possible withdrawal of funds by

Chase did the board develop the necessary paperwork. The project moved forward.

Over the next five years PCL matured into a professional-skills development program through which principals looked in depth at instructional supervision and curriculum development, strategies for dealing with special students, school-based management, and instruction in basic skills. In 1987 the New York State Education Department approved a grant to the Alliance to continue the work of PCL as a permanent arm of the state education system.

Two other Alliance programs are worth noting here. One involved oral communication skills. The first phase of this program served over 800 students in seven high schools and covered a wide range of skills and abilities. After two years of constant monitoring by selected professionals, a comprehensive curriculum guide was produced. In 1988 phase two of the program took the shape of a weekly course for teachers held at NYU.

The second program, called CAMI: Cadre of Advanced Mathematics Instructors, began in 1986 and sought to improve the quality of math instruction. It provided 20 CAMI Fellows with advanced math instruction at NYU. The Fellows then return to their eight high schools to share advanced course work and special projects with their colleagues. Several hundred CAMI Fellows are now acting as disseminators of advanced math instruction throughout the New York City system.

Flom has retired as the chair of the Alliance. She passed the baton with the knowledge that the programs she started are continuing, many as permanent components of the city or state systems. She remains active in the educational arena as a trustee of Fordham University, has rendered yeoman service as a member of a special task force of the state Board of Regents charged with assessing the management methods of the city's high schools, and was a member of the three-person selection committee directed to find a chancellor for the city's schools.

Flom is occasionally assisted by her son, Peter, who, after leaving Gateway School and attending regular elementary and secondary schools, was admitted to New York University. He was accepted early, skipping what would have been his senior year of high school. He obtained an M.A. from NYU, concentrating his graduate work in the field of special education. He shares his mother's knowledge and concern about education.

========= **The Gateway School** =========

Starting a school is not easy. Seeing one flourish and grow is highly satisfying. The Gateway School began in 1965 with three students, one of whom was Peter Flom.

The school used the innovative methods of Dr. Elizabeth Freidus to help students with learning differences learn, understand, and develop. Flom obtained space in the Madison Avenue Presbyterian Church building at 921 Madison Avenue. The school is still located there but today accommodates 34 students. Students are accepted at ages 5 through 7 and can remain through age 10. The principal is Dr. Davida Sherwood, a psychologist; there is one other administrator. The five classroom teachers typically work in groups. Four days a week, psychologists, speech pathologists, and adaptive physical education teachers are at the school. There are consultants in optometry and math, and part-time teachers in art, music, and occupational therapy. A person who specializes in transition to regular schools is also in attendance.

As it was when Flom and her partners founded the school, Gateway is very much needed. It plays a unique role in the New York education community.

Eunice Ellis and Arthur Gunther
Book It!

Eunice Ellis presides over Book It!, the largest partnership in which private enterprise plays a voluntary role in the public schools. Book It! is a reading incentive program that reaches 17 million children—more than half of the 26 million students who attend America's public elementary schools.

"The Book It! reading incentive program works for all children, even those who have difficulty reading or those who have never liked to read," says Ellis. "Best of all, the program has helped millions of children discover that the printed word is a great source of pleasure and information." The program, which is headquartered in Wichita, Kansas, is sponsored by Pizza Hut, Inc.

Book It! is frequently cited as an ideal program. It is brilliantly conceived, it confers a commercial benefit on its company while still achieving a significant educational goal, it has been designed and objectively evaluated by educational experts, and it is staffed by skilled professionals. All the more remarkable, therefore, is the fact that the program grew not out of a grand design but out of the personal experience of one family.

In the course of a game of pool in his family rec room, Arthur Gunther, chief executive of Pizza Hut, learned that his teenage son had a severe vision problem that he had managed to conceal from his parents, teachers, and peers for a number of years. This, in turn, had led to a reading problem.

In the next few months, as Gunther dealt with the disability that afflicted his son, he learned the shocking facts of adult illiteracy. Literacy Volunteers of America estimates that as many as 27 million adults are functionally illiterate, prohibiting them from effectively performing essential life tasks such as completing a job application.

The overwhelming majority of adult illiterates do not have vision problems, however. In general, they have a history of not being properly taught to read at an early age and of masking their inability through a course of conduct that only compounds the problem. Gunther decided to help.

Armed with a salesman's faith that pepperoni can move mountains, Gunther approached educators in Kansas, where Pizza Hut is headquartered. Together, Gunther and these educators designed a simple program. Each child would be given a reading goal, and if he or she reached it, the youngster would receive a Personal Pan Pizza from Pizza Hut. If the entire class met their goals, then the class would be given a pizza party. It is important to note that each student would be given an individualized goal by the teacher: one child might be expected to read a new book every month; another a single chapter. A child with a particularly difficult problem might only be assigned a few pages.

With the prize would come recognition: The school principal would sign the certificate acknowledging that the goal had been met, and the manager of the local restaurant would see that the accomplishment was duly noted, perhaps by making an announcement ("We have another winner") or by seating the winner with an appropriate flourish. Parents were encouraged to work with their children and to limit television-watching so as to expand reading time.

Gunther, of course, did not single-handedly implement Book It! Credit for much of the program's success goes to Ellis, who was transferred from the business side of Pizza Hut to administer the program. When Book It! was conceived, Ellis, who had a background in teaching at public and private schools, was an obvious choice to take the helm. Together, Ellis and Gunther forged good intentions into tangible results.

Schooled in his years with Pizza Hut and PepsiCo, the company's parent, to the harsh realities of the marketplace, Gunther was keenly aware that good ideas don't automatically succeed. For this reason he insisted on periodic evaluation's of the Book It! program in operation. Dr. John Boulmetis and a team from the Institute of Human Science and Services of the University of Rhode Island conducted the studies. The initial scope was the statewide pilot in Kansas, but by the third year of the program, the researchers used a 10 percent random sample of the 220,000 classrooms in which Book It! was in place. Gunther found he had a product that worked.

Look at the record: The average number of books read increased by almost 300 percent in a period of three months, 80 percent of the participating students reported increased enjoyment of reading, 69 percent of the participants raised their reading level, and 53 percent of the students who participated improved their grades across all academic areas. And virtually all of these figures increased even further as the students continued in the program.

The anecdotal information is also impressive. Ellis shared with me some of the letters received from students, parents, and teachers involved in the program:

- A teacher from Pennsylvania described the program as "probably the *best* thing to happen to education in the seventeen years I've been teaching."
- A thirteen-year veteran elementary school teacher wrote from Kansas that after fulfilling her requirements of four books and four book reports a month for five months, her students had their pizza party. "But even after the reward of the party," she continued, "I am still hearing from parents of how their children are continuing to read! Our library and bookmobile are still being used."
- The program coordinator at a juvenile detention facility in Lexington, Kentucky, reported that "Aside from the obvious reward, our kids benefited in ways that they themselves may not recognize. They gained self-esteem by setting a goal and

attaining it, they received recognition from others for accomplishments, and they took pride in themselves for perhaps the first time in their lives."

These letters indicate that the program has had its positive effect on both the very good students who achieved good grades but previously had no interest in reading and the weaker students whose literacy and accomplishments were at a low point before Book It! moved them to unexpectedly higher plateaus.

With its $20 million annual expenditure for administrative expenses and materials, millions of dollars in free pizzas, and thousands of hours of personnel time, Pizza Hut has made a major investment in Book It! The company has undoubtedly achieved a significant gain in terms of favorable public relations in the extremely competitive fast-food field. But who can criticize them for doing well when they have done so much good?

Regina Snowden
Partners for Disabled Youth

Regina Snowden is no newcomer to the field of human services. She holds a master's degree in social work and for many years has been involved with programs for at-risk youth. Her particular expertise lies in helping kids survive adolescence, a period of discovery that is both exciting and stressful. Snowden feels that given adequate support, at-risk youth can get through those tough times without becoming dropouts, drug users, or teenage parents.

It was in her role as director of a mentor program for adolescent girls, however, that she found a new focus for her efforts: children with physical disabilities.

In her work with youth services, Snowden often received requests from parents for programs that might help their disabled children. "It was then I realized that there are hardly any programs serving youth with physical disabilities," says Snowden. "I didn't have anywhere to send them.... The more I got involved with this population of disabled people, the more I realized that this is true for the disabled population as a whole. Adults with disabilities truly had to be the pioneers in advocating for themselves."

Snowden decided she would be an advocate for services for disabled children—adolescents in particular. "Kids with disabilities are often at risk of not achieving their potential because of self-esteem issues related to having a disability," she says. "And yet, they have so much to offer the world."

Many kids with disabilities live a very isolated existence, she claims. In fact, she once met a little girl at a hospital for the disabled who thought the world of disabled individuals began and ended at her school. "The only adults this child came in contact with were parents, doctors, social workers, and teachers, all nondisabled adults." As a result, Snowden decided that disabled children needed to be involved with successful adults who were also disabled. "These adults, I knew, were the ones to show them the way," says Snowden.

The first step was to put notices in newsletters that served the disabled community, both to explain her idea and to solicit would-be mentors. Nine adults responded, adults who were vision impaired, mobility impaired, and hearing impaired. "I realized when I met these individuals that I had a program," says Snowden. "Some of those adults told me they had never even seen an adult with a disability when they were growing up. They thought that when you grew up, you just died."

Once she began to match up the adults and youth, the program took off. "I knew I had tapped an unmet need," says Snowden. "These kids had never met disabled adults who managed careers, lived independently in their own apartments, learned how to access transportation for themselves, or had families and successful social lives." One reason for the program's success may have been her approach to preparing the partners for the reality of the relationship. "Like any relationship," she tells them, "you're going to hit it off or you're not. Expectations and idealism can be very high in this kind of thing, as well they should be, because exciting, idealistic things do happen. But you're going to have days when the relationship goes through times that just aren't as positive as other times."

In 1983 Partners for Disabled Youth (PDY) was established as an independent, nonprofit organization. Since then, it has gone quietly about its work, uniting growing numbers of disabled mentors and disabled youth. As word of its success spreads, PDY gets more and more referrals. Currently, approximately 40 youngsters are waiting to be paired with mentors. "It's amazing what has happened with so few resources and so little staff," says Snowden. "We do what we can based on the staff we have."

PDY now provides services beyond mentor pairings. It organizes, for example, Youth in Preparation for Independence, a discussion group that brings together disabled youth and a panel of disabled adults to talk about issues related to disability or adolescence. PDY also conducts support groups for the parents of disabled youth, many of whom were unwittingly passing their low expectations for people with disabilities on to their children. Upon meeting their child's mentor, many of these parents expressed renewed hope in their child's future.

The heart of the program, however, continues to be the mentor relationships. Julie Brown is a case in point. She was seven years old when she entered the program. Born with spina bifida, she sometimes worried that she would never be able to drive or hold a job. Of more immediate concern was her fear of using a wheelchair on ground that was even slightly uneven. Both her range and her confidence were extremely limited.

Now Julie is paired with Martha Donaghue, a former gymnast who became a quadriplegic when she fell from the uneven parallel bars eight years ago. Since that accident, however, Donaghue graduated from Boston University summa cum laude, learned to drive (she is a daily commuter who drives to work herself), and secured a job as an actuarial assistant at the John Hancock Mutual Life Insurance Company. The two meet every other week to bake cookies, shop, draw pictures, and practice wheelchair mobility.

Last year Snowden had the joyful opportunity of seeing the benefits of PDY come full circle. Now of college age, some of the young people who were early participants in her program are returning as mentors. During last year's Volunteer Appreciation Night, a former youth participant who is now a mentor addressed the group. "He was fantastic," recalls Snowden. "He talked about how he felt when he was in high school; about how his adult mentor, Mike, had been the first person to tell him about his rights and get him involved in justice and civil rights issues for disabled people. Mike, he said, helped him look at his abilities, not his disability. Excited now to be a mentor himself, he only hoped he could provide the encouragement and support that Mike had given him. That was a high for me."

Judith Berry Griffin
As Solid as ABC

Schooling confers many benefits. In addition to acquiring skills and knowledge, many of the young people who attend some of the finer public and private schools and are admitted into the "old grad" networks of those institutions often find it easier to gain entry to tracks toward leadership in government and industry.

Historically, minorities have been denied access in significant numbers to top schools and, therefore, to those exclusive networks. In 1963 Dartmouth College set out to do something about it. In cooperation with 23 heads of independent boarding schools, Dartmouth founded Project ABC, a program that offered high school minority group students who had high academic potential the opportunity to participate in summer programs at Dartmouth.

Selected students spent their summer in an academically rigorous environment designed to help them succeed in high school and be accepted to the better colleges. Upon completion of the summer program, each student would be enrolled at a selected preparatory school. The prep school heads also organized a program called the Independent Schools Talent Search (ISTS). Its intent was to identify and recruit students to join Project ABC. These two organizations merged to become an independent entity, A Better Chance, Inc. (ABC), which is located in Boston.

Judith Berry Griffin has been president of ABC since 1984. "My interest in education is primarily directed toward minority children who are not getting a good education," she says. "I want to give them a greater variety of opportunities, particularly if they are motivated and capable."

Berry Griffin herself is a graduate of the University of Chicago and of Columbia University Teachers College. "I'm a black person, and I was lucky," she says. "My father was a physician. When I was four years old, my parents sent me to the University of Chicago Laboratory School, which is a very progressive and wonderful school. Early on I determined that what I was going to do with my life was to make that opportunity available to as many other minority children as I could lay my hands on."

As a teacher, a principal, an executive assistant to the U.S. assistant secretary of education, an author of children's books, and as a

69

president of ABC, Berry Griffin, no doubt, has managed to lay her hands on a good number of fortunate minority children.

ABC's goal is simple: To substantially increase the number of well-educated minority people who can assume positions of responsibility and leadership in American society. In order to ensure equal opportunity, there are no charges to ABC students. The organization is funded by private sources and federal agencies participating in the U.S. antipoverty program. The participating prep schools include boys' and girls' boarding schools and day schools. The admitting school absorbs the cost of tuition for the ABC student; most are full-need students, approximately one-third are from welfare families. "The problem," admits Berry Griffin, "is finding qualified schools that have the financial aid available and the space available to take particular students."

ABC has definite criteria for identifying a "qualified school," and it takes much more than a promised scholarship to join the ABC membership. Before a school is accepted, it has to be passed by a board. Schools are evaluated as rigorously as student applicants. According to Berry Griffin, the schools must be committed to improving, understanding, and working constructively with children of color.

To complement the private school program, ABC introduced Public School Programs (PSPs) in the late 1960s. In essence, PSPs are public school systems with boarding programs. In them a community-leased or community-purchased house in a district with high-quality public schools becomes home to six to twelve students who normally do not reside in that district. Living in the home enables the children to attend those schools rather than the inadequate schools in their own communities. Each PSP has a board made up of community residents who select the students, raise the money to support the program, and provide academic and personal counseling.

The houses themselves are run by resident directors who may be professionals, graduate students, or couples who make their homes available after their own children are grown and gone. Each school night, resident tutors conduct mandatory three-hour study and counseling sessions. As of 1992, 24 PSPs are operating in 23 communities in Connecticut, Massachusetts, Minnesota, New York, Pennsylvania, and Wisconsin.

The application process for potential ABC scholars is highly competitive. Prospective students are required to complete lengthy application forms, supply ABC with recommendations and transcripts, take the PSATs, and undergo interviews. Unfortunately, demand far exceeds the spaces available. Of the 2,212 applicants in 1991, only 316 were placed in private and public schools. Upon acceptance the student faces another major hurdle. Being transported from the inner city to exclusive schools in suburban America is more than a geographic adjustment; it can be a culture shock. But ABC has a good record: 96 to 100 percent of ABC's alumni enter college year after year, and at least 90 percent graduate.

In support of Berry Griffin's unceasing drive to reach minority children, ABC also oversees several outreach programs. Serving as a recruiter, each year ABC provides access to educational supplemental programs to between 600 and 700 children. Information sessions held nationwide give high school students valuable information about the types of courses they need to take to stay on a college track. In addition, it directs Parents as Partners groups across the country to let parents know what they can do to increase their children's scholastic motivation.

ABC's most recent effort is Pathways to College, which began a pilot program this year in Newark, New Jersey. Pathways to College is an ancillary program for high school students that meets every Saturday throughout the school year. Alumni and others come to talk with the students about career options, self-esteem, study skills, and time management.

The problem ABC foresees for the future is not difficulty finding qualified students but finding adequate resources. ABC's operating budget for 1991 exceeded $1.6 million. In this period of economic uncertainty, its dependence on private donors makes unstable financial foundation.

As of June 30, 1991, ABC alumni numbered 7,317. William M. Lewis Jr., managing director of Morgan Stanley & Co. Inc., is an ABC alumnus. So is Robert H. Fayne, president of Consolidated Management Group. Through an enthusiastic network that includes more than 3,000 volunteers, ABC is now 7,317 steps closer to ensuring an America of equal educational opportunity.

Two Case Histories: Dmitri Bloodworth and Dale Allsopp

THE CONCERNED STUDENT

by Dmitri Bloodworth

Speaking from my experience, there are two types of students at Exeter: the concerned and the unconcerned. The concerned have qualities that set them apart from the others. They are always interested in those who are different from themselves and engage in conversations for knowledge, not for conflict. The unconcerned usually don't take part in diversity discussions and try to tell you that it's not important.

I first came into contact with a concerned student my freshman year. It was the week of Dr. King's celebration, and Exeter was showing the movie *Do the Right Thing.* Quite a few of my dorm mates saw it the same night I did. When I returned to my dorm, a discussion took place between my peers and myself. Soon the conversation deteriorated into an argument. Feeling frustrated and upset, I left the common room and went to my room.

In the midst of trying to do my homework, I heard a knock at the door and asked who it was. It was the senior with whom I had been arguing in the common room. I let him in. We apologized to each other and began talking about the movie and other issues of diversity. I label him a concerned student because out of the six or seven people in the initial discussion, he was the only one who actually thought enough of the knowledge that could be gained by finishing the conversation.

I have also had my share—or maybe more than my share—of encounters with unconcerned students. One that sticks out is an incident that happened in the spring of my [junior] year. No matter what grade you're in, spring term always means college talk. Everybody starts to fantasize about colleges. I was in a room with a bunch of people talking about college and what kind of "suck" they would have to do to help their applications look more appealing to the colleges of their choice. I began rattling off what I felt I needed to do. Halfway through, another guy in the room cut me off and said, "You're black. That's your ticket in." Needless to say, this angered me. I went on to explain why it angered me to all present in the room. The person who said it then tried to defend himself by saying I was being touchy, and that I should not have been offended.

I label him unconcerned because he did not listen to what I had to say. He did not try to understand where I was coming from. Many

Exonians have exhibited those same qualities when it comes to issues of diversity.

The administration of Exeter has set a tone of diversity that has begun to penetrate the student body, but we have a long way to go before everybody on campus can appreciate the contributions made by others different from themselves and will care enough to listen.

Bloodworth, a senior from Brooklyn, New York, writes a weekly column for the *Exonian.* This article first appeared in *The Phillips Exeter Bulletin,* Spring 1992.

A local program like ABC was initiated in 1979 in New York City by Gary Simons, then a doctoral candidate at Columbia University Teachers College. Called Prep for Prep, the program was designed as a rescue mission for gifted students in public schools who are in need of extra attention and more advanced materials to fuel their interests and develop their skills. These students are identified, given intensive academic training, and placed in some of New York City's most exclusive independent day schools. In September 1991, 110 such schools were participating.

TRANSITION

by Dale Allsopp

Reflecting on my brief life, I realize that there are certain individuals as well as organizations that were very instrumental in me being where I am now. My grandmother, Francina Trotz, my family, my primary school principal, Mr. Schaffer, and the Calhoun School's community all helped shape me into the mature, capable person that I am. However, the Prep for Prep organization, above all, prepared me for the rigors of private school academia and set the basic foundation that is still supporting the way I think.

Prep for Prep stands for preparation for preparatory schools. After "getting through" the program there is a commencement that symbolizes "the end," and each student who has "survived prep" goes on to a private school.

A rosy picture is definitely painted of Prep for Prep: however, this is not what is always observed by those closely affiliated with the program. To get the best out of these students, Prep administers a sometimes overbearing amount of homework. It is common for students to say, "If I can survive prep, I can do anything." Personally I had to divorce myself from the social atmosphere of the other kids around my neighborhood. I wasn't allowed outside until I had finished all my homework during the seven weeks each summer. Not seeing me regularly, the children started labeling me nerd and lambda geek (from *Revenge of the Nerds*). Luckily this did not really affect me, for my grandmother would always say, "Dale, you're not doing this for me, you're not doing this for your mother, and you're definitely not doing this for those children downstairs—you're doing it for yourself."

In this sense prep was an emotional strain as well as academically challenging. Not being able to go out and play baseball or whatever games the other children were playing was anything but satisfying. It was very hard to concentrate on studies when the kids outside could be heard screaming and carrying on in a seemingly enjoyable fashion. I definitely lost whatever popularity I had with the kids around the block; the ramifications of trying to get ahead in life were ridicule and the constant judging of my person. Although some have learned to respect me, to this day I still get the occasional "sellout" and "token negro" flung my way. One reason I was able to stay as focused as possible was the fact that there were other children experiencing the same situations—other kids had to deal with the strenuous task of doing both their school work and Prep for Prep work during the winter sessions. The transition was rough, but the edges were smoothed by influential people in my life.

The second transition was made from prep to private school. Of course the work was challenging, and we were prepared for that. What I was not prepared for was the ratio of white students to minorities. We had all heard about the number of white students in private school, but seeing was definitely believing. In prep there was always someone "covering your back"—looking out for you—if not someone in the administration, then a particular student you could confide in. My first few minutes at Calhoun were probably the loneliest I have ever spent in my life. I felt I was locked in a small space by these "strange" people around me with no escape. Fear and hate encompassed me, and I felt that I would certainly be picked on because I was smaller and different. These ill feelings were quickly alleviated by three people who I consider to be among my best friends. Oliver Chase, Zeke Edwards, and Josh Israel took it upon themselves to approach me and make me feel welcome. Their altruism is one reason why our bond is as strong as it is. The transition from prep is not as hard as the transition to prep, but it was a very trying experience.

I would have to consider prep a rewarding experience, for it has helped sculpt my character. Intellectually prep has supplied me with the will to learn, to accept challenges, and made me believe I could succeed. The great thing about prep is that it doesn't end after the second summer. Students are provided with counselors, summer jobs that are so important to students facing college, and opportunities that allow one to give back to the program. It has even "hooked" alums up with permanent jobs once they have finished college or graduate school. The prep process continues to grow as long as kids need it, and neither prep not Gary Simons will turn their back on you.

Dr. Virginia Leibner
Homework Hotline

In the fall of 1991 McDonnell Douglas Corporation announced a merger of unprecedented size. Citicorp was involved, and so was KPLR-TV, a major St. Louis television station. In addition, before the merger could be completed, an agreement had to be worked out with one of the nation's largest unions. In spite of the number of participants, the diverse nature of the companies involved, the unusual role played by the union, and the emergence of the largest entity of its kind, the merger received virtually no national media attention. Cosponsored by Citicorp and KPLR-TV and operated by volunteers from the Missouri National Education Association (MNEA, a branch of the nation's largest teacher union) and McDonnell Douglas, the hotline will reach an estimated 500,000-plus students in the St. Louis bistate area alone. Students located in other parts of Illinois or Missouri can access it through a toll-free number, and hotline officials estimate that some 25,000 calls will come in on that line this year.

Six years before the merger, as curriculum director of University City High School, Dr. Virginia Leibner was constantly searching for ways to help improve learning conditions for students. She knew of a program in Atlanta in which teachers stayed after hours to answer questions about homework. While she recognized the value of such a program, Dr. Leibner felt her school did not have the resources to do the same thing. That's when she started paying attention to the representatives from McDonnell Douglas, University City High School's business/school partner.

"They were always asking how they could help us," remembers Leibner, "I knew McDonnell Douglas encouraged a lot of volunteer work among their people, so one day I suggested the hotline."

Working with McDonnell Douglas employee Gayle Clung Proffitt, Leibner formed a solid idea of what the goals and functions of the Homework Hotline would be. The hotline doesn't provide answers; it coaches students through solutions to homework problems. It doesn't replace classroom teaching; it emphasizes the importance of school and learning. Hotline volunteers are not responsible for teaching skills to the students but rather for providing guided practice that allows them to master skills. "Gayle and I clicked," Leibner says. "We shared an interest in developing the program, and her enthusiasm really helped the program take off."

According to Leibner, not all teachers were in favor of the hotline. "I heard every excuse in the book about why this wasn't good for the students. Teachers who were against the hotline felt we would be providing the students with an easy way out."

In the mid-1980s, when the hotline was just starting up, students were given Leibner's office number, and their calls were forwarded to a volunteer room at McDonnell Douglas. In this way, volunteers—engineers and computer specialists—could participate without leaving the complex. Volunteers were invited to visit the school during lunch to meet with the children, and the children had the opportunity to match faces with voices. The volunteer room still exists, but now it's also linked by an 800 number to the rest of Illinois and Missouri.

Today's hotline headquarters has more than just phone lines, however. There's a library of textbooks, and volunteers are prepared to provide help with reading, language arts, English, and social studies as well as math and science. And in addition to McDonnell Douglas volunteers there are volunteers from the MNEA, retired teachers who enhance the group's ability to talk directly with teachers and reassure them that the hotline can be a useful supplement to their work.

In a typical call students are asked to give their first name, grade, school district, subject, and then the problem. Volunteers begin by clarifying methods and procedures. Since the problem may simply be that a student has not understood the directions, there is first a general review of what needs to be done. In general, volunteers frame questions in a way that entails more than a simple yes or no response. The textbooks available in the hotline library also enable volunteers to turn to the exact page and problem. If the query runs into roadblocks, a student may be asked to speak to his or her teacher or referred to sources such as the public library. In some cases volunteers ask for the caller's phone number and call back after locating further information.

Although the hotline covers kindergarten through twelfth

grade, the majority of callers are between the ages of 12 and 14, and most of the questions involve math or science. Jim Mason, Homework Hotline coordinator and volunteer, reports that the hotline received 8,622 calls between September and December 1991, for a nightly average of 141.

According to Ted Tunison, director of special programs for the National Education Association, the Homework Hotline is "a program designed to help students move through their homework and not get discouraged by the frustration they may feel when a problem seems overwhelming."

So far the program is well received; the volume of phone calls bears this out. If students feel a sense of relief and comfort, however, just think how parents—years away from geometry, chemistry, and the subtle meanings of Silas Marner—must feel!

Sanford McDonnell
A Valued Program

Dr. Leibner drew on the assets of the McDonnell Douglas Corporation, University City High School's partner, to enhance a program that she developed to assist student scholastic development. Interestingly, a few years earlier, under the leadership of the corporation's chairman, Sanford McDonnell, the corporation initiated a program to assist school children citywide in another aspect of their development—ethical behavior—with its Personal Responsibility Education Program.

The program grew out of McDonnell's desire and work to get his boys to follow the Boy Scout code of ethics. Having encouraged them, however, he wondered how well he himself was following those noble principles, and, further, how well they were being followed by his company's employees. Since McDonnell Douglas is a major defense contractor, it needs to avoid even the appearance of unethical conduct. Government contracts can be waived or delayed for long periods if any questions of impropriety arise.

Convinced that McDonnell Douglas's future rested on the responsibility of his employees, he decided to establish a code of ethics companywide. "Not many businesses have a code of ethics," he says. "For me, a code of ethics is an 'I will' code. Most companies have a code of conduct, which is usually a long list beginning 'I will not.' " The first step was what McDonnell refers to as an indoctrination program: "We feel that since we push them so hard to meet the bottom line, we must push them equally hard to do it in an ethical manner." To this end, the company held employee seminars on ethical decision-making and distributed a series of pamphlets entitled *Taking the High Road.*

At first, employees didn't believe the program was to be taken seriously. "But over time and through example," says McDonnell, "we showed them we were serious. And the proof of its effectiveness lies in the number of letters and phone calls I've received from employees telling me how glad they are that the company takes such a firm stand on ethical decision making."

Encouraged by the program's reception throughout the company, McDonnell wondered whether the city's school system might benefit from similar instruction. His motivation to implement such a program in the public schools was based on two stated beliefs: "that young people want to know what is right and what is wrong" and "that when a person graduates from high school, it is more important that they be team players and have character than that they be brilliant. Brilliance is important, too, but a brilliant person who is unethical isn't worth much to the company."

Working with local educators and school administrators, McDonnell and other community leaders developed a program for youth that was initiated in seven St. Louis school districts in 1988. PREP (Personal Responsibility Education Program) is premised on "a critical—and increasing—need to help young people take positive responsibility for themselves and their community." To satisfy concerns over whose ethics are being taught, school principals ask teachers and parents to come up with a list of unanimously endorsed character traits. Trust, honesty, hard work, respect, and caring for others are just a few of what seem to be universally desirable traits in participating districts. Teachers have been pleased by the business community's interest in promoting character building and personal responsibility. "It makes it a heck of a lot easier," says McDonnell, "when teachers are able to work with kids who have learned to take personal responsibility not only for themselves but also for others."

Over the past three years PREP has flourished. Individualized programs have now been instituted in 21 school districts attended by a total of more than 160,000 students, and they enjoy strong community support. Participating faculty and administrators have also formed an organization called the Network that supports other initiatives (such as a 15-month Teachers' Academy for the training of master teachers).

PREP is supported by 30 corporations and foundations. Founders McDonnell Douglas, Emerson Electric, and the Danforth Foundation have been joined in their support of the program by a veritable Who's Who of St. Louis institutions—Anheuser-Busch, Pulitzer Publishing Company, and United Way, among others. Costs are shared by participating districts and private funders. City-wide the 1990–91 annual operating cost was $258,000.

PREP's full-time coordinator is Linda McKay. The organization is in the process of publishing *Personal Responsibility Education Program Handbook*, a comprehensive guide intended to be used by other communities interested in initiating a similar program. Princeton University's Class of '55, well known for its active involvement in social causes, is reviewing the possibility of implementing PREP nationwide.

Anyone who has taken an ethics course (at law school, business school, or at some earlier level of schooling) knows that the subject can be preachy and just plain dull. PREP avoids these pitfalls. Using such things as storytelling (particularly in the early years), colorful posters, music instruction, and professionally produced videotapes—all developed and implemented by experts—the program makes students enthusiastic participants.

And the hard work has paid off. Somewhat cautiously (a detailed, formal evaluation is still in progress), PREP released the following statement: "improvement has been noted in school drop-out rates, absenteeism, and academic performance." It's a result that echoes PREP's theme, a quote from the original education president, Thomas Jefferson: "Teach responsibility—they'll teach themselves the rest."

Wendy Kopp
Teach For America

Princeton University's Foundation for Student Communication publishes one of the largest student magazines in the country. As a former editor of that magazine, Princeton graduate Wendy Kopp remembers having a terrible time finding student contributors who could construct grammatically correct sentences. "As I put in all-nighters rewriting articles, I became more and more frustrated and began blaming our education system for not teaching these really bright people to write."

The idea for Teach For America (TFA) came to Kopp during a conference on the plight of American education. Based on the model of John F. Kennedy's Peace Corps, Teach For America's goal is to enlist outstanding, committed individuals to teach America's children. "Most graduating seniors don't even think about teaching as an option," notes Wendy. "All their lives they hear that teaching is not something you do if you have other opportunities. School districts, furthermore, don't recruit people who major in something other than education, so most people think that only education majors are allowed to teach. Yet there are lots of college seniors with strong academic and extracurricular backgrounds who would be wonderful teachers and who would love to assume a real responsibility and to make a difference in the lives of children."

Kopp decided to write her senior thesis on her vision of Teach For America because, she says, "I personally had the privilege to attain a wonderful education. Over the years I have come to feel really strongly that everyone should have that same opportunity and that many of society's problems would melt away if they did."

What Kopp describes as "an almost obsessive belief in the concept of Teach For America" drove her to move forward with her vision. With a well-thought-out plan in hand, Kopp believed the next logical step would be to establish Teach For America as a nonprofit organization. When Kopp mentioned this to Professor Marvin Bressler, chairman of Princeton's sociology department and Kopp's thesis adviser, he asked her where she thought she was going to come up with $2.5 million. "I told him that I didn't know, but that I was sure that Ross Perot would fund it," remembers Kopp. "After all, Ross Perot has the entrepreneurial spirit, and he's into education reform, and he's from Dallas, which is my hometown."

After approximately 10 letters to Perot, Kopp was surprised one day by a call to her office. When someone yelled out, "Ross Perot is on the phone," Kopp took it to be a joke. "I could hardly articulate a sentence. But I told him I was planning to be in Dallas the next week and would love to meet with him. He said yes, and on April 10—exactly one year after I turned in my thesis—he committed to give me a challenge grant of $500,000."

Today Teach For America is a national program, and Kopp serves as its principal fund-raiser and chief executive. Initially funded by major American corporations and foundations to the tune of $1 million, TFA's budget projections over the next five years reach an annual figure of $16 million. By the fall of 1990 Teach For America had a full-time staff of 10 and a board of advisers that included the CEOs of Equitable, Xerox, and Union Carbide. It also had more than 500 trainees—selected from among more than 2,500 applicants—placed in school systems in Los Angeles, New York City, Louisiana, North Carolina, and Georgia.

"Public schools in underresourced urban and rural areas have a desperate need for enthusiastic, committed teachers. So our goal was to recruit outstanding college seniors to fill that need," says Kopp. "We build an aura of selectivity, service, and status around teaching; we aggressively recruit individuals of all academic majors and ethnic backgrounds; and we facilitate their training and placement and provide ongoing support."

After its first successful year, Teach For America published a profile of its corps. It pointed out that Teach For America's "demographics defy national averages at just about every turn. While 82 percent of teacher education students are female, the corps is 56 percent female, 44 percent male. While 7.8 percent of teacher education students are people of color, 27 percent of the corps is. While teacher education students average 950 on the SAT, corps members average 1251." Clearly, Teach For America is reaching beyond the traditional pool of teacher talent.

Teachers are corps members for life, says Kopp, who hopes someday to see thousands of Teach For America alumni working to effect positive educational change in communities throughout America. "In the long run we hope to change the mindset of America—to influence them to view education as a challenging field that demands the attention of the nation's best minds, and to increase their commitment to providing all children in this country with equal opportunity to quality education."

Yet, for all its initial success there are clouds on TFA's horizon. As her thesis had predicted, financial demands expanded as recruitment, training, and fund-raising needs grew. What was not as clear when the initial plan was drafted in 1989, however, was how severely contracted public funds for education would become, particularly in the inner cities and poor rural areas, where the need for teachers is most pronounced. Often the first victims of budget cuts are the most junior teachers, members of Teach For America and other recent graduates among them. This problem is compounded by a shrinkage in private funding, brought on by the current recession. It is to be hoped that the program will succeed in spite of these problems. But then again, Teach For America has a history of confounding the experts.

Kopp's goals for Teach For America are lofty, but there can be little doubt that she will follow the advice she offers any beginning volunteer: "If you have an idea that you really believe in, don't let anything stop you from implementing it. Just create a concrete plan and stay true to your vision and move forward."

Teaching: More Than I Ever Imagined

I thought I had found the perfect answer to the question "What are you going to do when you graduate?" An organization was starting called Teach For America. It sounded a little unstable, but right up my alley. I applied and a few months later committed to teach two years in inner-city New Orleans.

Five hundred charter corps members were flown out to the University of Southern California's campus for an eight-week training program that involved numerous workshops, lectures, and a five-week student-teaching apprenticeship in the Los Angeles unified school system. For me it was all very informative, especially since I had only ever had one education class at Vanderbilt University [and it] actually scared me away from teaching.

The workshops on classroom management, discipline, and other aspects of teaching were based on theories that sounded great in an auditorium yet seemed very far removed from the actual classroom. In fact, not knowing what I would be facing in August, it was difficult to differentiate necessary or applicable information from everything else. Even the student-teaching experience, which for me involved teaching sixth-grade math and social studies to predominantly Latino students, did not prepare me for the challenge I would face in New Orleans.

I arrived in New Orleans, found a place to live, and began teaching seventh-grade math at Fannie C. Williams Middle School in early September. The school was a new facility in a fairly nice-looking neighborhood in New Orleans East. Its racial composition was roughly 85 percent African American, 12 percent Vietnamese, and 3 percent white.

The first day I faced my students, I was jerked into the reality of the situation. All of a sudden, I was the adult. Approximately 30 little faces looked up at me each class period, waiting for instructions. So I promptly fell into the role. I started explaining the rules and procedures as I'd been told to do in the workshops. I'd also been told not to smile until Christmas—I blew that the first day. Based on my own schooling experience, I came to this job with certain expectations.

I soon found what a different world I had come to. I started too soft. And kids, being very perceptive, started to take advantage of my naivete. I was constantly assaulted by stories that I just couldn't believe to be true: how this was Latoya's second year in seventh grade; how it was Lasundreia's third; how students cut class, "jumped" each other, and stole from one another.

And I found the problems weren't just with the students. Faculty absenteeism was a great concern. Effective administration was scarce. No sooner had I begun teaching and adjusting, organizing an educational environment within my classroom, than the threat of a teacher's strike became a reality. Their contract was up for renewal, and teachers were fighting for better pay. I decided I was there to teach and crossed the line. Outside, teachers were picketing, calling names, and even putting nails and glass under our car tires. Inside, things were even crazier. Students were just placed in classrooms, regardless of grade. Due to the shortage of teachers and substitutes, we were asked to keep one class all day and teach all subjects. All records in the front office were frozen. I taught students that weren't even enrolled in our school!

For three weeks this madness continued, until, finally, the school board and the union reached an agreement. This strike created a division, a great chasm, in the faculty. It continues even now and has weakened the faculty immeasurably. To this day, I have students say to me, "You were really mean during the strike, Ms. Schuh." Unfortunately, I had to be. With all the chaos outside the classroom, I tried to maintain a semblance of order inside.

That first year was filled with challenges, joys, and heartaches. One particularly painful incident occurred when I returned from Christmas vacation and was greeted by several of my students. "Ms. Schuh," they told me, "your boy's (sic) dead." Shawn James, a student I'd become close to over the last few months, had been shot by a carful of boys in a rival gang as he walked home from a Christmas party. Being only 23 years old myself, I was not accustomed to dealing with death, especially the death of someone I had taken for granted. Shawn was one of those students who constantly popped up at odd moments. I would be in the middle of a lesson when I would hear a knock on the door, only to open it and see Shawn's grinning face. "Just stopping by to say hey, Ms. Schuh."

For the summer of 1991 I applied to be a Teacher-in-Residence for TFA. TIRs, as we were called, were to go to the institute in Los Angeles and help new corps members better prepare themselves for teaching. In addition, we assisted new corps members upon their arrival at their teaching site. During a two-week induction, corps members are introduced to the city, find housing, jobs, and cars, and become established. I thought this would be a great opportunity to share the knowledge I had gained over the past year. While '91 corps members were eager to hear war stories and had many questions, anything we told them could not and would not substitute for their future classroom experiences.

TFA captures intelligent, confident corps members who all think they'll be "the one"—"the one" to go into the classroom, inspire and motivate the students, and change everything. This belief is what enables TFA's idealistic corps members to be successful, but it's also what makes it difficult to prepare them for the challenges that lie ahead.

My second year of teaching has been easier. They say experience is the best teacher. But it's still very challenging, at times overwhelming, and I catch myself losing sight of the big picture. These kids are in need of a good role model, of basic things like hugs, compliments, and a little caring. It's difficult to keep a focus just on education. Teaching in an inner-city school, I'm aware of tremendous inadequacies: financial, educational, and fundamental needs of these children have to be addressed. Despite all this, however, it would be difficult to ever secure another position in which I'd feel so needed, so challenged, so delighted and disappointed, so loved, so hated, and so very satisfied.

Sometimes I am very frustrated with Teach For America—how the program is run, how I feel dumped into this incredible, impossible situation with no easy answers. But then I remember Teach For America is just starting out. Recently I was at the Southeastern Regional Conference for TFA, and I heard a wonderful analogy. Just as idealistic first-year teachers want to do everything, help everybody, and reach each student, so TFA is a first-year organization, still trying to learn, unable to fix everything or help everybody.

—Christina Schuh,
Charter Corps Member,
Teach For America

Barbara Bush

Leadership and Literacy

At the first National Symposium on Partnerships in Education, Barbara Bush joined the small band on the Georgetown University campus to hand out partnership flags to everyone in attendance. She delivered a brief spontaneous talk that was received with great enthusiasm. Those who attended that symposium viewed Bush as one of their own: she had worked for decades on various projects to improve education in America.

A few years after that pioneering conference, Bush accepted the honorary national chairmanship of the newly formed NAPE and attended two more symposia. She is best known, however, for her work in promoting literacy.

Of the 23 million American adults who lack basic literacy skills, a significant number are parents. Within these family units, a child may never enjoy the experience of being read to, and the parent may never experience the joy of reading to his or her child. The resulting cycle is known as intergenerational illiteracy. On March 6, 1989, the Barbara Bush Foundation for Family Literacy was established to break this cycle. As the First Lady points out: "Parents are their child's first teachers, and the home is the child's first school. One of the most important things parents can do to help their children succeed in school is to read to them at an early age."

Bush serves as honorary chair of the foundation, lending her name and initiative to its success. During her husband's eight years as vice president, she participated in more than 500 literacy events across the U.S. Traveling to day-care centers, single-parent classes, classes for high school dropouts, centers for the homeless, libraries, and schools, Bush became intimately acquainted with America's illiteracy. As a result, she chose to dedicate her first official trip as First Lady to the fight against illiteracy. Before an audience of 200 at the Free Library of Philadelphia on February 7, 1989, she read Judith Viorst's *Alexander and the Terrible, Horrible, No Good, Very Bad Day*. That same year she served as chair of the Year of the Young Reader. Its motto: Give Them Books, Give Them Wings.

The mission of the Barbara Bush Foundation for Family Literacy is threefold. The foundation seeks, first, to support the development of family literacy programs, second, to break the intergenerational cycle of illiteracy, and third, to establish literacy as a value in every family in America.

Children love to be read to, Bush says. And children who are read to learn to read more easily than those who are not. Reading encourages the development of a child's curiosity, imagination, and vocabulary. Moreover, children who are read to develop longer attention spans, expand analytical skills, and are more successful communicators.

In December of 1991 Linda Katz and Marcia Moon, organizers of Philadelphia's nonprofit Children's Literacy Initiative, persuaded Bush to participate in "Mrs. Bush's Storytime," 10 half-hour radio programs featuring the First Lady reading children's stories and offering advice to parents. Approximately 200 radio stations, almost all Capital Cities/ABC-radio affiliates in large cities, broadcast the Sunday night series.

Moon, a teacher, notes that one out of two children entering kindergarten in urban areas is labeled "at risk" educationally. "It's because they don't have the vocabulary," she says. "That's why we're saying you have to get kids while they're young. The first five years are so critical." Katz, a librarian, adds this: "Reading a book and hearing a story on the radio is the same mental process. There's the same idea of imagining, the same comfort of hearing a voice and being able to embellish."

In the recently published *Barbara Bush's Family Reading Tips,* Bush relates an experience she had while visiting a library. "I met a young father in work clothes and boots, holding his daughter in his lap and reading to her. We talked about raising children, and he said, 'I wish I could give my daughter more—a nicer home, prettier clothes.' And I told him, "You're already giving her the most valuable gift of all. You're reading to her!"

A great deal of the foundation's work involves identifying successful family literacy programs. Once it has identified them, the foundation supports these programs through grants. In 1991 13 grant recipients were chosen from more than 600 proposals. The winners received grants that ranged in size from $14,000 to $50,000. A total of $500,000 in grants was distributed in 1991.

To continue its work the foundation has set an endowment goal of $25 million. This endowment will ensure the continuation of yearly grants as well as provide funds to cover the foundation's minimal operating costs. By encouraging programs that allow functionally illiterate parents to learn along with their children, the Barbara Bush Foundation for Family Literacy hopes to reduce America's illiteracy rate now and in the future.

Celebrities
as Mentors

In the course of working with partnerships in education, I have often seen students come in close contact with celebrities. At one point President Reagan visited a class at the Martin Luther King Jr. Elementary School just outside Washington, D.C., and later spoke in the auditorium. The students were fascinated. More recently, I saw Charles Ogeltree, a Harvard professor and trial lawyer, answer questions asked by a group of wide-eyed, teenaged moot-court competitors from Virginia about his experiences as Anita Hill's lead counsel in the Clarence Thomas confirmation hearings. When he finished his remarks, the students wouldn't let him go. But do these fleeting impressions have any lasting effect?

In 1990 a group of 10 students from Franklin K. Lane High School in Queens met with Marilyn Quayle, wife of the vice president and a former practicing lawyer, and Judge Randolph Jackson of the New York State Supreme Court. After the meeting, two of the students, both Hispanic males, said that "their lives were changed" by this contact. "You know," the first said, "the judge isn't such a bad guy. Maybe I'll go into the law field myself." The second agreed, adding that maybe the long years of study were worth it.

Both students were part of a program called SOAR (Student Outreach for Achievement and Retention). They hardly ever went to school, and when they did, they were highly disruptive. One came to the meeting with Ms. Quayle sporting a Mohawk haircut, and the other was visibly up for the occasion. But their teacher believed they had significant potential and could be reached by the visit. Two years later, while writing this book, I called that teacher to see if the meeting had truly touched their lives.

The teacher reported that both students had undergone significant changes in behavior and attitude. One received passing grades in all subjects for the first time ever; he is still in school. The second started writing for the school paper immediately after the meeting, greatly improved his attendance, and graduated from high school last year.

Whether the changes were caused by the meeting or the daily efforts of SOAR's excellent teachers and counselors we'll never know. But one thing is clear: although many programs involving celebrities are purely public relations gimmicks, some achieve significant results, as you will see in the stories in this chapter.

Marjorie Vincent

When Marjorie Vincent came to work for our law firm in the summer of 1990, we had no idea that she would soon become a future Miss America. She was a second-year law student at Duke with an impressive resume. In addition to earning fine grades, she was a member of the Black American Law Students Association (BALSA) and had done well in moot court. Her record also contained some unusual accomplishments. She was a concert-grade pianist, for example, and spoke fluent French. Her interviews, both on campus and at the firm, received outstanding marks: she was a highly articulate person with a genuine enthusiasm for the law. Her work in our corporate department revealed fine writing skills and high intelligence.

In the middle of that summer with the firm, she asked for permission to take a long weekend off in order, as it turned out, to compete for the Miss Illinois title, which she won. She went on to become Miss America in September (fortunately, we had already offered her permanent employment). The next spring, at my invitation, she spoke to the students at the Law and Justice Institute at Martin Luther King Jr. High School in Manhattan. She opened with a short talk and followed up by taking questions from students. They wanted to know just how she got where she was. Oddly enough, many of the questions centered on why she was interested in the law and what it was like to practice on Wall Street, not on what it was like to be Miss America!

Was Vincent's message received with greater interest because she was Miss America? Of course. Young people need heroes and heroines. This is particularly true for minority children, who until recently have been faced with a paucity of information about the heroic achievements of minority figures. A major part of being a mentor is being a role model. If the mentor is a person whose achievement has led to national acclaim, the impact may be all the greater.

The message of Vincent's speech at the Law and Justice Institute seemed to my ears to be particularly demanding. She talked again and again about hard work. She emphasized the time she had spent doing homework, concentrating on her studies, and practicing the piano. She spoke about the care with which she was determined to handle the responsibilities brought to her by almost instantaneous fame.

Bill Cosby

Bill Cosby's message to students is as unrelenting as Marjorie Vincent's. "Kids are too busy asking for $70 sneakers when they can't even play ball," he says. "But education is where your minds have got to be. The world is not going anyplace whether you pass or fail. It sits where it sits. You fall off." Also like Vincent's, though, Cosby's presentation ends with an element of hope. Education goes beyond school, he tells his audiences: "You all missed the point about education. It's not just to learn how to read, write, add, and subtract but to challenge yourself, to learn to express yourself creatively. College is not a place where you get a degree so you can get a job. You get an education so you can enjoy your life and improve the quality of your life. That's very important."

The remarks quoted above were recently delivered to more than 3,000 students and parents at two Rochester, New York, high schools. As spokesperson for Eastman Kodak's Color Watch System, Cosby was invited by Kay Whitmore, Kodak's chief executive, to speak in the city as part of the Rochester Brain Power Project (RBPP). Even with RBPP's full bill—sponsoring mentors, teacher salary increases, counseling, science and math tutoring, and a total restructuring of the schools—Whitmore recognized the influence celebrities can have. He knew that Cosby's frank talk would have an impact that hardly any other individual could achieve. And this is especially true when the message is delivered in the context of a system that can follow up on that emotional high.

Cosby has a great interest in education. He holds a doctoral degree in education from the University of Massachusetts and often weaved important educational themes into his television comedy series, "The Cosby Show." Together with GMI Group, Inc., a public relations firm, he developed "Bill Cosby's Picture Pages," videotapes and workbooks designed to help preschoolers hone their learning skills at home. He and his wife Camille have funded scholarships to predominantly African-American colleges (for full tuition, room, board, and textbooks for four years). In each of the college grants, which are among the largest college scholarships granted to public school students, Cosby's message is implicit. A 3.0 grade point average is required to gain an initial interview. A 3.0 average is needed to retain the scholarship in the first two years of college, and a 3.5 must be maintained during the last two years.

Cosby's best-known educational initiative is probably the $20 million he and Camille gave to Spelman College in 1988. More than half of this fund will go to establish the Camille Olivia Hanks Cosby Academic Center, and the remainder will endow chairs in the fine arts, social sciences, and the humanities. The Cosbys' gift—one of the largest ever given to an educational institution— brought deserved attention to Spelman and spurred giving to other African-American colleges, many of which were in financial difficulty. Johnnetta Cole, Spelman's dynamic president, commented at the time: "Quality in education is surely a process, but great God almighty, it sure is wonderful when a couple of folks come in and say, 'Let this push you along.' "

Arturo Barrios

Three world-class milers were introduced to the kids packed tightly into the high school cafeteria: Joe Falcon, 1990's top-ranked miler; Steve Scott, who had run 132 sub-four-minute miles; and Arturo Barrios, who has been described by *Runner's World* as "the first Mexican runner to hold a world record." Falcon and Scott received perfunctory recognition, but when Barrios was introduced there was an outburst of applause that rocked the room's foundation. Kids stood, shouted, and pumped their fists into the air. The high school where this took place is located in Chula Vista, California, just north of the Mexican border. Most of the students are Hispanic, which explains the outpouring of affection.

Later that day in the auditorium, Barrios told the assembled students about his own background: of his having come to terms with the fact that without education, many doors would always have been closed. Running gave him his opportunity, he said. Through running he earned a scholarship to Texas A&M and graduated with a degree in mechanical engineering. "Education is the only way you can improve yourself," he told the students.

He described why he and his fellow milers had come to Chula Vista High School: "We want to do what we can to help these kids, give them a hand so they can motivate themselves and do something with their lives."

In addition to using his time to help motivate kids, Barrios has created the Barrios Invitational, which since 1989 has raised more than $42,000 to provide college scholarships to students in need. Mexican Americans relate extremely well to his efforts because they know he understands their plight. And while he is keenly aware of his impact as a role model, Barrios also knows there's only so much he can do.

But in the true spirit of a mentor, he accepts this as a challenge and an opportunity. "If I can reach only one kid, then it's okay," he says. "Who knows? It might be the beginning of the beginning."

Arnold Schwarzenegger

Arnold Schwarzenegger now serves as chairman of the President's Council on Physical Fitness and Sports (PCPFS). At the time of his December 1989 appointment (when President Bush referred to him as "Conan the Republican"), Schwarzenegger stated that "personal fitness ought to be a national priority, just as it was 2,500 years ago when the ancient Greeks declared the importance of mind and body." He said that his mandate was "to reignite in this country the importance of physical fitness in the schools, at home, and in our workplace." He believed that he could "get physical fitness and physical education classes back into schools."

Of all the people who have held this position since President Dwight D. Eisenhower established it in 1956, Schwarzenegger may be the best suited. He brought himself to prominence first as a champion bodybuilder and then as a physically commanding movie star through an almost superhuman commitment to physical fitness and nutrition. He is now a major box-office attraction. Schwarzenegger's visibility is important to the PCPFS because of what he calls "America's well-kept secret"—the country's inattention to physical fitness education and the poor state of health of the nation's children.

Many people who are aware of the failings of our education system do not know that our public schools make hardly any effort in the area of health, where a great deal of attention is needed. As Schwarzenegger points out, "It greatly disturbs me that there is only one state, Illinois, that has a mandate on its books calling for daily physical education for all youngsters from kindergarten through grade twelve." The remainder of the states require physical fitness classes once or twice a week, if that.

Schwarzenegger differentiates between a school with a fine sports program and one with a fitness program. The idea that one student can lift 500 pounds or run 100 meters in 9.9 is no excuse for not having a program for the remainder of the students—for the cardiovascular systems, flexibility, and strength of all youngsters. He points out that the United States is barely among the top 20 nations in the world in terms of youth fitness.

Schwarzenegger acknowledges the significant recent increase in fitness programs for older people and the attendant proliferation of health clubs. He also comments on the president's personal commitment to jogging and physical fitness. But all of this interest, he points out, has had little or no effect on the health and nutrition programs for our young people.

In an era when so much attention is, deservedly, being focused on the nation's health costs, scant attention is being paid to early intervention. Schwarzenegger likens this situation to the television commercial in which a garage mechanic holds up an oil filter and says, "You can pay me a little now or a lot later."

To date, Schwarzenegger has focused significant attention on the need for fitness. He convinced President Bush to hold a "Great American Workout" on the south lawn of the White House to kick off National Fitness Month in the spring of 1990. Celebrity-athlete participants included Bruce Jenner, Rafer Johnson, Carl Lewis, Dorothy Hammil, and Carl Weathers.

Schwarzenegger has also undertaken a national tour and visited more than a dozen states to date. Typically, he meets with the governor (who, like Governor William Weld of Massachusetts, generally admits that he could lose 20 pounds and promises to undertake a personal fitness regimen) and visits local schools. While there, one of the things he points out is the junk food being sold in the school's vending machines.

As important as it is, PCPFS has very modest funding. Its annual appropriation of $1.5 million is buried in the Public Health Service budget. Schwarzenegger supplements this with a considerable expenditure of his own money. In addition, he has allied himself with groups such as the national Parent Teacher Association, the Governors' Council on Physical Fitness and Sports, the American Alliance for Health, Physical Education, Recreation and Dance, and many others.

Schwarzenegger has also thrown his considerable weight behind the Presidential Sports Award Program, in which individuals can obtain a certificate of achievement and various awards by meeting certain minimal standards. Although fewer than 25,000 Americans currently qualify annually for the awards, the number is growing. During Schwarzenegger's term the minimum age for qualifying for the award has been lowered from 15 (where it has been since the award was established in 1972) to 10. The first requirement in this campaign for fitness is to increase public awareness of the problem. Schwarzenegger may be just the man to do it.

Mentors
or Merchants?

Although standards for acceptable advertising in public schools have been developed, not all educational organizations have accepted them, and even those that have often ignore the standards. As a result, the inevitable advertising that occurs in the course of business-school partnerships often hovers near limits that are quite indistinctly drawn. How far should such advertising go? The names of sponsoring corporations become known to the students, as do the corporations' products. Students working at AutoZone locations, for instance, or at Rich's Academy when it was located in Rich's Department store, those working with Lego toys in the LEGO/Logo program, or students whose reading achievement earns a free pizza at Pizza Hut all become familiar with corporate partners as companies that sell products. This recognition ultimately adds up to positive public relations for the businesses involved.

Consider the controversy I first encountered at a board of directors meeting of NAPE (National Association of Partners in Education). At that meeting Dan Merenda, NAPE's executive director, reported on the "Milwaukee Conference," where standards for acceptable advertising in public school had been devised and debated. The NAPE board ultimately decided to table their decision on the Milwaukee standards until more information could be gathered.

Is there a point at which the line is crossed and the negative intrusion of the commercial component outweighs the educational benefit? Decide for yourself as you read the pages that follow.

Chris Whittle
The Whittle Companies

The NAPE board decided to deal with the advertising question in the course of developing broader general guidelines for partnerships between the public and private sectors. The company whose aggressive activities had unwittingly provided the major impetus for the development of the advertising guidelines was Whittle Communications of Knoxville, Tennessee, and its innovative chief executive, Chris Whittle.

Whittle Communications is one of the fastest-growing media companies in the United States. Known for developing innovative ways for advertisers to reach select audiences, Whittle Communications sends hundreds of thousands of short hard-covered books without charge to business people each year. The books present well-known authors—George Plimpton writing on the X-factor that all winners possess or Arthur Schlesinger Jr. writing on multiculturalism—and include ads from a single company.

Whittle Communications has also developed publications that are displayed on special racks in controlled locations such as doctors' offices. Doctors are offered the publications (and even the racks) without charge on the condition that very few competing publications will also be in the office. This form of advertising, the company argues, increases the advertisers' impact per dollar because they can direct campaigns to specific audiences. But what does this have to do with education?

Whittle has now directed its special kind of marketing at public schools.

The Whittle Education Network, according to its press packet, is "a comprehensive package of educational programming and video equipment designed to provide teachers with innovative tools to help meet the needs of today's students." The network reaches more than 6 million students and 400,000 teachers. Secondary schools receive the programming free plus $50,000 in satellite and video equipment needed to view the programs.

Education officials in California, Massachusetts, and New Hampshire have denounced Whittle's efforts as an attempt to buy the minds of America's children. The controversy revolves around Channel One, a daily news program designed to make world news relevant to teens. The program is produced by Susan Winston, a former producer of ABC's "Good Morning America." A typical show contains several news stories relevant to high school students, a profile of someone in the news, one segment of a multipart series on a topical issue such as the environment, and a trivia quiz. The news stories are reported by young professionals who often introduce stories by locating the area of concern on a map.

So far so good. Critics do not object to the ten minutes of Channel One programming devoted to news. What has caused the uproar are the two minutes devoted to advertising. Advertising dollars support the program and enable Whittle Communications to provide the satellite and video equipment without charge to the schools. In return, advertisers know they are getting the innovative, concentrated Whittle approach. They are marketing to a specific audience, 12- to 17-year-olds in a captive environment. The "captive" aspect is nonnegotiable; to receive the equipment, schools must agree to air nine out of every ten Channel One shows. By the fall of 1993 the Whittle Educational Network is expected to reach 12,500 schools and eight million students, which represents almost 40 percent of American teenage students. If participating schools choose not to air a program, administrators at the school must explain why.

Channel One offers students the opportunity to become aware of world events; it is also the first in-school program to be close-captioned for the hearing impaired. Other benefits to the school include Whittle's International High School Assemblies: the "Sharing Freedom" program linked U.S. and Soviet teenagers for a live discussion in November 1991. And the television equipment used by school systems in return for airing Channel One may be used for other purposes as well.

But many educators and parent/teacher groups argue that advertising in schools is unethical—no matter what the benefits. Students, who are required by law to attend school, have no choice but to watch Channel One. Susie Lange, a spokesperson for California Education Superintendent Bill Honig, put it this way: "[Whittle Communications is] in it to make money, pure and simple. I'm sure there are lots of commercial ventures out there that would like to get their hands on millions of little minds, just like Whittle."

Whittle supporters remind critics that advertising is not new to schools. Every time a student looks at a sponsored scoreboard, he or she is being exposed to advertising. Free book covers are sponsored by banks, and local advertisers support school yearbooks and newspapers. Whittle salespeople point out that the teenager watches an enormous amount of television each week. Will four more commercials each day, they ask, have such a powerful impact?

Many of the commercials that air on Channel One are often identical to those broadcast on regular TV, but increasingly commercials are being made specifically for Channel One. One of Channel One's advertisers, Burger King, appears to be approaching their advertising opportunity with a sense of responsibility. The Burger King ads feature teens living with the issues of unemployment, hunger, and homelessness. Problems depicted include everything from drug abuse to crime to boredom. Clearly these ads have a message: Stay in school. Each commercial ends with a voice-over stating, "Sometimes breaking the rules means staying in school," a variation of the Burger King slogan.

While education is controlled at the state and local level, Whittle has waged a street-by-street campaign to bring the program into public schools. Whittle has been careful to buttress its sales efforts with a prestigious twelve-member board consisting of educators and public figures who offer advice and direction to Channel One. The panel is headed by Terrel H. Bell, secretary of education under President Ronald Reagan. Other board members include industrialist H. Ross Perot and Albert Shanker, president of the American Federation of Teachers.

In order to prove the educational impact of Channel One, Whittle commissioned a study by Jerome Johnston of the University of Michigan covering 900 teachers and 4,400 students at 24 schools (half of which received Channel One). Although teachers rated the program highly for student interest and 60 percent would recommend it, the report found that the impact of Channel One newscasts on student knowledge was really "quite small." While participating A students averaged 6 percent better on a current events test than nonviewing A students, viewing added nothing to the scores of C students. Whittle Communications said it was "pleased" with the results of the study, but it was candid enough to admit that the report "presents clear challenges for improving our program and making it even more usable."

Channel One is only one segment of the Whittle Educational Network. The Classroom Channel, a nonprofit agency owned and operated by 43 public television stations, provides schools with more than 250 educational programs that are commercial free. Operation is made possible through a grant from Whittle Communications. The programs on The Classroom Channel are designed as a resource, and program information and teacher guides are sent free of charge to all participating schools. In addition, Whittle Educational Network launched The Educator's Channel in 1991. Its programs are designed to keep educators in touch with new developments in their field, in the form of classroom materials or teaching techniques.

Recently Chris Whittle went even further in his effort for reform by employing a blue-ribbon committee of leading figures (not all of whom are professional educators) to design new schools that Whittle intends to market to communities in place of conventional public schools. Whittle Communications and its corporate partners are prepared to spend up to three years and $60 million on this study. With characteristic flair, Chris Whittle has called this "The Edison Project."

Chris Whittle is now pressing his campaign for acceptance of Channel One in the classroom. Many school systems, desperately short of funds as state and local governments tighten their budgets, view Channel One as the only way they can obtain valuable television equipment. Ten thousand schools throughout the country now subscribe to Channel One. Educators, meanwhile, continue to debate the ethical considerations involved and the effect of the program on children. Although Whittle has established the audience for Channel One at eight million teenagers, the *New York Times* reports that the channel is "banned in New York and Rhode Island." Organizations such as NAPE and school boards at various levels will attempt to establish appropriate standards.

Supporters of Channel One see it as a perfectly appropriate enterprise in a free market economy. Meanwhile, fertile ground has recently been found in another geographic area. Russian Education Minister Eduard Dneprov has announced that Channel One will begin airing in six pilot schools in Moscow and St. Petersburg.

═══ Greener Academic Pastures ═══

Members of the Yale Corporation were shocked to learn that in late May of this year, immediately after the university's commencement ceremony, that Benno C. Schmidt Jr., Yale University's president, was leaving to become president of what the *New York Times* called "an untested venture" in the field of academia.

Schmidt indicated that he planned to leave his post no later than January 1, 1993, to become chairman and chief executive officer of Whittle Communication's Edison Project, a business venture financed with $60 million from Whittle and its partners Time Warner, Philips Electronics N.V. of the Netherlands, and Associated Papers of Britain. It is assumed that Schmidt's compensation for the post will be significantly more than the $187,000 per year he received at Yale.

The goal of the Edison Project is to design completely new schools and operate them at a lower cost than public schools. The company hopes to make substantial profits by charging tuition. It plans to build and open 200 schools combining day care and elementary education by the fall of 1996 and a total of 1,000 campuses offering day care through high school classes by the year 2010.

Whittle sources say yearly tuition will be less than $5,500, the estimated average cost per child in public school. Even though 20 percent of the students at these schools would be on scholarships, Whittle principal Chris Whittle anticipates the venture will have a high yield. This would have to be so, because Whittle estimates that it will have to raise $2.3 billion before it can open the first 200 schools. Chris Whittle believes the schools could produce nearly $700 million in revenues in their first year of operation. If the project reaches its goal of 1,000 schools, he maintains, revenues could reach $10 billion.

While a major premise of the new school system is "parental choice," the experts picked by Whittle to design them will be considering revolutionary pedagogic methods and technology. In discussing the venture, Schmidt says he knows he is taking a risk. Certainly, the project could fail. "It will have been a noble effort," Schmidt observes, "and I will no longer have tenure."

Ann Moore
Sports Illustrated for Kids

Can you imagine a sports magazine that features Bo Jackson relaxing by the fireplace reading Hemingway's *The Old Man and the Sea*? We all know Bo knows baseball. And football. And track. But how many adults know that Bo knows the American Library Association? Kids know. The ad featuring Bo Jackson reading Hemingway is just one of many proliteracy and proeducation ads to be found in *Sports Illustrated for Kids*.

Another ad, credited to the Children's Defense Fund, pictures a high school athlete in the locker room with his helmet on the floor and his books beside him on the bench. The caption reads "Develop your body and you could be a football player. Develop your mind and you could own the team."

The mission of *Sports Illustrated for Kids* goes beyond educating America's youth for sports trivia battles. Time Inc., publisher of *Sports Illustrated for Kids*, wants to prepare young Americans for life. According to Literacy Volunteers of America, 27 million American adults can't read. For a company whose survival depends on a literate public, these statistics are frightening. Executives at Time Inc., therefore, were faced with a choice: rely on the already overburdened public education system to reverse the trend, or put company dollars to work finding a solution. They chose the latter.

J. Richard Munro, chairman of the executive committee of Time Warner's board of directors, explains: "We sell more reading matter than any other company in America. But our efforts go beyond mere self-interest—they reflect our commitment to learning for its own sake and for the good of society. They also reflect our insistence on the ideals of equality of opportunity and government by an informed electorate."

The School in the Home

In 1973 Harper and Row published my book on home schooling, *The School in the Home.* Focusing primarily on the home schooling of preschoolers, the book is based on the techniques of A. A. Berle. His book by the same title was published in 1912, about the same time that the work of Dr. Maria Montessori was first introduced in this country. Berle wrote for a decade more, but unlike Montessori's, his methods were largely forgotten until I reintroduced his method to the small audience who read my book.

My own interest in the Berle method was fostered because his son, A. A. Berle Jr., had been a professor of mine at Columbia Law School. He was a remarkable man who had served as an aide to Woodrow Wilson at Versailles, as a member of Franklin Roosevelt's Brain Trust, and as an ambassador under Harry Truman. He was also a successful lawyer and law professor. He did all of this after entering Harvard at the age of 13 and earning his bachelor, master's, and law degrees all before he was 20. His brother and two sisters had similar academic careers (at Harvard and Radcliffe, respectively), and all of them had interesting and productive lives.

Although Berle's method of utilizing a child's curiosity as the touchstone of informal instruction could be practiced anywhere, I came to the conclusion that the dinner table was a productive venue, particularly for word games. This was often supplemented with reading materials found around the home. Today sociologists tell us that many homes, particularly in the inner city, do not have dining rooms or dinner tables or much reading material. The family area is frequently in front of the television set. Too often the children are there all day, except for the hours they spend at school.

"Sesame Street" supplies learning for very small children through the medium of television. Inducing one's children and other youngsters to watch that show and programs like it can be a useful entry into a number of subjects. The Discovery Channel and public broadcasting can furnish worthy shows for older children as well. The national Parent Teacher Association estimates that by the time a youth graduates from high school, he or she has spent 11,000 hours in school and 15,000 hours watching TV.

One hopes the dinner table may some day return not only as a place for eating but as a place for family discussion. In the meantime, while television reigns, TV sets and computer games can provide an even more direct form of learning. Classroom, Inc., is a computer-assisted learning system used in the schools at the present time and developed at Columbia's Teachers College. It can undoubtedly be replicated in the home. In addition to that, Dale Mann, a professor of education and education administration at Teachers College has devised computer games that can be played at home through television or on a computer and that can be a powerful method of instruction. Mann believes that by 1993 a new generation of technology will make this resource even more productive.

Enter Ann Moore, the assistant publisher of *Sports Illustrated*, who was asked to take charge of the new magazine. Moore's initial idea was to create a product that would help children establish a lifelong reading habit. She also wanted to make the product available to kids who couldn't afford it. Her viewpoint encompassed another factor as well. "I am a mother," she says, "and I suppose I share the concern of parents across America who have school-age children. We see a terrible lack of motivation. It's not that the kids can't read, it's that they're bored to death. At Time Inc. we thought that if we waved something as wonderful as *Sports Illustrated for Kids* in front of them, we could get them interested."

The magazine was launched in January 1989. Using interest in sports as a hook, it attempts to transfer kids' enthusiasm for sports into an enthusiasm for reading. With a target audience of children age eight and up, *SI for Kids* enters the lives of children at a critical period in their reading development. "I'd say anything that gets a kid to read and turn off the television is a good addition to a home," says Patricia Berry, *SI for Kids* assistant managing editor.

Early results show the venture to be highly successful. *SI for Kids* has an estimated monthly readership of 4,474,000 kids age 13 and under. The magazine reaches nearly one third of the almost 21 million Americans between the ages of 8 and 14. "One of our biggest challenges was to convince the backers that *SI for Kids* deserved the same quality of writers and photographers that *SI* uses," says Moore. "A big risk—and one that paid off—was taking people who knew sports and teaching them children; we didn't take people who knew children and teach them sports."

One of the reasons for the magazine's success has to do with its respect for its readership. "We hire consultants who advise us on what works with kids and what doesn't," says Craig Neff, managing editor of the magazine. Focus groups with kids were conducted to help the launching team discern what kids want from a magazine: no-nonsense features about kids' favorite sports figures combined with eye-catching, action-packed photography, cartoons, puzzles, and posters.

The magazine's regular departments include "Hotshots," a profile of a young athlete; "What's the Call?" a play-by-play section that allows kids to test their knowledge of game rules; "My Worst Day," a personal account contributed by a famous sports figure; "Tips from the Pros"; and "Letters," which prints reader responses to articles.

In addition to fun and games, *SI for Kids* is committed to covering serious issues in a responsible manner. The January 1992 issue covered Magic Johnson's announcement that he is infected with the HIV virus. The article informed kids accurately and reassuringly about AIDS: "It is almost impossible for any kid to get AIDS from doing everyday things, such as playing with friends or going to school. However, teenagers and adults do have to be careful about some of the things they do. If you are confused or worried about AIDS, you should talk about it with your parents or teacher. The best thing you can do for someone with AIDS is to give him or her lots of love and support."

Missing from *Sports Illustrated for Kids* is the condescending tone that kids too often perceive in their relations with adults. Neff asks his staff to write articles on a fifth-grade level but confesses he's not quite sure what that means. A team of three educators reads each story and offers advice concerning vocabulary and writing style.

══ The Milwaukee Conference ══

NATIONAL PRINCIPLES FOR
CORPORATE INVOLVEMENT IN PUBLIC SCHOOLS

Business/school relationships based on sound principles can contribute to high-quality education. However, compulsory attendance confers on educators an obligation to protect the welfare of students and the integrity of the learning environment. Therefore, when working together, schools and businesses must ensure that educational values are not distorted in the process. In an attempt to establish guidelines for the relationship, the Milwaukee Conference, a meeting of educators, business personnel, and partnership professionals held in November 1990, developed the principles listed below. Adoption of these principles by individual schools and school districts has been sporadic.

1. Corporate involvement shall not require students to observe, listen to, or read commercial advertising.
2. Selling or providing access to a captive audience in the classroom for commercial purposes is exploitation and a violation of public trust.
3. Since school property and time are publicly funded, selling or providing free access to advertising on school property outside the classroom involves ethical and legal issues that must be addressed.
4. Corporate involvement must support the goals and objectives of the schools. Curriculum and instruction are within the purview of educators.
5. Programs of corporate involvement must be structured to meet an identified education need, not a commercial motive, and must be evaluated for educational effectiveness by the school/district on an ongoing basis.
6. Schools and educators should hold sponsored and donated materials to the same standards used for the selection and purchase of curriculum materials.
7. Corporate involvement programs should not limit the discretion of schools and teachers in the use of sponsored materials.
8. Sponsor recognition and corporate logos should be for identification rather than commercial purposes.

Time Inc. has done more than put a quality children's magazine on the shelves. To ensure that their publication would reach 250,000 of the children who can't afford the $18.95 yearly subscription rate, Time Inc. solicited corporate sponsorship from 32 advertisers who collectively form the Reading Team. The Reading Team provides the funding necessary to allow children at risk to receive their own copies of the magazine each month of the school year. The program involves children at more than 1,400 schools selected from impoverished districts identified by the U.S. Census Bureau.

The economics of the children's magazine business are tricky, explains Moore. An 11-year-old child cannot consume a magazine of more than 100 pages. In order to maintain a healthy balance between copy and advertising, each issue shouldn't contain more than 30 pages of advertising. "We were very fortunate that the IBMs and Pepsis of the (advertising) world accepted the premise that reaching the underprivileged child was as important as reaching the upscale kid," admits Moore. "I worry that in times of recession, efforts such as the Reading Team won't get start-up approval."

Teachers in the 10,000 participating classrooms receive *Chalk Talk*, a free companion guide to the monthly issue. The guide, prepared by Bank Street College of Education in New York City, offers suggestions for incorporating *SI for Kids* into school curriculums. For example, when Scott Norwood, place kicker for the Buffalo Bills, was the guest columnist for "My Worst Day," he recounted his disappointment when he missed the game-winning field goal in Super Bowl XXV. *Chalk Talk* suggested that teachers ask students, "If you were one of Scott Norwood's teammates, how do you think you would have felt when he missed the field goal that could have won the Super Bowl?" The *Chalk Talk* companion to the January 1992 issue contains a section entitled "Talking with Kids about AIDS." Teachers are given advice such as "Listen carefully for signs of misperceptions and underlying fears." AIDS information resources for teachers and children are also provided.

SI for Kids has changed the way many kids view reading. Subscribers report reading each issue an average of seven times, and 85 percent of subscribers save every issue. In a study of Reading Team teachers, 99 percent said that the magazine is a good motivator in their classrooms. Ninety-eight percent of teachers felt the magazine helps their students develop a positive attitude toward reading. With results like these, it is clear that Time Inc. is not the only beneficiary. "*SI for Kids'* success proves that if you invest in a product and price it right, you've got a business," says Moore. "It is possible to do something good and have it pay off as a business decision."

Creating a
New School

Many educators believe that the basic problem in America is that our schools simply don't work anymore. Designed for the nineteenth century, they fall far short of dealing effectively with contemporary problems. The New American Schools Development Corporation (NASDC), a component of President Bush's America 2000 strategy, is trying to take on the problem of outmoded schools by selecting teams to draw blueprints and create models so that communities can "reinvent their schools."

Many of the 700 ideas NASDC chose from are based on work already in progress. ATLAS Communities of Providence, for example, is expanding on reforms started by Ted Sizer and James Comer (both are discussed in detail in this chapter). Some of the schools focus on particular subject areas: the Co-NECT School of Cambridge, for example, deals largely with math and science. Others, like the Modern Red School House in Indianapolis, where former Secretary of Education William Bennett heads the design team, tend to emphasize broader approaches like "classical education," with "old-fashioned" ideas about schooling often augmented with more recent pedagogic notions like multiage and multiyear homerooms where students have teacher-advisors.

These initiatives will pass through three phases on their way to becoming reality: search and design (through summer 1993), testing in school settings (culminating in spring 1995), and a nationwide implementation of a "new generation of American schools" (through spring 1997).

While most of these initiatives appear to be sound, we do not have to wait until 1997, 1995, or even 1993 to establish "break the mold" schools. As becomes clear in this chapter, such schools are

106

here now: promising public and affordable private schools are already achieving remarkable results. They did not depend on a wave of reform or a national program. In each instance they "started small." Based on a variety of educational theories, in some instances their operating premises appear to be in direct conflict. All of them, however, share the hallmarks of effective teaching and learning. In short, these are ideas that work.

Whether your community has been selected for the design and implementation of a new school, you and other like-minded private citizens can begin now to put an innovative school in your neighborhood and to transform your area's educational environment. Many of the model schools described here have already been replicated in various cities and states. You can start a school with space in a school building in your neighborhood, in your company's office building, or even in your own home. Although it may seem like a daunting project, it's being done in communities across the country—and it's making a difference *today*.

Marva Collins
Chicago's Westside Preparatory School

Westside Preparatory School in Chicago seems old-fashioned in its concentration on the classics. The students in grades one through nine read Milton, Chaucer, and Euripides and other Greek classics. They memorize and recite the poetry of Shakespeare. They study Latin and geometry. When asked whether this fare is too demanding, the principal responds: "What I teach now is no more than what was expected of students a hundred years ago."

Marva Collins had been teaching in the inner-city public schools of Chicago for 14 years when she established Westside Prep in 1975. The school was begun with $5,000 from her pension fund and the carpentry skills of her husband, Clarence, who converted the second floor of their home into a classroom. Textbooks were salvaged from schoolyard trash bins and supplemented by hand-copied versions of the cherished classics. Other school supplies were financed by Clarence's second job. The school was located in West Garfield Park, one of Chicago's poorest neighborhoods. Tuition was charged, but the couple often subsidized families who could not meet even that meager fee. From the start, Collins rejected federal grants, stating, "I don't want any experts telling me what's good for these kids or telling me how to teach."

Within two years Westside Preparatory School began to draw attention from the local media. Although many of the pupils had been performing far below their grade levels when they got to the school, one periodical reported that: "under [Collins's] firm tutelage [they] often jumped to as much as five years above their grade levels in most academic areas."

Collins was born in Monroeville, Alabama, in 1936. Her father, Henry Knight, was "the moving inspiration in [her] life." He instilled in her, she says, "a stubborn streak, self-reliance, and a strong work ethic. We grew up memorizing Bible verses, repeating The Lord's Prayer, and praying before each meal." Asked to compare her upbringing with that of a typical modern child's, she says only that "for almost every ill in our society, we can realistically point back to a loss of values.... Values such as determination, perseverance, keeping your word, honesty, and integrity."

Collins graduated from the all-African-American Eschambia County Training School in 1953 and four years later earned a B.A. in secretarial sciences from Clark College in Atlanta. She then moved to Chicago, married Clarence Collins, and began a 14-year stint as a teacher in the Chicago public school system.

Her experiences in Chicago's public schools—among the worst in the nation—introduced Collins to the difficulties faced by today's urban youth. "We must not forget the slaves who taught themselves to read in the dark," she says. "It was against the law for them to learn to read. But then today, in the light, in the name of progress, we produce boys and girls who cannot read and write." It is precisely because of such inner-city problems that Collins is a traditionalist.

"During the 1800s," she notes, "the readers had no giant pictures that dominated the text; books of the nineteenth century concentrated on strong stories that taught valuable lessons or detailed the lives of great thinkers, writers, and teachers. Teaching today has become too dependent on cutting edge theories as to what children can and cannot learn. Today's educators have drawn their focus too thin; hours of psychological probing are no match for a simple pat on the head or a truly affectionate hug."

Collins also teaches self-esteem. Her students learn a creed that she has composed, which includes such lines as "I was born to win if I do not spend too much time trying to fail" and "I will ignore the tags and names given me by society since only I know what I have the ability to become." Collins believes that such labels as slow, incorrigible, unteachable, and unmotivated have become "life sentences that incarcerate far too many children in a sea of failure." She lashes out at multiple-choice tests ("idiot workbooks") and the practice of seating children in "militaristic rows." Although she insists on high standards, she is also patient and spends considerable time with her students. She trains her teachers to do the same.

Collins is justifiably proud of her training work. "We have trained 2,600 teachers from all over the world and have thereby touched a million children," she said in 1989. The second school in the U.S. based on the Collins Method has been established in Cincinnati.

Today Collins travels throughout the country instructing teachers and lecturing on her beliefs. Her speeches are dotted with quotations from John Donne, T. S. Eliot, Martin Luther King Jr., John F. Kennedy, and countless references to great books. She's most frequently questioned about the classic nature of her curriculum. "Some ask, 'Why teach classical literature?' And I answer that though these works are old, they are not without merit in today's society. In the epic tale *The Iliad* warriors fought patiently for ten long years. In *The Odyssey* Ulysses's men learned that evil does exist, and overcoming it can be as simple as shutting it out of your life. Much in the same way Ulysses's men shut out the sound of the sirens' song by stuffing their ears with wax, our children must learn to shut out the lurid siren of drugs, alcohol, and sex in today's world."

She insists that "America cannot produce literate, thinking leaders of society by reading such banalities as 'See Sue, See Dick, See Jane.'... We must once again give our children substance, stories that deal with steadfastness [and] determination."

Joseph Kellman
Chicago's Corporate/Community School

On May 17, 1990, an op-ed article by Joseph Kellman appeared in the "Voice of the People" section of the *Chicago Tribune*. The headline read "Run School System Like a Corporation." Kellman's article supported the paper's editorial calling on Mayor Daley to resist pressure to name anyone other than the finest people possible to the local Board of Education. He also made some recommendations as to the composition of the board—he wanted a full-time paid board with varied experience—and called for an oversight authority to ensure that the full-time board performed in a businesslike and efficient manner. He summed up his position: "We Chicagoans must introduce the most effective management approaches known to business to run the $2.2 billion enterprise on Pershing Road [Chicago's Board of Education]."

Kellman's article might have been dismissed as just another letter by a businessperson frustrated with education's bureaucracy except that he has put his money where his mouth is. Kellman and the Chicago business leaders recruited by him have established their own corporate school dedicated to efficient management and businesslike methods.

The Corporate/Community Schools of America (C/CSA)—a single school with a pluralized name reflecting the national expansion ambitions of its founders—was established in 1988 in the Lawndale section of Chicago's west-side ghetto. More than half of Lawndale's residents receive public assistance, and more than a third of the housing is substandard. The murder rate in Lawndale is six times the national average; the infant mortality rate almost three times the national average.

Kellman is no stranger to the area. He grew up in the Lawndale neighborhood and left school after eighth grade to join his father's glass business. Kellman firmly believes that schools—even in a depressed neighborhood such as Lawndale, in an old building like its weathered two-story brick headquarters, and with the same or less financial support than is currently allocated per pupil in public education—can be made better if they are run using corporate management techniques. Kellman is putting his beliefs to the test. C/CSA is very much a research center, a pilot project dedicated to proving that Kellman is right.

Certainly Kellman knows how to succeed in business. He started with one retail store. Now he owns 80 in Chicago and has branches in 16 states. Last year Kellman's company, Globe Glass & Mirror Co., had sales of $100 million and "sound profits."

Kellman dreamed of a corporate school for more than 20 years, and in 1988 he had the good fortune to team up with Vernon R.

Loucks, chief executive of Baxter International Inc., the giant hospital products manufacturer and one of Chicago's corporate in-crowd. Loucks and Kellman raised the $2 million necessary to open C/CSA that September. The 105 sponsors they enlisted in the second $5-million phase of their fund drive reads like a Who's Who of corporate America. In addition to Baxter International, other leading Chicago-based corporations such as Sears Roebuck, Quaker Oats, and United Airlines climbed aboard.

The fund-raising effort drew considerable publicity, and more than 1,400 applications were received for the initial student body of 200. Kellman insisted that the pupils be chosen by lottery, not screened. He wanted no built-in advantage. In the same vein, he decided that the school would operate with the same class size—typically 25 students—as the inner-city Chicago public schools. By 1994, when C/CSA reaches its planned maximum enrollment of 300 students, it will, according to Kellman, operate at the same cost per pupil as the public schools.

Kellman's corporate jargon is sometimes a bit much: "The CEO [i.e., the principal] hires executives called 'teachers.' And they work on a product called 'students.' The bottom line is student achievement, as measured by the same tests used by the public schools." Kellman's sound business management includes keeping the school open year-round (closed only for three weeks in August) and insisting that the teachers can be fired if they do not do the job; there is no tenure). Although his carefully recruited teachers receive salaries that are 10 percent higher than their public school counterparts, Kellman insists that raises be tied to performance.

Although C/CSA's policies may seem like good old-fashioned business notions, many of the practices are highly innovative. The school stays open from 7 a.m. to 7 p.m., allowing the building to be used as a day-care center for working parents and giving the kids a place to work or play as an alternative to the often dangerous neighborhood streets. The school also serves as a center for vital services for the children and their families, with counseling and drug treatment programs and close links with hospitals and social, community, and welfare agencies. The staff includes a full-time nurse/social worker. School principal Elaine Mosley believes that the "greatest failure of the public schools" is the lack of similar on-the-premises outreach programs.

Because Kellman and his teachers believe that early intervention is essential, many of the children begin school at 2 years of age, a practice that Kellman maintains will reduce their future dropout rate by one third. Each room has a teacher and an aide. Children up to 9 years old are grouped in two-year clusters. C/CSA students receive no grades. Instead, progress reports are given at parent/teacher conferences. There is no formal curriculum. "Our approach," says school principal Elaine Mosley, "is to present children with experiences that are appropriate to them and that will generate success in learning."

There are skeptics. Chicago school reformer Don Moore wonders, "How long are these corporations willing to put up this much money? The history of these kinds of efforts is they fall on hard times after awhile."

It is too early to tell whether the C/CSA will succeed. But Kellman maintains that they'll "get the job done." His mission takes on a greater urgency in light of his view that without a turnaround in America's system of education within five years, democracy cannot survive. Some observers admit that good things are happening at C/CSA but doubt that the school can be replicated elsewhere. Kellman has an answer for this, too: "Sure, critics say we're achieving success with only one school. But you have to begin somewhere. It's like my business. I began with only one store. Now I have 80."

Leo Jackson
Atlanta's Rich's Central

The sixth floor of Rich's Department Store in Atlanta, Georgia, once housed a bakery. In 1982, however, Rich's Academy was established there, and the floor was closed to shoppers and opened to students. The name, Rich's Academy, somewhat grand, evokes images of an elite school rather than what it is: a "street academy" where educators seek to provide some of Atlanta's high-risk teens with viable alternatives to lives of crime, drug abuse, and welfare. The name and location of the school have changed, but the objective has remained the same: to bring into the mainstream young people who might otherwise not participate in the community at all.

The school began when Rich's chief executive noticed an increasing number of teenagers hanging around the store—kids who were spending their days on the streets rather than in school. "If we don't address this dropout problem today," he told himself, "we'll be taking care of these kids tomorrow."

Last year Rich's closed its downtown store, but the company's sponsorship of the school continues. In need of new facilities, the academy opted to unite with two Atlanta alternative schools, the Downtown Learning Center and Central, both of which were experiencing financial difficulties. Combining resources, the three entities became one and formed Rich's Central. Three hundred students are enrolled.

Schools such as Rich's Central, often referred to as alternative schools, are called into play when conventional schools aren't able to meet the needs of all youths in the community. Most likely, a Rich's Central student has already dropped out of school. Upon examining his or her transcript and file, a school social worker may recommend that the school system try to get this child back into school through the alternative education system. If, during an intake interview, the student expresses an interest in continuing education, the student is admitted to Rich's. The school's goal is to mainstream these youngsters back into regular public high schools within two semesters.

In addition to former dropouts, Rich's is also home to students who display behavioral problems such as fighting, substance abuse, or truancy. Rather than expel the youngster, the school system places the student in an alternative education site to receive more individualized instruction and attend counseling sessions. The third category of students at Rich's are those who have experienced some type of trauma or mental stress—the death of a parent or, perhaps, a friend who was shot. For whatever reason, the child is unable to function in a large group and is in need of therapeutic attention. Instead of being in a classroom with 32 students, he or she is placed in a class of 15. Whatever the reason for being there, the students at Rich's Central most likely would not have stayed in school were it not for the special curriculum and attitudes at Rich's. It is truly a school of last resort.

Barbara Vobejda, a *Washington Post* education writer familiar with Rich's Central, estimates that "as many as one third of the nation's 40 million school children were born into poverty, unstable homes, non-English-speaking families or minority groups with lower academic performance...." Without intervention, many of these children are destined for failure. The Education Commission of the States estimates that at least 15 percent of young people ages 16 to 19—about 2.4 million teenagers—will fail to become productive adults because they will drop out of school, become pregnant, abuse drugs, or violate the law. Vobejda believes that this group may be half of the high school population in some cities and that their number is growing.

Leo Jackson, who served as the administrator/principal of Rich's Academy, holds the same position at Rich's Central. Jackson was trained as a psychiatric social worker. "All our kids have one thing in common," he says, "poor academic performance. And, of course, that's understood. If you don't go to school, you can't learn. If you come to school and are constantly being put out of class, you can't learn. And if you've got other stuff on your mind, you can't learn."

The faculty and counselors at Rich's know that their students require more attention than average students. Until Rich's students are able to focus their attention and overcome the social or psychological problems that engulf them, no learning will occur. Rich's support staff, which is larger than that of public schools, helps to ensure that the kids will get the counseling they need. "Once we have addressed the psychosocial maladies," reports Jackson, "then maybe we'll see a grade point average increase."

Rich's Central also provides special social services such as health care and counseling. The programs are available largely because the school is administered by Exodus Inc., a privately funded agency that operates four alternative high schools in Atlanta. Exodus is associated with Cities in Schools, a national organization that runs similar programs in 22 other cities, including Washington, D.C. Cities in Schools founder William E. Milliken sees schools as more than educational institutions; he sees them as a delivery center where social services can be provided to children in need. Counseling and support are a major part of the Cities in Schools program. "It is not about reading or writing or arithmetic," Milliken says. "It's about loneliness."

From its inception Rich's Central teacher salaries have been paid by the Atlanta public school system. The public school system also supplies all the materials needed to educate the students. The courses offered are the same as those available in a mainstream school; and when a student graduates, he or she receives an Atlanta public school diploma.

Canveta Burke, Rich's Academy Class of 1988, was a typical student. She became pregnant at 14 (about 15 percent of Rich's students are teenage mothers) and would be classified as poor by any economic measure. Concerned about her pregnancy and ashamed of the fact that her clothes were old and no longer fit because of the weight she had gained, Canveta dropped out of school. It wasn't until she was introduced to Rich's that she learned she could avoid welfare, might go to college, and might even have a career as a singer (her dream). "They brought me out of my cocoon," she says.

Each morning students begin their day with an informal counseling session known as family group. Male and female staff members are paired as "parents" in an attempt to fill a void in the lives of many of the students whose single parents are unwilling or ill-prepared to counsel or comfort them. The family group tries to set the tone for the day by encouraging the students to deal with their problems and frustrations. Counselors help students face troubling issues and feelings by conducting activities such as "lemon squeezes." The lemon squeeze begins with the statement "What I like most about you is...." and ends with "However, what I like least about you is...." By engaging in role playing, students are able to sharpen interpersonal skills that may not develop at home.

When students first arrive at Rich's, they are told not to worry about academic performance. "We say, 'Let's get you together. Let's deal with some of these needs that you have. I'll stick you in an environment where you're guaranteed to learn,' " says Jackson, who doesn't overwhelm the emotionally fragile students by making heavy academic demands. When students are ready, he says, they put forth the extra effort. Instead, he tells them, "Come to school every day. Pay attention. I guarantee you'll pass. You've got all this brain power that just absorbs knowledge. It'll happen."

Jackson's attitude toward grades has developed over time. He relates an experience early on in his career at Rich's with a young girl who came running into his office to show him her report card. "I looked at the report card and said, 'Big deal. This is straight D's.

You've got to do better.' She put her hand on her hip and told me, 'I don't know what you're talking about, but this is the first report card I ever got that ain't had no F's.' So I said, 'Well, this is progress! Let's celebrate this report card!' " Jackson recognizes that success at Rich's Central takes many forms and must be recognized at every level. "Applaud the D's," he advises, "because if we never applaud the D's, we'll never get an opportunity to applaud the A's."

Rich's rejects the rigid age-bound grade levels that prevail in most public schools; ability and progress define its classes. The school goes to great lengths to avoid categorizing students in a way that will make them appear to be above or below their peers. The rate at which academic material is presented is often exceedingly slow, and students are given ample opportunity to make up assignments. Whenever possible, there is focused one-on-one contact between staff and students. Teachers frequently take their students home with them, letting them play with their own children, taking them out to eat, even buying them clothes.

Although the social services component of Rich's Central is responsible for professional counseling, Jackson maintains that teachers have to have a high level of understanding, tolerance, and patience. "Every one of our kids represents a potential disruption," he says. "Every child is here because he or she has had some kind of problem." When students express anger, frustration, or hostility in the classroom, Jackson sees those emotions as symptoms of deeper problems. Often, he says, outbursts are the result of embarrassment: an 18-year-old is not going to admit he can't read. "He's carrying this horrible secret around," he says, "and misbehavior is the result."

Rich's Central does not have funds for detailed tracking of students after they graduate, but preliminary results are encouraging. With a population of almost all at-risk students, Rich's has a graduation rate of 65 to 70 percent. But the school also measures itself in terms of what has been avoided: lives of crime, unemployment, and welfare. Whatever the criteria, the school does have its successes. Sharrod Brown, a 1987 graduate, graduated from Columbia University in 1992 with a B.S. in political science. Pending acceptance to the program, Brown hoped to join the ranks of the Teach for America corps in the fall of 1992 to teach disadvantaged urban high school students.

The Dean of the New Professionals

Cities in Schools is a philanthropic enterprise established in 1976 to assist schools and businesses establish effective partnerships. Rich's Academy is one such enterprise. Burger King Academy, which since 1979 has opened alternative programs in 17 communities from West Palm Beach to Anchorage, is another. A third, the Metropolitan Corporate Academy, an alternative school in Brooklyn based in part on the Rich's and Burger King models, was spearheaded by Goldman Sachs, the international investment banking firm.

The founder of Cities in Schools is William E. Milliken, who, after years of experience as a street worker in Harlem and New York's Lower East Side, was able to multiply his own effectiveness through a number of organizational frameworks. Milliken was involved in the formation of Exodus Inc. in Atlanta in 1971 and in the establishment of Postal Academies, staffed by U.S. postal workers in the 1970s.

During the Carter administration he served as White House advisor on youth issues and believed then as he believes now that the needs of potential dropouts go far beyond education. Those needs include health care, counseling, and job training—all services that can, and should be, available through schools. Cities in Schools operates more than 60 dropout prevention programs, most of which are located in existing schools. Some, however, such as Rich's and Burger King, work through corporate academies.

If his job as a street worker has helped Milliken understand the problems of today's troubled youth, his familiarity with many people who work on Wall Street has helped make him more effective. The chairman of Cities in Schools for most of its existence has been Robert Baldwin, formerly the head of Morgan Stanley, a premier investment banking firm. Milliken's friendship with Geoff Boisi, who recently retired as managing director of Goldman Sachs to devote his full time to working with public schools, has proved to be a boon to the numerous public education partnerships supported and operated by Boisi's former firm.

Jim Renier

Minneapolis's New Vistas School

Dr. James J. Renier is chairman and chief executive officer of Honeywell Inc., a manufacturer of, among other products, home thermostats and aircraft instruments. His office in Honeywell's corporate headquarters in Minneapolis is much like any other executive office. His daily routine is similar to that of other busy corporate chiefs too, except that on many mornings, he likes to position himself to see the school van arrive and drop off students who attend the New Vistas School located in Honeywell's building.

The father of eight, Renier has had an interest in children that has led to an unusual effort by his company and to his persistent speeches and congressional testimony on the need for federal aid for children. In Minneapolis Renier chaired a special committee of 22 community leaders who worked in conjunction with the United Way of Minneapolis to assess the barriers to adequate early childhood development within the community. It's solution was Success By 6. Launched in 1989, the program is a comprehensive community initiative that targets early childhood development. It unites business, government, labor, education, and health and human service organizations and has three goals: to obtain widespread community understanding of the crisis and commitment to the healthy development of young children, to increase participation and improve service access for all families with young children, and to expand public/private collaborative efforts that develop an integrated and culturally sensitive system of service.

A man of action, Renier founded the New Vistas School, which is modeled after the much larger New Futures public school in Albuquerque, New Mexico, and is funded in part by Honeywell. The profile of students at both schools is similar: young mothers who bring their babies with them to the school.

Thirty-one students are enrolled in the school, and they have 34 stroller-age children. Their day at New Vistas begins at 9 a.m.—almost two hours later than the starting time at the city's conventional high schools. This gives the young mothers more time to get themselves and their children ready to begin the day. On arrival at New Vistas, the students deliver their children to the day-care center adjacent to the classroom and give the children breakfast. Classes run from 9:30 a.m. until 4 p.m. in space donated and renovated (at a cost of $200,000) by Honeywell.

In addition to a basic core curriculum, New Vistas students take classes in family planning and child development. Students also spend one day a week helping in the day-care facility. The school format does not include lectures or classes as such. The students work at computers (donated by IBM) and set their own pace. Two teachers and various textbooks are supplied by the Minneapolis public school system. Volunteers provide assistance.

Sixty-two-year-old Renier justifies the company's special effort in economic terms: "For every dollar spent on child care and education the taxpayer saves $6." He cites a five-year-old study by the Minneapolis Planning Department which found that 50 percent of adolescent mothers were on welfare five years after their pregnancies. "To the degree that we can avoid these things, we are helping all industries' bottom lines," he explains. "It's one of the most self-serving things in the world for a corporation."

Furnishing special services for the poor, early childhood education, and social and health services at one school is not unique to New Vistas. The same effort is being made at New Futures (and Rich's Central, as you read earlier). At New Vistas, however, the students get daily exposure to the business world, including unpaid internships in the credit union and paid summer jobs. Honeywell employees also volunteer as mentors to the students.

The New Vista students represent a distinct minority of the teenage mothers and pregnant students in the Minneapolis school system. There were 1,331 girls in this category in 1989, most of whom preferred to attend regular schools where they could enjoy conventional high school life. Students who have volunteered for New Vistas are, in the words of one observer, fiercely focused on just two things: taking care of their babies and obtaining a diploma.

Interestingly, being unwed teenage mothers—until now a virtual guarantee of life in the welfare cycle both for themselves and, most likely, for their offspring—has led many New Vistas students to enhanced self-esteem and a desire to help others similarly situated. For example, 17-year-old Tammy Stofferahn had dropped out of school at 15, run away from home, become involved in drugs, attempted suicide, and given birth. Currently a tenth grader, Tammy entered school after emerging from a rehabilitation clinic. At first she was withdrawn and depressed, but she liked the teachers. "They talked to me," she said. "They made me feel good. They taught me to take care of my baby." She has found her course work easy. "I've been zipping through everything." Now she is looking toward graduation and after that a career. "I kind of want to work with children and errant teenagers," she says.

Another 17-year-old, Angela Carter, the mother of a year-old son, is also bent on a career in which she may be able to help others. "I'm going to college next spring to be a nurse," she says.

Although most of the students receive Aid to Families with Dependent Children and food stamps, and in some cases have avoided getting married in order to stay on welfare, they now set their sights higher than a lifetime of maintenance at government expense. Even their public aid is being used more productively. Three of last year's graduating class of five will use public assistance to enter the University of Minnesota. The fourth has enrolled at a local community college. The fifth is already off welfare, working as a retail store clerk. While the dropout rate for teenage mothers in the city's other schools is between 40 and 50 percent, it is only 25 percent at New Vistas. The students seem to gain a new energy; they want to move through their courses as quickly as possible and get on with life. Sixteen-year-old Quantina Beck intends to graduate next year and hopes to work with animals. She knows that her education will not end with her schoolwork, however. "I want to go to work and help my daughter grow up," she says. "We'll just have to finish growing up together."

Ted Sizer
The Coalition of Essential Schools

Horace Smith is well-known to America's teachers. His subject is English. His school is in the suburbs. He is responsible for 120 students in his various classes (and feels fortunate that he doesn't have the 175 for whom city teachers are often responsible). Smith's day begins at 5:45 a.m., which allows him 40 minutes to drive to school (he can't afford to live in the suburb where the school is located) and another 40 minutes to relax and review the day's lesson plan before classes begin. After his classes end at 2:30 p.m., Smith generally does some extracurricular work with the school theater group, puts in two hours behind the counter at a family store, and spends another hour after dinner reviewing papers.

Smith believes that it's important to review a short piece of writing by each of his students but is able to spend only five minutes per week on each student's work. Even this adds up to ten hours a

week. Added to his 32 hours of class work, administration, preparation, and extracurricular time, Smith puts in a 42-hour work week
(not including lunch periods, supervisory duties, coffee breaks,
and travel, of course). For this he receives $27,300, plus some con-
tribution to his pension fund. Smith has been teaching in the public schools for 28 years.

Horace Smith is not a real person. He is famous, particularly
among America's teachers, because he is the central figure in
Theodore R. Sizer's book *Horace's Compromise: The Dilemma of the
American High School.* Although Smith isn't a real person, his di-
mensions are grounded in hard fact. Ted Sizer's book is one of several emerging from a five-year-long national inquiry into adolescent education called "A Study of High Schools."

While his colleagues in the study concentrated on in-depth in-
quiries into particular areas, Sizer attempted to gain a broader view
in his visits to 80 schools. He describes Horace Smith as "a blending
of people and places ... all [his] classes are 'real' classes.... My device ends up somewhere between precise journalism and nonfic-
tion fiction."

Sizer brings a variety of relevant experiences to his work. In his
midfifties, he has a personal curriculum vitae long enough to encompass three or four careers. He has served as dean of the Graduate School of Education at Harvard University, headmaster of Phillips Academy in Andover, teacher of history, author, and editor
and is currently chair of the education department at Brown University and a trustee of Columbia University Teachers College. Recently Sizer embarked on still another career: director of the Coalition of Essential Schools.

After the publication of *Horace's Compromise* in 1984, Sizer was in
tremendous demand as a speaker. He was not content to be a critic
of the system, however. Instead, he organized the Coalition of Essential Schools, which initially involved seven public and private
schools from Maine to Texas. Although the exact nature of their
curricula and administration may differ, all of the coalition schools
attempt to implement the nine common principles detailed in the
book. Today, the coalition includes more than 200 schools.

Amid the plethora of proposed reforms and the fads that often
engulf American education, Sizer's view appears surprisingly simple. "Curiously, most of us, lay people and educators alike, tend to
underrate teaching," he observes. "We rarely underestimate the

difficulties of learning. Having had to learn, we know that it is a complicated and unpredictable business. Likewise, the craft of provoking us to learn—the act of teaching—is itself complicated."

Sizer places teachers in a triangle together with students and the subjects of their study. He states his basic premise as: "We know that the game of school learning is won or lost in the classroom, and we feel that America's present system of schooling makes winning often very difficult indeed. Any improvement in American high schools must take into account the stubborn realities of this triangle. Understand the triangle and the subsequent necessary steps become clear."

Sizer would restructure the basic academic program of public schools into four large departments: inquiry and artistic expression, mathematics and science, literature and the arts, and philosophy and history. He believes too many courses are offered today. Their objective is coverage more than mastery of intellectual skills. His goal is "to teach students to think." If secondary education is to be truly effective, he maintains, high schools should be open only to students who have demonstrated basic competence in literacy and mathematics and who possess an understanding of civic responsibility. Sizer abhors lectures; his proposed classes would use the Socratic method. The average school day of seven 40- to 50-minute classes—a system born of America's industrial revolution in the nineteenth century—would give way to subject-oriented exercises that might last a day or an hour. Teachers would plan the week's classes in faculty discussions at the beginning of the week, and classes would often involve more than one subject.

Sizer's ideas are revolutionary. They represent a huge change from the way schools have been conducted in this century. When he announced his plans for the Coalition of Essential Schools, the *Christian Science Monitor* described him as a "visionary former headmaster and Ivy League dean." The paper also observed that a "common response to *Horace's Compromise* was that Sizer had "both feet planted firmly in the air." Still, more schools join the Coalition of Essential Schools each year, and Sizer's supporters include an abundance of respected educators from all over the country. His new book, *Horace's School: Redesigning the American High School*, which focuses on the design process and lessons learned from the Coalition of Essential Schools, should bring even more schools into the coalition.

Although it is difficult to precisely measure the results to date, some of the schools that have been involved for nearly five years in the coalition find that students have higher self-esteem, sharper thinking skills, and a confidence they didn't have before.

In an "essential" school a number of the pillars of contemporary education would disappear. These include the teacher standing in front of a blackboard; students sitting in row after row of chairs, referring to textbooks designed not to offend anyone; and the taking of multiple-choice tests that in Sizer's words, "come in hermetically sealed packages and go puff when you open them." Bells would not ring every 50 minutes. Instead, schools would concentrate on teaching a few essential subjects well, and teachers would be coaches who inspire, prod, guide, and otherwise help students learn. Students would sit in small groups, or the classroom might be forsaken for the school lawn or a nearby park. Since no teacher would have to get to know more than 80 students, English teachers might have to help out in social studies, math teachers with science, and so forth. Diplomas would be awarded not on the basis of accumulated courses or time and place but on exhibitions of what the students had learned. "We have learned much and changed much since the 1800s," Sizer says, "and we can do better than continuing to operate a school designed when Henry Ford's Model-T was new."

The Coalition of Essential Schools includes a wide spectrum of institutions. On one hand we see a pioneering effort in East Harlem reinvigorating a school in an area where simply getting the student to attend is a major challenge. On the other hand there is Lindblom Technical High School on the southwest side of Chicago, which announced in 1990 that it was joining nine other Chicago high schools in the Illinois Alliance for Essential Schools.

What is remarkable about Lindblom's decision is that it was already viewed as one of the top five high schools in Chicago. It had one of the lowest dropout rates in the city and above-average achievement scores. A large percentage of its graduates went on to college. In announcing the school's participation in the coalition, principal Lynn St.James made it clear that she was not pleased with the status quo. "We're going to stomp out frustration, apathy, discouragement, burnout, absenteeism, anger, and withdrawal," she said. Under the new system, Lindblom's teachers have a lot more flexibility and have more expected of them.

In emphasizing intellectual development rather than coverage of information, Sizer acknowledges the rapidly changing technology of the modern world. New industries and new jobs are created more frequently now than in the past. Governor Garrey Carruthers of New Mexico, one of the nation's "Education Governors," focuses on this point: "Most kids in school today will have to be trained and retrained half a dozen times. We've got to teach them to learn."

Debbie Meier and the Central Park East Schools

On a recent visit to Manhattan's Central Park East Secondary School, where Deborah Meier and Paul Schwarz are codirectors, I was impressed with the effectiveness of this school—a member of the Coalition of Essential Schools—as a learning center. When Debbie Meier asked me whether the school was different from what I had expected, I answered that it was less raucous than I had anticipated. With everything that had been written about the excitement of these schools, I had expected more noise. There was a definite enthusiasm, but there was also a sense that each student was involved in very serious learning. In one physics class the students were seated at tables in twos or threes planning a field trip to Great Adventure Amusement Park. Under discussion was how to develop a device to measure the speed of the rides.

The atmosphere is different at the Central Park East school. The teachers have, in effect, "reinvented" it. They have done so by starting small, while school was in session. As Meier points out, "unlike most industries, we cannot retool by closing down the factories and sending all the workers back to school. We need to do everything at once. It is driving while changing the tires, not to mention the transmission." While money is needed for this process, Meier reverts to a military analogy that is so often pursued in the education wars: "Unpaid volunteer armies can defend their homeland better than highly trained and equipped mercenary troops."

There are no bells, no seven-period days, no changing courses midyear. The faculty gets to know students. They are on a first-name basis. There is a collegial atmosphere. The students are made to feel safe. Teachers work in a number of disciplines rather than just a single specialty.

In the course of my tour I learned that progress is measured by a system of 14 portfolios (rather than standardized tests) used to show what students have learned in such areas as creative thought, lucid writing, self-expression, and reading skills. The portfolios provide a basis for student evaluation by performance-based assessment methods.

One day each week, every student participates in community service, some of which involves keeping track of hospital reimbursement forms or working with older people. Every day begins with a "Family Group" (something like the homeroom I remember from decades ago but far more interactive). Every teacher seems to be a generalist and part-time counselor. Parental involvement is expected and encouraged.

The results are impressive. Ninety percent of the students in the Central Park East school complete high school. A far higher than average number are going to college. And the students, in learning to learn, seem to get more out of their lives and appear, in Meier's words, "far better able to join society as productive and socially useful citizens than are their counterparts."

James Comer
The Comer Method

The central figure in *Maggie's American Dream* is not, like Horace Smith, fictitious. Maggie is, in fact, the mother of the book's author, Dr. James P. Comer. Maggie made it her business to become involved in the education of her four children, who collectively hold 13 academic degrees. And now Maggie is the inspiration for an educational system that has brought thousands of African-American children from despair and failure to success in school and in life.

The School Development Program, equally well known as the Comer Method, began in 1968. Dr. Albert Solnit, then director of the Yale Child Study Center, invited Dr. Comer, who was then associate dean of the Yale University Medical School, to become involved in a school-intervention project. Solnit was especially concerned about two schools in New Haven: the Martin Luther King Jr. School, which served about 300 students in kindergarten through fourth grade, and the Katherine Brennan School, which served 350 pupils from kindergarten through fifth grade. Almost all the children in these schools were African-American and poor. The schools had high dropout rates, low test scores, and ranked near the bottom among all city schools. The staff turnover rate was an alarming 25 percent. Chaos prevailed in the classrooms.

A graduate of Howard University Medical School and a practicing psychologist, Dr. Comer brought considerable expertise and an intimate knowledge of the New Haven community to the task. Nevertheless, he was shocked at what he saw when he first visited the two inner-city schools where his work would begin. Children were yelling, screaming, and fighting with each other and openly insulting the teachers. "What I saw was almost unbelievable," he wrote. "I just couldn't bear to admit the extent of the problem."

Still, Comer could not have been entirely surprised. An African-American, Comer grew up in East Chicago, the son of an Indiana steel worker who died when Comer was six. His own boyhood schooling was certainly no guarantee of success. In fact, he remembers the very different fates of three classmates whose backgrounds and aptitudes were similar to his own: one died at an early age from alcoholism, the second spent most of his adult life in jail, and the third spent virtually all his life in mental institutions. Looking back, Comer felt that the difference in his life was brought about by the active role his mother played in both his life and his schoolwork.

If Ted Sizer's system could be described as teacher-focused, James Comer's system would certainly be characterized as parent-focused. After his early visits to the target schools, Comer found much more wrong than classrooms that yielded low test scores and high dropout rates. He also detected a disturbing attitude among the teachers: they held much lower expectations of their students than did teachers in more amenable situations. To Comer this condition was most troubling of all. "If these kids have been made to feel dumb," he said, "then they have low expectations and little self-confidence—and these things affect performance."

With the full support of local school officials and supplemental funding from private sources, Comer set about establishing a new model at the two schools. He hoped to turn them into effective schools, a key element of which would be parental involvement. Another principle was the establishment of higher expectations. "If a car rolls down the assembly line and doesn't have a wheel," he says, "you don't assume something went wrong with the car and give it an F or a D. The assumption in this model is that all kids can do better."

Washington Post education writer Barbara Vobejda has described the Comer method as follows: "Team management of each school by the principal, teachers, and parents who, together, identify problems and decide how they should be corrected; increased parent involvement by hiring parents as teacher's aides; a mental health team of school personnel to deal with attitudes, morale, and other issues that affect students and the school environment; a new curriculum and a calendar of events designed to help low-income students learn the social skills that make them better able to participate and be accepted at school. Students read newspapers and telephone books and learn such things as how to participate in elections and how to write letters and speeches."

Once the Comer method had been implemented, Diane Garber, supervisor of early childhood education for the New Haven schools, noticed an immediate difference. "I saw a dramatic change," she reports, "in parent participation and student performance. I was a teacher; I could feel the change." In addition to the social skills curriculum for inner-city children, the Comer method employs a full basic academic program. When Comer first visited the Martin Luther King Jr. and Katherine Brennan schools, they ranked 32nd and 33rd in test scores among New Haven's 33 schools. Twenty years later, they rank third and sixth.

Parental involvement is a key feature in the Comer strategy. Parents are enlisted to help turn around the schools in which their children have been trapped by circumstance. They attend potluck dinners, "Welcome Back" nights, holiday parties, and graduation ceremonies. They also come into the classroom as visitors, aides, or tutors. As a result, the program often has a salutary effect on parents as well. Comer cites the example of one parent who, at the outset, could not understand the value of her showing up at school. "She felt she had nothing to contribute to professionals," he says. "But after getting involved in some activities, she recognized she had ability." Buoyed by her new attitude, she eventually finished high school, went to college, and is now the dean of a community college. In 1990 the Comer method was made a part of the renewal plans at three San Diego Unified District schools.

Today there are Comer models in all of New Haven's schools and in at least 100 additional schools in eight states. Although it normally takes at least three years to achieve significant improvements in test scores, Comer says that the school climate, not test scores, is his yardstick for measuring success. "You know when a school works and when it doesn't," he relates. "You feel better when you walk down the hallway."

Reform! Reform!

Across the country, many corporate executives are fed up with what they perceive as the overwhelming mess in our public schools. What's necessary, they say, is more than just another effort aimed at shoring up already existing programs, efforts that generally fail. Instances of job calls that uncover only a few qualified applicants and examples of high school graduates who cannot read at the eighth-grade level abound. For these reasons some business leaders are prepared to settle for nothing less than the complete reform and restructuring of the entire educational system.

This chapter examines the reform initiatives of two authors whose books have had a significant influence on current activities (both are now officials in the U.S. Department of Education) and an effective statewide organization that has seen its hard work rewarded in legislation. Interestingly, the latter example includes the story of a former member of that team who now believes that the initiatives he once called for are not sufficient and whose current efforts for reform have separated him from that organization. To repeat a point I made at the outset, "reform" can mean entirely different things to different people.

David Kearns
Winning the Brain Race

David T. Kearns is Deputy U.S. Secretary of Education. Before entering government, when he was chairman and chief executive officer of the Xerox Corporation, Kearns found time to serve on countless boards of educational institutions and community organizations bent on improving the schools. "I did not become involved in the education issue as the result of any esoteric or social concern," says Kearns. "Rather, during my tenure at Xerox, I found that a key part of our work force did not have the skills to compete in our increasingly international marketplace. I recognized that if America wants to remain the leading economic force in the world economy, we must lay the foundation with dramatically improved education for all our citizens."

In time, though, Kearns became disenchanted with piecemeal changes in education. He genuinely believed that many well-meaning efforts were feel-good enterprises, incapable of producing genuine improvement. So he did what few business people have done for the field of education. He wrote a book.

With coauthor Denis Doyle, a senior research fellow of the Hudson Institute, Kearns wrote *Winning the Brain Race: A Bold Plan to Make Our Schools Competitive.* In its opening pages he makes his feelings clear: "The task before us is the restructuring of our entire public education system. I don't mean tinkering. I don't mean piecemeal changes or even well-intentioned reforms. I mean the total restructuring of our schools."

Kearns was one of the first business voices raised in favor of restructuring the schools. Now virtually every business leader cries the same refrain. Although he lauds business leaders and organizations such as the California Business Roundtable for the work they have done in education, Kearns laments that to date "the business community has treated the schools with kid gloves." He takes the gloves off. He believes that business leaders have been lulled by educators into thinking that incremental change will be enough. He disagrees.

After his book was published in 1988, Kearns took to the road. He claimed no special credentials in the field of education (although coauthor Doyle had written widely in the field) and frequently referred to his business experience, particularly the example of Xerox's rebound from a period of decline. "The largest challenge facing education reform today is to develop an atmosphere to support real change," Kearns reported. "No major institution has ever undergone dramatic change without outside pressure. Xerox would not have reacted without the challenge from foreign competition. And yet, without action, Xerox would not have survived the 1980s as a major corporation. Education needs to tap into that same instinct, if only to support the hundreds of teachers and others who are striving for change."

In urging Americans to commit to a total restructuring of its public schools, Kearns set out a six-point Education Recovery Plan for America. The program offers the following:

1. **Choice.** Children would be given the opportunity to attend any public school in their district or region. State funding would follow students to the school of their choice, and teachers also would have the ability to market their skills to any school in their district or region.

2. **Restructuring.** Every school district of 2,500 or more children would reorganize into a year-round universal magnet system. Kearns would like to see the district office reduced to a service center, with principals and teachers given complete academic and administrative autonomy in running their schools. Individual schools would determine their own specialties (e.g., performing arts or math and science) and their own curricula. An attempt to maintain racial balance would be made by a special effort to inform minorities and the poor of their ability to attend the schools of their choice. Students would complete their education at their own pace, and traditional grade structures would be eliminated. States would ensure a minimum level of school performance by testing annually. "Schools that persist in poor performance," he says, "would be closed."

3. **Professionalism.** Standards for teachers would be raised for licensing, employment, and retention. These new standards would "emphasize academic knowledge over methodology—what a teacher knows is far more important than how he or she is going to teach it." Undergraduate degrees in education would be eliminated. After attaining a bachelor's degree in an academic subject, the new teacher would spend a year in the classroom preparing under a master teacher. A national certification board would be created, and salaries would be based on a combination of performance and longevity, not on longevity alone. Board-certified teachers and teachers whose specialties are in short supply would be paid more.

4. **Standards.** Student promotion would be tied to performance. Elementary schools would introduce foreign languages, music, geography, history, and computer technology. In high school students would master basic skills in core

subjects that would enable them to function easily in society. At a minimum, high schools would require a core curriculum of four years of English, three years of math, three years of history, two years of a foreign language, two years of natural or physical science, and one year of computer science.

5. **Values.** Students would understand the great documents of American citizenship and the standards of a democratic society. While "schools should not proselytize religion and morality," they should not ignore the important role of these things in American history.

6. **Federal responsibility.** While limited, it would be more than it has been. Limited matching funds would be given to school districts that design universal magnet systems, and a venture capital fund of $40 million would be created to help finance innovative experiments in teaching and school organization. College loans would be forgiven for those teachers who specialize in critically needed skills or teach in hardship areas. The federal government would triple its $100-million research budget, and the National Assessment of Educational Process (NAEP) would be more fully funded so that it could truly function as "the nation's report card," testing more subjects and compiling a state-by-state database for the first time.

Kearns believes that the federal government should fully fund Chapter 1 and Head Start. Interestingly, many of the points in his plan are included in America 2000, the program he champions today. Certainly choice, testing, and a federal venture capital fund appear in both programs, although Kearns's plan would have limited choice to the public schools and emphasized testing on a state rather than a national level. Still, Kearns should be given significant credit for having raised the level of debate.

As education has become a major issue on the national agenda and business people are becoming more involved, so has Kearns provided the model for the new business leader. None are exempt from Kearns's call to action: "Everyone must recognize that they share responsibility for a solution. We must recognize that all children can learn and that there are no good excuses for not taking an active role in education. You need to go to bed each night thinking about what you are going to do the next day to transform education in your community. You need to build a coalition of stakeholders to push for change, including parents, businesses, and community-based organizations. You need to embrace and support risk. Above all, you need to set extraordinarily high expectations. Don't settle for tinkering around the edges; go out and break the mold."

Across the nation people are responding to his call. Executives who had previously shown no interest in the public schools—or had, at best, either provided corporate T-shirts for a career day or entered into very limited adopt-a-school programs—have now entered the fray and taken to the podium. Addressing chambers of commerce, trade associations, and countless education summits, they have demanded nothing short of total reform and the restructuring of our public schools. Again and again, a single word is rising from the swelling chorus: Reform!

Diane Ravitch
What Every 17-Year-Old Should Know

In the mid-1960s Diane Ravitch was living in a townhouse in Brooklyn Heights, New York, with her husband and four children. A 1960 graduate of Wellesley College, she was doing some freelance writing, but her life centered on taking care of her family. When her second son died of leukemia in 1966, it brought about a sea change in Ravitch's life and a desire to commit herself to something important. Looking back, she says, "I guess because I was a young mother, I chose education."

She selected the history of education as her field. Working with Lawrence Cremin, the historian and president of Columbia University's Teachers College, she obtained a Ph.D. from Columbia in 1975. From 1977 to 1978 she was a Guggenheim Fellow and later served in various positions on the Teachers College faculty. In 1983 she became an adjunct professor. Since then she has written six books and in 1991 was appointed U.S. assistant secretary of education and director of research of the Department of Education.

In 1983 Ravitch's book *The Troubled Crusade: American Education, 1945–1980* drew considerable—and favorable—attention. More recently she has become known both for her work in helping to design the history and English curricula for the State of California and for her criticism of the Afrocentric curriculum proposed by a special committee headed by City University of New York professor

Dr. Leonard Jeffries Jr. An extremely bitter debate followed the latter. Ravitch maintains that while she is strongly in favor of multiculturalism, she does not favor distorting history nor does she view it as a help to any group to do so.

Even in the heat of controversy, Ravitch was easily confirmed as assistant secretary of the DOE. Her primary responsibilities include providing research for various educational programs and attempting to develop standards by which to determine whether a given program is working.

Two of Ravitch's books are having a significant influence on American education today: *What Do Our Seventeen-Year-Olds Know?*, coauthored with Chester Finn in 1987, and *The American Reader,* published in 1990. *The American Reader* is a collection of speeches, poems, songs, and readings (including Patrick Henry's speech to the Second Virginia Convention and Henry Wadsworth Longfellow's "Paul Revere's Ride") that Ravitch considers to be "words that moved a nation."

What Do Our Seventeen-Year-Olds Know? placed Ravitch and Finn in the middle of the debate on whether a school's central purpose should be to teach a student how to think or coverage—teaching a student information that defines an educated person. Finn, who is a professor at Vanderbilt University, held the jobs in the Reagan Administration that Ravitch now holds in the Bush Administration. Like Allan Bloom, who wrote *The Closing of the American Mind,* and E. D. Hirsch Jr., author of *Cultural Literacy,* Ravitch and Finn reveal in their book how little high school seniors know in specific areas of learning; they targeted American history and English literature. To many American leaders the findings were shocking.

Working with the National Assessment of Education Progress (NAEP) and a panel of teachers and experts, the authors composed a multiple-choice examination on American history and English literature. It was distributed to 8,000 high school juniors throughout the country. These 17-year-olds were carefully selected to reflect the nation's overall population in terms of region, gender, race, type of community, and type of school. The authors chose history and literature because they believe the humanities are important in that they teach students to think and stimulate students with ideas that have evolved in the past. (Also, the paucity of knowledge in math and science was already well documented.) Based on their study, the authors concluded that society "is breeding a new strain of cultural barbarian ... who cannot read or write except at the most rudimentary level and who possesses virtually no knowledge except that conveyed through the television set."

The average score the students received on the history test was 54.5 percent; on the literature test it was 51.8 percent. The distressing headlines at the time, however, pinpointed specific gaps of knowledge: 70 percent of those tested could not identify the Magna Carta; nearly 68 percent could not place the Civil War between 1850 and 1900; only 30 percent could date Columbus's discovery of the New World before 1750; 35 percent did not know that Watergate occurred after 1950.

The authors believe that their findings, while not a perfect survey, lead to certain inescapable conclusions. "We do not assert that American 17-year-olds are stupid," Ravitch and Finn maintain, "[or] that they are apathetic, or that they are short on savvy, creativity and energy.... We merely conclude that [they are] ignorant of important things that [they] should know, and that [they] and generations to follow are at risk of being gravely handicapped by that ignorance."

The NAEP survey also explored the backgrounds and study habits of the students. Random findings are interesting. More minority students read poetry than do nonminority students, for example, and suburban students who watch more than two hours of TV daily fared poorly on the test, while Hispanic students watching equal amounts of TV did better than their counterparts who didn't. The more literate their parents, the better the students performed on the test. The presence of a computer in the home was likely to be correlated with higher scores. Attending preschool seemed to provide an advantage, as well. Students who were living with both parents tended to do better. Those who read for pleasure scored better than those who didn't. And top students were just as likely to pass an entire semester without reading a novel or a play as those at the bottom.

What Do Our 17-Year-Olds Know? provides significant justification for the views of the educators who believe covering material is more important than teaching students how to think. Something must be done, they insist, to reverse this descent into ignorance. The students will not or cannot do it themselves; adults must play a role in establishing the right kind of schools. In their book and in articles and speeches stemming from the survey, Ravitch and Finn speak out for national testing as recommended by America 2000; both contributed to the development of that program.

Where does this lead us? And more particularly, what role will Ravitch and the DOE play in the crisis of public education today? Since Ravitch has not hesitated to speak out on most education issues, we may gain some notion of her role from a statement she made in 1986. In an article published by the *Washington Post*, she called federal research essential to assessing reforms in the nation's locally controlled schools. "We can't begin to judge which reforms work and which have failed," she said, "unless there is solid research and responsible assessment of the programs."

Sam Ginn and Joseph Alibrandi
The California Business Roundtable

In his plea for total restructuring, David Kearns singled out certain individuals and organizations credited with making a difference in education. Prominent among them was the California Business Roundtable, which Kearns noted as having spearheaded major reform in California.

The California Business Roundtable is an organization of more than 90 chief executive officers of California's major corporations. Education, primarily the state's public elementary and secondary school system, is a major priority in its work. Those used to thinking of California as being near the top of state education systems—a belief fostered by the state's fine university system—may be surprised by how the Roundtable begins its pamphlet *Restructuring California Education:*

California Tomorrow?

With over one third of its students dropping out, California's school system now ranks 44th in the nation. Without great improvement, well over a million students will have left before graduation between now and the year 2000; another 50,000 high school graduates per year will be barely literate, adding to California's 5 million functionally illiterate adults. But even these numbers understate the problem. Most of the future's increase will be students from poor, single-parent, and minority backgrounds—a population truly "at-risk" in the current system.

The California Business Roundtable puts its mission in stark economic terms. It believes that it is necessary to educate the state's citizens so that they can move into jobs with a minimal amount of retraining. Educational reform is necessary, they say, to reduce unemployment and somehow manage the expanding financial demands of the education system. The Roundtable estimates that K–12 enrollment in California will increase by 142,000 students per year over the next decade. If expenditures per pupil remain constant, funding to public schools will double to more than $40 billion during this period; if expenditures rise to the New York per-pupil level, this sum could be $65 billion. California's business leaders, they say, can no longer stand aside and let an inefficient, inadequate, and extremely expensive education system grow out of hand. The Roundtable has taken a stand, one strikingly similar to the position spelled out by David Kearns in *Winning the Brain Race:* "Small improvements are no longer acceptable. To meet the challenge of the 21st Century, California education needs to operate at a new plateau of student performance, teacher productivity, and cost effectiveness."

The Roundtable has promulgated six guidelines for the recommended restructuring. They are set out here in full for ready comparison to the America 2000 goals and Kearns's program:

Principles for a New Education System

1. **Performance.** Students, teachers, administrators, schools, and districts should be evaluated according to their performance and held accountable for results.

2. **School Autonomy.** Principals and teachers should have the authority and support to provide quality education attuned to community needs and characteristics.

3. **Parental Choice and Flexible Alternatives.** Parents should be able to choose schools and schooling appropriate to their children, including small-school, flexible environments in which parents are actively involved.

4. **Incentives and Innovation.** Teachers and administrators should have incentives for high performance, productivity, efficiency, and the use of modern technologies.

5. **Professionalism.** Teaching should be an honored, respected, and well-paid profession in which teachers are compensated

according to their ability, experience, and responsibilities.

6. **Pluralism.** The learning gap between poor minority and other children should be eliminated, and ethnic, linguistic, and cultural diversity should be treated as a strength.

One of the hallmarks of the California Business Roundtable is that it does not leave much to chance. The statement of principles set out in *Restructuring California Education* is followed by detailed recommendations on each of the six points, complete with supporting data and a step-by-step guide to implementation. This plan of action was followed by a subsequent pamphlet entitled *The Status Quo Is Not an Option: A Call for Education Reform,* which elaborated on the need to restructure the school system and set forth a comprehensive action plan.

But the Roundtable was not satisfied with pamphleteering. Under the effective leadership of Pacific Telesis CEO Sam Ginn (and his capable aide Jere Jacobs) and other top corporate executives, Roundtable-supported legislation that paved the way for a comprehensive new pupil-assessment program was passed by the state legislature. This was a critical first step to setting up demonstration projects around the state that addressed student performance needs and specific school accountability applications.

===== To Choose or Not to Choose? =====

According to the American Legislative Exchange Council:

In total, more than 36 states are currently engaged in some type of activity relating to public or private school choice, including pending legislation and task force recommendations promoting choice.

At least 20 states are considering specific legislative measures on public/private school choice, and several other states will introduce choice measures when their legislative sessions begin.

At least 10 states have acted on or are considering proposals to permit the use of taxpayer money for private school tuition.

Legislators in Arkansas, Colorado, Iowa, Massachusetts, Minnesota, Ohio, and Utah have already enacted statewide open enrollment legislation.

America 2000, 22, March 16, 1992.

Unlike many other organizations of business leaders, the Roundtable has been able to move from a call to action to action itself. But the organization—and its actions—are not without critics. Interestingly, one of the most vocal is one of its former members.

By almost any standard Joseph Alibrandi would seem an ideal member of the California Business Roundtable. He is chairman of Whittaker Corporation, a $190-million Los Angeles–based aerospace supplier. He is a strong believer in the public schools and in public aid to education. He himself is a product of the Boston public schools and attended the Massachusetts Institute of Technology on the G.I. bill. In fact, he had long been an active member of the Roundtable and oversaw its study, *Restructuring California Education.* As the Roundtable shifted its emphasis from support of public education to the next plateau—restructuring the entire system—Alibrandi became a central figure.

As I said earlier, reform means different things to different people. And now Alibrandi finds himself in direct opposition to many of his former colleagues. He has moved out front on a particular issue, one which many of the Roundtable members do not support.

Alibrandi advocates choice. Instead of limiting choice to the public schools, he wants to include private and independent schools as options. Tuition, he says, will be funded, in part, by a voucher for public funds. In this Alibrandi agrees with the America 2000 program. But he is not content simply to endorse the federal program. As this book went to press, he was involved in a bitter, costly campaign to put the matter of choice and the issue of the voucher on the November 1992 California state ballot. Revolutionary tax proposals have been instituted by this method in the past, and Alibrandi sees the referendum as the way to bring vouchers from the drawing board to the school system now.

Alibrandi knows he has a battle in front of him. He believes, however, that he will soon have other chief executives on his side. "It's only a matter of time," he maintains, "[un]til they reach the same level of frustration that I did. I think I know the business community quite well. Fundamentally, they believe this is the way we've got to go. You know, we've had 20 years of reforming. What have we accomplished?"

Alibrandi is also looking beyond the business community to win this fight. He envisions a coalition of interested parents, minority activists, and conservative populist groups carrying the day. He notes that a similar Oregon referendum, on the ballot in November 1990, failed by a two-to-one margin but points out that the initiative did better among voters with incomes under $25,000. He believes that his new coalition, mobilized by a suitable campaign, will garner sufficient local support to ensure victory.

If Alibrandi's group EXCEL (Excellence through Choice in Education League) succeeds in getting the issue on California's November 1992 ballot and is victorious, the movement begun by the Roundtable will be significantly altered.

Transforming a City

New York City Schools Chancellor Joseph A. Fernandez recently committed his administration to establishing at least 30 "smaller, more thematic high schools" over the next three years. Such an effort, while long on impact, calls for very little increase in expenditures of public funds. Instead, it encourages corporations, community-based organizations, and private citizens to make these schools a reality. At the heart of this program is a recognition that starting small is a move in the right direction, and that choice among public schools is a highly productive option.

Actually, the movement toward small, theme-oriented schools that offer students and their parents an educational choice has been a successful initiative in New York for almost 20 years. The most commonly cited example is District 4 in East Harlem, where a group of schools that were previously at the bottom academically rose to the middle of the city's schools (and beyond) on reading and computation achievement tests. All this was achieved because a persistent district superintendent was able to implement an innovative program as a local initiative in his district, with virtually no guidance (or, for that matter, interference) from the central board.

That district superintendent was Anthony Alvarado, who was assisted by Alternative Schools Director Sy Fliegel. Now a private citizen, Fliegel works for the Center for Educational Innovation advising school districts in the East on how to establish alternative schools along the District 4 model. When asked to summarize his approach, he gives the following advice:

> We always say create small, diverse schools with different philosophies. If you accept the idea that there is no one best school and no one best way to learn, then you better have diverse schools. Give them an identity. Make sure they have a clear vision, high expecta-

tions. Extend ownership and give the school autonomy. Focus on learning.

If your local school system is not educating its students and refuses to change itself, it's up to you to move it. Virtually every informed educator, administrator, and mentor will tell you that effective reform must come from the ground up. If you can build on the current reform movements (like America 2000), so much the better. You will be capitalizing on their recruitment of community leaders, and you will be supplying a grassroots ingredient that they must have to succeed.

If your community lacks any impulse toward reform, and you are unable to mount the small efforts that can be so effective working within the system, then consider how you might launch a citywide reform movement. Mentors who have already been involved in the public schools provide fertile ground for recruiting. Business and community leaders can be brought in—this could be you, an executive from the company you work for, or the chair of a community-based organization.

On the road to transforming a city, you may very well encounter false starts. Issues and opponents you never expected may rise to defeat you. And the restructuring that you put in place may not work as you had hoped it would. But as you will see from the Boston Compact and the Rochester Experiment described in this chapter, a major city *can* be turned around. In both cases significant public and private funding was part of the package—a major achievement. And the children in these two cities have been the beneficiaries of change.

Ken Rossano
The Boston Compact

In 1989 Ken Rossano, a key figure in the development of the Boston Compact, spoke at the annual National Symposium on Partnerships in Education sponsored by the White House. Although his was one of several simultaneous presentations, the room was packed to overflowing. The Boston Compact, the partnership that had guaranteed support of Boston's public schools by the business community in return for improved results in education, was widely known. At this presentation, however, this zealous pioneer's message was slightly different from what listeners had come to expect from him. The theme was accountability. It was imperative, he said, that partnership programs be measured by appropriate standards: if they do not measure up, they must be rejected.

What most of the listeners didn't know was that Rossano's message was inspired by an uneasiness with the program. What had seemed an ideal plan on paper had turned out to be exceedingly difficult to accomplish. The *Boston Globe* reported that in the fall of 1988, "[T]he business community balked at renewing the Compact, saying that while business had more than exceeded the goals set six years before, the schools had fallen short of theirs." When renewal negotiations between the compact steering committee and representatives of the school system took place, the *Globe* reported, "Business leaders have questioned whether the schools are fulfilling their part of the original Boston Compact by improving test scores and lowering the dropout rate." Test scores, the paper reported, had not improved; and while the dropout rate had improved over previous years, it did not even approach the 5 percent per year reduction target established in the original compact. In addition, in one two-year period (1985–87), the dropout rate actually rose from 43.6 percent to 45.1 percent.

In the course of the 1990–91 renewal negotiations, business leaders pressed for a true restructuring of the schools. "The redefinition of the Compact's goals is essential to progress," Mike Taylor, executive director of the Private Industry Council, said at the time. Before they would sign a new agreement, the Compact steering committee insisted that there be full implementation of a new student-assignment plan, completion of a collective bargaining agreement with teachers, and adoption of a school-based management plan that would ensure accountability by school teachers and principals for reaching the new goals.

The divergent elements that had united to form the Compact years before—school officials, labor leaders, spokespersons for the minority community, university presidents, and corporate chief executive officers—were each complaining that while they had met their goals, others had not kept their end of the bargain. Corporations maintained that they had given job preference to graduates of the Boston public schools but questioned whether the schools had done their job in properly preparing the students. School officials, in turn, complained that the trade unions had not met their obligations to train students, which provoked the following response from Joseph Joyce, secretary and treasurer of the Greater Boston Labor Council AFL-CIO: "It's a two-sided contract. The agreement was that the kids would arrive [in the training program] prepared.... But some of these kids had no mathematical comprehension." He also pointed out that reading levels were far below what was needed to learn a trade.

The mayhem was not altogether unexpected. If ever a city was destined for failure, it was Boston. With a Byzantine political system, it is one of the few cities in America where a mayor has been reelected while serving a jail sentence. After a federal judge ordered the schools desegregated in 1975, a number of political careers were made by individuals who steadfastly opposed busing, an essential part of integrating the schools. While Boston's public school population of 59,000 students represented less than 10 percent of the public school students in the state, 49 percent of all the state's African-American students were located in Boston, along with 37 percent of the state's bilingual students, 24 percent of its Hispanic students, and 12 percent of all students who had special education needs.

In Rossano's prepared speeches, he often mentions that in 1955, 60 percent of the households in the United States consisted of a working father, a housewife mother, and two or more school-age children. He points out that in 1985, only 7 percent of Boston's homes matched that 1955 norm. In the 1980s approximately 1,000 girls left Boston's school system each year because of pregnancy. Drug problems abounded. In short, at that time the city had a long list of problems.

The possibility of some resolution was foreshadowed in the 1970s, when a group called the Tri-Lateral Council for Quality Education brought together the Greater Boston Chamber of Commerce, the National Alliance of Business, and the Boston School Department to establish partnerships between major businesses and high schools. This arrangement still exists; but more importantly, it provided a hospitable background for the development of the Boston Compact.

The compact rose from three bilateral agreements. The first was signed in September 1982 by the Private Industry Council (representing business leaders) and the Boston School Board. A year later the Boston Higher Education Partnership and the school board entered an arrangement whereby colleges and universities would provide scholarships, jobs, and counseling to public school students. The third agreement, between the trade unions and the schools, was signed in December 1984. The letter of intent signed by each corporate participant describes the fundamental agreement embodied in the Boston Compact in the following terms:

> If the Boston public schools will improve the quality of secondary education, the business community in Boston will endeavor to provide job opportunities to Boston public high school graduates with respect to vacancies for which they are qualified. Improvement in the quality of secondary education will be measured through year by year improvements in five categories: attendance, drop-outs, achievement in reading and mathematics, college placements, and job placements.

In 1984 the Boston Compact was supplemented by the Boston Plan for Excellence in the Public Schools. On the bicentennial of the founding of the Bank of Boston, the bank contributed $1.5 million to establish an endowment for the Plan for Excellence. The endowment now stands at more than $30 million. Rossano, who by then had become a senior vice president of the Bank of Boston, described the Plan for Excellence in the following terms:

> The Boston Plan for Excellence currently sustains six major programs. These programs include grants to individual schools to support innovative teaching and curriculum ideas, fellowships to teachers for self-improvement, grants to sustain basic skills instruction and athletic programs in the middle schools, a model system of financial aid advising and last-dollar scholarship assistance for students going on to higher education, a community service program, and a program ... to support programs in early childhood education.

The Boston Compact and the Boston Plan for Excellence have yielded significant results. Jobs have been made available for virtually every student who graduates from the public schools. Colleges and universities are supplying significant numbers of scholarships. ACCESS, a "last dollar" scholarship program in which volunteer counselors instruct students on to how to apply for aid, makes up the difference between aid received and the funds needed for college by drawing from the endowment established through the Plan for Excellence. ACCESS guarantees that every public school graduate with a C average or better who is accepted to college will

144

receive sufficient financial aid to attend. A new school superintendent was put in place. As a result of a new state law, in January 1992
the thirteen-member elected school committee, which, in the view
of its critics, had been given more to debate than action, was replaced by a seven-member board appointed by the governor.

Still, Boston is Boston. In 1991 a bus drivers' strike paralyzed the
public schools for a number of months. The mayor and the new
superintendent of schools were at odds over budget matters. Critics have complained that by appointing his former director of operations and close confidant as acting executive secretary of the
new school committee, the mayor has gained turf at the expense of
a smooth-running system. And the schools have still not met the
targets set for achievement test scores and dropout rates, although
there are some bright spots.

Star-studded coalitions with grand visions have learned that
many good ideas falter when politically connected interest groups
find that they must give up something in the process of reforming
schools. Community leaders such as Rossano have been frustrated
but not defeated. They have come to realize, as Otto von Bismarck
once observed, that politics is the art of the possible.

The Most Bully Pulpit in Atlanta

The Atlanta project has many things going for it. It has capital-
ized on the city's enthusiasm for the upcoming Olympic Games to
address the problems of impoverished inner-city areas.

In addition, leading educators such as Dr. Jim Laney, president
of Emory University, and Dr. Johnetta Cole, president of Spelman
College, have agreed to give major portions of their time in leading
their respective clusters. (Each of the city's 20 clusters, or districts, is
organized around a high school, which is the focal point of efforts in
that area.) The city's religious and business communities have
agreed to play major roles in the project. A Collaborative Training
Center has been established in some 2 million square feet of the old
Sears Roebuck Building to train loaned executives and others to
participate more effectively in the project. Ample funding has been
targeted, with a $26-million price tag ($18.5 million in cash and $7.5
million in kind) over a five-year period.

And the project is being coordinated by Dan Swett, an experienced former city administrator who is universally acknowledged as
an effective executive of nonprofit organizations. Still, Swett can-

didly admits that the project would not be possible without the leadership of former President Jimmy Carter.

Until recently the Carter Center has been primarily engaged in international work, including immunization for children throughout the world and conflict resolution. The center is now turning to the inner city of Atlanta, where it is located. Former President Carter has recognized that there are two Atlantas—one rich and successful, the headquarters of major corporations and the site of many beautiful homes, and the other the "second-poorest city in the United States, ranking only below Newark, New Jersey, with incomes less than half the minimum poverty level."

Mr. Carter has now made the Atlanta Project his highest priority and has infused the project with his own brand of hands-on leadership. As Swett observes, "When talking at one of our early meetings about when work on the project would begin, we all took out our calendars. President Carter looked at his watch."

Kay Whitmore
The Rochester Experiment

In the late 1970s the city of Rochester, New York, found itself gripped by economic crisis. Its businesses were being overwhelmed by Japanese and other foreign competition. Although local corporations acknowledged the need to undergo massive internal revision, the local work force did not appear up to the demands imposed by city's largely technological industries. As business leaders tightened their belts and made hard decisions regarding their own companies, they found it necessary to begin to play a role in the city's public education system, or else give up to the international competition completely.

Melles Griot, a California-based optical component manufacturer, is a case in point. While Rochester has been dominated by a few giants, including Eastman Kodak and the Xerox Corporation, a significant portion of its employer base came from the smaller, technologically oriented companies that had, prior to the late 1970s, found the city a hospitable environment. Facing competition from abroad, Melles Griot questioned whether to expand its manufacturing operations in Rochester.

"We can't find workers with enough education to do even basic manufacturing work," James Van Kouwenberg, the company's production manager, noted at the time. "Either their reading comprehension is too low or their math comprehension is too low." The general manager reported overall job applications were "pretty depressing."

Kay Whitmore, Kodak chairman, president, and chief executive officer and a key figure among Rochester's business leaders, seconded Melles Griot's concern. "The only thing this community can do proactively," he concluded, "is to provide a more educated pool of people."

The Rochester community did not differ significantly from most other major urban areas. The student body was 52 percent African American and 13 percent Hispanic. The teaching force was about 20 percent African American and 2 percent Hispanic. About a third of all ninth graders could be expected to drop out before graduating from high school. Nearly two thirds of the ninth graders were one or two years below grade level. About a fifth of the students were absent at least one day a week. Only 25 percent of those eligible took the Scholastic Aptitude Test (as compared with 37 percent nationally), and test scores were below the national average. A large majority of the city's 33,000 students came from low-income families, and nearly half came from single-parent households. There was a high rate of teenage pregnancy. Corporate personnel managers estimated that 10 percent of the community's work force was functionally illiterate.

Two reports published in the mid-1980s led the community to move toward a program of reform and restructuring. The first, in 1984, was a study of the Rochester public schools. It showed that of 1,200 graduates that year, a bit more than half of whom were African American, only thirty-nine African-American students had maintained a B average or better. This led to a call by Rochester's African-American leadership for a unified community response. The school superintendent, the president of the urban league, the president of the teachers union, and a number of business leaders, including Whitmore, wrote a report that became the focal point for educational reform in the city.

A second report was promulgated in 1986 by the Community Task Force on Education. Entitled *A Call to Action,* it called for a massive change in the public school system. It stated, "Picture, if you will, 100 children entering a Rochester public school this year. Almost half of them are below the national norm in language development and number recognition, the basic school readiness skills.... The enthusiastic commitment of the business community is essential if the problems of the schools are to be solved."

Soon after that report was issued, the Rochester reform leaders went to Washington, D.C., to meet with Marc Tucker, who had directed the Carnegie Corporation study *A Nation Prepared: Teachers for the Twenty-First Century*, which had just come out. The Carnegie report called for sweeping changes in education, and Tucker was more than pleased to review them with the group from Rochester. While Tucker was not surprised that he and the group had drawn the same conclusions, he was amazed at the diversity of the group. "What was utterly remarkable was that in Rochester it wasn't just one group that was committed to this vision," he recalls, "but a number of them from different segments of the community. And they were willing to work together." Tucker was so impressed that two years later he moved to Rochester to establish a thinktank called The National Center on Education and the Economy to monitor the Rochester effort.

The community task force program—now called The Rochester Experiment—began in 1986. It included one of the country's early efforts in school-based management. Among its components was to expand teacher duties to include counseling. In effect, teachers were expected to act as social workers as well as to fulfill their traditional role. Veteran teachers would be called on to act as mentors to their less experienced colleagues. The expanded responsibilities led to a commitment from Rochester's business leaders to significantly increase teacher salaries. The pay-for-performance schedule that was implemented would place Rochester teacher salaries among the highest in the nation (exceeded only by those in Alaska). Annual compensation ran from $26,000 to $57,000 in early years of the plan, rising to $69,000 as the plan entered its second three-year phase. In its first stage the increases represented a whopping 40 percent hike over the three-year period of the teacher's contract.

In its first four years the Rochester Experiment showed gains. In 1989 the average reading scores on the California Achievement Tests for each Rochester high school grade improved marginally over the previous year. The number of students who passed the New York State Regents competency test in science increased steadily: In 1988, 55.2 percent of those who took it passed; in 1990,

72.2 percent passed. The high school dropout rates declined for the first time in eight years.

But by 1990 it showed strain as well. Many teachers found that they had neither the skills nor the aptitude for the counseling function they had undertaken. "I have never seen morale lower among teachers, because of the unrealistic expectations that are being pressed upon them," noted Bill Read, a teacher in his mid-fifties who was about to retire. Adam Urbanski, the dynamic president of the Rochester Teachers Association and one of the architects of the original reform, found himself opposed for reelection by a dissident group within his own union. After two failed efforts, a new three-year contract with somewhat more realistic pay-for-performance standards was agreed on. In addition, cutbacks in the state budget led the school superintendent to propose that several administrative positions be eliminated, resulting in protests from that quarter.

Interestingly, with reform firmly in place but not quite meeting the expectations of its architects, the city's corporate leaders decided to add a more traditional partnership element to the mix. Wegmans, a leading Rochester supermarket chain, provided after-school jobs for students who might otherwise drop out and offered a $5,000 college scholarship to students who chose to continue their education. Students were required to maintain passing grades; and if they fell behind in their schoolwork, the work commitment was suspended for one grading period. Each student was assigned a mentor from Wegmans. In 1990 thirteen of these at-risk students composed the first graduating class of Wegmans Scholars. Nine of the students planned to attend college in the fall, and three of the others planned to attend college the following year.

Kodak's action was more widespread. About 2,500 of the company's employees (5 percent of its local work force) volunteered to go into the schools to work directly with local teachers on science and math. As in successful reform efforts in other parts of the country, effective work by mentors continued and expanded after reform had begun.

Transforming a State

From time to time, states become the battleground for significant educational reform. But as efforts transcend individual schools and school districts and extend beyond the boundaries of cities into larger arenas, citizen involvement becomes that much more difficult to obtain. As a result, many states are left with pronouncements from on high but very little action in the schools themselves.

This chapter presents the stories of reform efforts that transformed three states. In each instance there was widespread controversy and persistent government inertia; but eventually new statewide funding was approved, and genuinely significant positive changes took place in the public schools. Most important, there was widespread citizen involvement in each state.

The first state is Texas, where Ross Perot, legendary businessman (and would-be president), raised confrontation to a new level. Aided by Mark White, a governor who was willing to risk his political career (and later paid for it) to help the schools, and aided further by an expenditure of millions of dollars of his own money, Perot and his allies toured Texas, developed support, and eventually achieved major school reform. Taking a different tack, Jack Moreland, superintendent of a small school district in Kentucky, began a legal action to improve the lot of poor districts across the state, including the one he administered. This litigation led to a complete reform and restructuring of the state's education system, an initiative that continues today. The effort enlisted educators, administrators, and private citizens throughout the state.

In South Carolina two governors, Richard Riley and Carroll Campbell—one a Democrat and one a Republican—realized that a better educational system could be good politics, good government, and good for the state economy. A key ingredient to this successful statewide effort was a poll, paid for by funds raised by a

150

prominent businessman, that showed the political leaders they could in fact resolve educational issues long thought insurmountable.

In each of these states dramatic reform packages passed by the state legislatures carried some of the largest ever one-time increases in state funding. Voters had to be convinced that tax money would be used not to perpetuate failed methods and ineffective policies but to build new approaches to education.

Different roads were followed to achieve reform: a well-financed statewide commission and lobbying effort, constitutional litigation that forced the issue of reform and a state supreme court that spelled out its mandate in no uncertain terms, and governors who made education reform a pillar of their political programs. But in each case private citizens were marshalled at every level for funding, leadership, and motivation to change.

Ross Perot: Texas

Consider this hypothetical situation: A business person with virtually unlimited financial resources decides that his state school system needs restructuring. Of the 22 states that keep track of scholastic aptitude test scores, his state is ranked 17. Can the business person marshal the financial, professional, union, and political forces necessary to bring about a revision of the state school system from top to bottom? This situation did in fact occur. The state was Texas, the time was 1982, and the business person was Ross Perot.

In 1981 Texas Republican Governor Bill Clements appointed Perot to head the "Texas War on Drugs." "The Governor asked me to head this panel," Perot wrote me, "and I couldn't think of a higher, better use of my time than to have a positive impact on the lives of the three million school children in Texas." Touring the state and visiting a large number of schools, Perot came to the conclusion that drugs were only part of the problem. There was also far too much emphasis in Texas high schools on pep rallies and football games. He lamented an expenditure in Odessa of $6.1 million for a football stadium at a time when money should, in his view, have been channeled into improving curriculum. Perot concluded that the entire state education system needed to be overhauled.

Perot got his chance to make a difference in the schools in 1983, when Democrat Mark White, who had succeeded Bill Clements, chose Perot to head a new state commission on education reform. Perot put up $2 million of his own money to ensure that the commission was fully staffed. In 1984 Perot's commission filed its report with the governor. Sweeping changes were recommended, including the following: an appointed State Board of Education to replace the larger, elected board; mandatory tutoring sessions for failing students; intensive English language training for preschoolers; lower teacher-pupil ratios in elementary grades; competency testing for teachers; the elimination of pep rallies during the school day; an end to the practice of excusing students from class to participate in extracurricular activities; and a summary exam for seniors to qualify them for graduation. The most controversial reform—and in Texas the most shocking—was a rule that took effect in the spring of 1985 requiring junior and senior high school students to pass all of their courses in each six-week grading period or forgo extracurricular activities (e.g., football) for the next six weeks. The shorthand term for this recommendation was "no pass, no play." The first state tax increase in 13 years, a multibillion dollar tax hike that was the largest in Texas history, accompanied the reform proposals.

Under the leadership of Governor White and with the persistent campaigning and lobbying of Ross Perot, the commission's recommendations became law. The comprehensive program was passed in June 1984. By the spring of 1985, 15 percent of the 39,000 high school varsity football players in Texas and 40 percent of all junior varsity and freshman players were precluded from play by the no pass no play rule. Some schools were hit especially hard. Eisenhower High in Aldine, near Houston, lost 90 of its 190 players. King High School in Corpus Christi lost 13 of its 22 starters.

Hostility to Perot, which had surfaced during the legislative debate on his bill, became more widespread. Bumper stickers soon appeared proclaiming: "I don't brake for Ross Perot" and "Will Rogers never met Ross Perot." The criticism did not deter Perot, and he continued encouraging Texas legislators to enforce the necessary scholarly discipline among students that so many of their families would not. Perot is aware that what would help students is "a strong family unit in every home, with parents actively involved with the schools. In that environment," he says, "we would have a great improvement in education overnight. Unfortunately, at this point we have a weak, disintegrating family unit."

Prosper, Texas, may be as good a place as any to capture the flavor of the debate on Perot's plan. Even though its football team had lost all 10 games in 1984 and found themselves trailing 61 to nothing at half-time in its 1985 opener, football was a major event in the town. Almost all of its 675 residents could be found on a Friday night at Eagle Field, hoping for divine intervention. As a result of the no pass no play policy, Prosper had to cancel football at mid-season. Now the stands at Eagle Field are empty. Still, the end of football in 1985 did not lead Prosper's residents to universally condemn the new policy. Prosper school board president Jerry Standerfer readily acknowledges the problems caused by the end of football in Prosper. "But for every one kid it hurts," he says, "it will help ten. I'm now hearing kids say they've really decided to buckle down and study, and that's a good sign. I think it's time the image of sports is changed. With this rule there won't be any reason for the 'dumb jock' label any longer."

Not everyone has accepted the change without a fight. Lori Patterson, a sophomore, is a clarinetist planning a music career. Although she has a 3.0 grade point average, she is having trouble with geometry, and a failing grade in that subject would mean she could no longer participate in the band. The school administration made an exception in her case based on a doctor's note stating she was experiencing worry and sleeplessness as a result of her fear of failure. In spite of this exception, Lori Patterson filed a suit to have the law overturned. Nelson Arnes, a ten-year-old learning-disabled child, had maintained a perfect attendance record in hopes of winning a trip to Astroworld. Although he attended every class, he was declared ineligible for the trip because he hadn't passed all of his courses. His mother complained to the school board and, after her appeal was denied, joined other outraged parents in a suit to have the law declared unconstitutional. In July of 1985 the Texas Supreme Court upheld the no pass no play provision, although Nelson Arnes's case had caused enough public interest and sympathy to bring about an amendment that exempts learning-disabled children.

Besides litigation, Perot's program has been altered by administrative and governmental moves. The teacher competency examination, according to a recent *New York Times* update, has been "watered down" so that it "only tested whether teachers could achieve the literacy level of an eleventh grader." Economic constraints have forced the state to cut back on the anticipated level of financing; and three years after the package passed, the voters changed the state board of education back from an appointive to an elective board.

Governor White justified his push for reform in terms of global competition. "For years Texas has been putting winning athletes on the playing field and didn't really focus on how well we were doing in the classroom," he said. "Japan doesn't care how many football games we win.... They play hardball economics. The real issue for our children and grandchildren is not going to be no pass no play; it's going to be no learn no earn." Dr. Harriett Arvy, director of psychological services for the Houston School District, supported the reforms in these terms: "Most of the kids are failing not because they lack intelligence but because they are not turning in their homework. The one thing kids have control of in their lives is their schoolwork, and it is important for their development that they learn mastery of some area in their lives. If the parents won't enforce the standards, the schools have to."

While others continue to debate the merit of extracurricular activities, Perot focuses on the old-fashioned educational staples: a demanding core curriculum, homework, classroom size, teacher training, and compensation. His vision of education is clear: "School is for learning," he says. "School is for work."

Jack Moreland: Kentucky

Jack Moreland is superintendent of schools in Dayton, Kentucky. He is regarded as a leader in his profession and a dedicated school administrator. He has been part of Kentucky's educational system for 22 years and has been a superintendent of schools since he was 31 years old. And yet, for a period of years in the 1980s, Moreland was the object of a number of personal threats, and his schools were subjected to an unexpected audit by the state.

What had Moreland done to incur such hostility? He was one of a handful of people behind a celebrated lawsuit against the state of Kentucky and the entrenched interests that for decades had supported the state educational establishment. In 1985 Moreland's and 65 other "poor" districts sought a judicial decision that would proclaim every educational law in the state unconstitutional and that would order a complete reorganization of the school system. During those difficult years Moreland was not popular. "Educational reform is like a Russian novel," he said. "It's long, it's boring, and everybody dies at the end."

Moreland defines his district in precise terms: "It is made up predominantly of blue-collar, working-class people. The property value here is next to the lowest in the state, and approximately 60 percent of our kids are eligible for the federal free-lunch program." These statistics are entirely at odds with those of the neighboring Fort Thomas district. Moreland says, "We're worlds apart in terms of the kind of clientele that we have and the amount of available dollars for programs." The Fort Thomas district services children whose parents are, for the most part, professionals. Only 3 percent of its student population is eligible for the free-lunch program.

The inequity between the two school systems most frustrated Moreland in that it hampered his ability to retain quality teachers. The pay rate for teachers in Kentucky was established as a minimum salary; districts with more funds were able to offer higher salaries. "We would get a teacher out of the local university whom we would put to work as a first-year teacher and train for a period of time," Moreland remembers. "And then, once we were able to get them to a position where they were up and going and ready to do some really good things in the area of education, they would jump to the other side of the fence where the grass was undoubtedly greener. We lost a good number of teachers not only to that district but also to others that have the same relative characteristics."

As his frustration mounted, Moreland became increasingly intent on working to ensure that kids in poor districts got the same educational opportunities as the children in affluent districts. In 1976, two years before Moreland became superintendent, Kentucky's general assembly passed the Power of Equalization law (POE), which, in effect, was a public recognition of the inequalities among school districts. "Theoretically speaking," says Moreland, "if that mechanism had been fully funded, there would never have been an equity suit." But funding was granted only at a constant level. From 1978 until 1984 the same number of dollars were put in the program, thereby preventing the Power of Equalization law from securing long-term change. "To [have the general assembly] acknowledge that there is a problem and, over a period of about six or eight years, to never make any more real progress toward solving that problem was very frustrating for those of us who are in property-poor school districts," says Moreland.

In 1984 Moreland and his fellow crusaders decided to take action. The Kentucky House had voted to put an additional $12 million into the POE program; the Senate had allocated nothing. To settle budget disputes assembly members debated the issue. "I remember it just like it was yesterday," says Moreland. "The committee took the $12 million out of the final budget allocation, and we wound up with zero again. The Kentucky General Assembly meets on a two-year basis, so in effect, we'd been said no to for another two years. That frustration was just more than we could deal with."

"I wish I could tell you that I was the prime mover [behind the equity suit]," says Moreland, "but I can only say that I was one of four or five people." Superintendents of property-poor school districts met to discuss their options with top-of-the-line finance person Dr. Kern Alexander, a professor at Virginia Tech. As a result of the meeting, the superintendents agreed to form an organization and press on. The Council for Better Education, consisting of 66 superintendents, was soon incorporated. "The next thing we did was probably the most important thing we did in the entire equity suit," he says. "We retained the services of former federal judge and former governor Burt Combs as our lead attorney. We had been sort of laughed at as the rabble-rousers whose suit would never amount to anything. But Governor Combs brought credibility and major-league attention to our organization."

Though the Council for Better Education's lawsuit didn't receive the full-scale endorsement of superintendents in property-rich school districts, neither was it the target of full-scale opposition. Moreland says he doesn't know whether to attribute this to luck or to the fact that Kentucky was one of the very first to take their case to the courts. "One of the platforms of the Council for Better Education was that we didn't want to level down, meaning to take the money away from the rich and give it to the poor. I know they've done that in Texas a little bit, and Ohio is getting ready to do some of that, but Kentucky was adamant that we didn't want to do that," says Moreland. He gives a lot of credit to the superintendents of schools who were able to look beyond their own needs and take all of Kentucky's children into account. "The posture taken by the more affluent school districts was: How can you be against every child having an equal education? And because of that," says Moreland, "there was no groundswell of negative support against us."

Moreland and his coplaintiffs won. In 1989, after prolonged litigation, Chief Justice Robert F. Stephens wrote for the majority of justices on the state's highest court: "Lest there be any doubt, the result of our decision is that Kentucky's entire system of common schools is unconstitutional." Every component of the educational system—be it finance, governance, or curriculum—had to be reevaluated.

After much effort, Kentucky's new educational policy rose from the ashes. "There's going to be some pain and suffering until we get the equity question resolved," notes Moreland, "because there are some school districts at the top who are either going to have to mark time or progress very, very slowly so the rest of us can catch up. Then we'll be able to press on together."

To date, the United States Supreme Court has found no right to education in the U.S. Constitution. But many state constitutions do provide for such a right. In the lawsuits pressed on the basis of these state provisions, the underlying issue is generally whether the state's funding system—which typically yields better schools in the affluent suburbs, where real estate taxes produce higher revenues—causes the urban and rural poor to suffer inadequate facilities and underpaid teachers in violation of their constitutional rights. Thus far there have been 28 such cases. In 14 it has been held that the particular constitutional provisions involved did not provide a sufficient basis to overturn the states' educational systems. Twelve of the cases have been won by plaintiffs. In two states, Colorado and New Hampshire, suits were abandoned before trial because agreements were reached to ensure more equitable bases of funding.

Successful lawsuits do not necessarily bring changes that satisfy every proponent of reform. This goes back, of course, to the fundamental truth that "reform" means different things to different people. When asked to counsel a group in another state that was considering an equity case, Jack Moreland observed, "We're going to get a lot of money, but we're also going to get some things that you might not necessarily want. You need to be aware of that." Nevertheless, the changes brought about by Jack Moreland's lawsuit are impressive.

"In terms of scope, no other state has made such broad changes," Chris Pipho, director of state relations for the Education Commission of the States, has observed. "Kentucky is in a league by itself." Unlike in other states in which financing systems were overturned, the Kentucky Supreme Court ordered a complete revision of curricula and methods of state and local administration. The governor and the legislature promulgated a five-year plan, with a price tag of $1.3 billion in the first two years alone. This was financed by a reworking of the state income tax and an increase in the state sales tax from 5 to 6 percent. Additional revenues were garnered by an expansion of the state's utility tax and a provision for local districts to receive matching state aid if they increased their taxes.

The five-year plan passed by the Kentucky General Assembly in March 1990, based on the state Supreme Court decision, went into effect in January 1991. It mandated preschool classes for four-year-olds from low-income families, more teachers, higher salaries for teachers, and school management changes that would take administrative responsibilities away from state and regional boards and place the running of schools in the hands of local principals, teachers, and parents. As a result, the state's Department of Education would no longer be in the business of regulating textbooks, curricula, and other details of day-to-day school operation. Other changes included plans for some schools to experiment with ungraded primary classes for pupils in kindergarten through third grade (along with special teacher-training sessions). Kentucky's compulsory school age was raised from 16 to 18, and a system of accountability was mandated, including a battery of tests to measure school and student performance. The measurement of student's academic performance, health, and attendance will be the basis of a system of rewards and penalties for schools and their staffs.

Under this system those schools judged successful will be rewarded with greater leeway in personnel and curriculum selection, as well as with bonuses for the teachers and administrators deemed responsible for the success. On the other hand, for those schools that do not succeed, possible sanctions include dismissal of individual teachers and even closing the schools.

Implementation of the five-year plan was nothing short of revolutionary. At the time of the Supreme Court decision, Kentucky ranked thirty-ninth nationwide in per-pupil spending. Under the new plan, the per-pupil cost of the preschool program alone, while considered relatively inexpensive by national standards, was almost as much as the total state and local per-pupil expenditure prior to the five-year plan.

The transition has had its painful moments. Kentucky experienced its first teacher strike in 14 years. Thirty-one superintendents left the state to take jobs elsewhere in the initial year of the plan, a record number of departures for a single year. "It has been very, very demanding," says Mary Ann Bueso, director of special education in Hardin County, a middle-class school district of some 12,500 students about 40 miles south of Louisville. "We have to do our regular jobs, and then we have to do this. It has been an awesome effort."

Movement to school-based management has also had its difficulties. "We were all a little leery of one another," reports fourth-grade teacher Bill Woolridge, a member of the management committee of an elementary school. "The principal thought we were teaming up on him, and we thought he was teaming up against us. It was tense." All in all, however, progress has been made. In Dayton, Moreland feels the school-based management teams have "taken to their tasks pretty well." He emphasizes that the program is only in its first year and advises management teams in his district to "take small bites. I told them individually and collectively that I was willing and, I think, the board was willing for them to have the authority to control spending, curriculum, facilities, and extracurricular activities—those things that, by law, they have the authority to do. Most of the management teams have not taken on the total responsibilities yet; but as they get more and more accomplished, they will get more involved." Moreland anticipates that once implemented correctly, school-based management will be a successful vehicle for increasing parental involvement in the schools.

"We still have some differences between the top and the bottom," acknowledges Moreland, "but that gap is closing rather quickly. We never asked that all of this be taken care of in one year. We knew that there would be a gradual phasing in until equity was accomplished." And even as the state struggles with the equity issue, Moreland advises that they must look forward to yet another issue: adequacy. Though the courts did not define the term, they ruled that no school district in Kentucky was "adequate." "I would submit to you," says Moreland, "that what we're trying to achieve should not be limited to regional or nationwide adequacy but global adequacy. It's not just in terms of education or in terms of dollars spent on education. If the reason that Japan is successful is because of the discipline they exhibit within the family structure, then we've got to find a way to get that structure back into that four-year-old child we have coming through the door. I would say that if we were very successful, then clearly we wouldn't be changing. But we've got some things that need to be worked on, so Kentucky is really grappling right now with the concept of equity. But as soon as that fight is over, then we're going to have to go back into the fray and deal with the concept of adequacy. I see us all rising together."

Carroll Campbell: South Carolina

What does it take to be an "education governor"? Generally, the label implies a long-standing interest in education. Tom Kean, for example, who served two terms as governor of New Jersey and played a major role in educational reform in that state, holds a master's in education from Teachers College at Columbia University and taught school for two years. After his two terms as governor, Kean became president of Drew University. Lamar Alexander, who is now U.S. Secretary of Education, served two terms as governor of Tennessee, during which time he instituted a master teacher program and other major elements of educational reform. He was an exceptional student, making Phi Beta Kappa at Vanderbilt University and going on to hold a Root-Tilden scholarship at New York University Law School. After Alexander left the governor's mansion, he became president of the University of Tennessee.

Richard Riley, who implemented one of the most sweeping statewide educational programs in the nation as governor of South Carolina, was a cum laude graduate of Furman and held a juris doctor degree from the law school of the University of South Carolina before entering the statehouse. Carroll Campbell, who succeeded Riley and during whose administration the South Carolina legislature passed "Target 2000," a major education reform bill, would also be labeled an "Educational Governor," but his personal history is markedly different.

When Carroll Campbell graduated from high school, he was unable for financial reasons to attend college. He went to work and took courses when he could. At age 19 he and a partner founded Handy Park Company, which was to become a successful chain of parking facilities. Eight years later, Campbell was a principal in the formation of Rex Enterprises, which developed into a chain of 13 Burger King restaurants before it was sold in 1978. During these years Campbell put his business and administrative skills to work as a manager of political campaigns of friends who were running for office. Then he served in the South Carolina House of Representatives and state Senate, as an executive assistant to the governor of South Carolina, as the representative to the U.S. Congress from South Carolina's 4th Congressional District, and as governor of South Carolina since 1988.

Throughout his meteoric career in business and politics, Carroll Campbell maintained his interest in acquiring an education. He took courses whenever he could and during his years in Congress continued his schooling at night, going on to earn his master's degree in political science. At American University he received the award for Outstanding Scholarship at the Graduate Level and was elected to two national honor societies, Pi Sigma Alpha and Phi Kappa Phi. He how holds four honorary doctoral degrees as well.

South Carolina's educational reform is centered on two pieces of legislation: the Educational Improvement Act (EIA) of 1984, passed under Richard Riley, and the "Target 2000" legislation, which builds on the EIA and was passed under Carroll Campbell in 1989. When the EIA was passed and funded, a banner headline appeared in the Columbia, South Carolina newspaper: "THEY SAID IT COULDN'T BE DONE, BUT RILEY WORKS A MIRACLE." Riley's leadership was a major factor, but the miracle would never have taken place without the active involvement of South Carolina's business community. Jack Rogers, speaker pro tem of the South Carolina House, put it this way: "Our business community didn't just watch the sausage being made, they were willing to get in and do some of the grinding themselves."

Significant educational reform with full funding is a miracle. The EIA included 61 initiatives, all of which have been implemented. They include such things as early childhood development programs, programs for the gifted and talented, a teacher loan-forgiveness program, and extra assistance in basic skills. The success of the EIA is due, in part, to work done before the bill was even drafted. W. W. (Hootie) Johnson, now chairman of the board of NCNB of South Carolina, raised money for early studies and polling, work that was performed by the Education Commission of the States. This preparation proved invaluable, particularly in the area of incentive pay. In other communities aggressive opposition to incentive pay on the part of certain teachers or the teachers union has led to failure on this issue. And failure on a critical issue can frustrate implementation of an entire reform package. The poll commissioned by Hootie Johnson identified a way to reward productive teachers that was favored by both the public and the teachers. In addition to such blue-ribbon leadership by the business community, citizens participated in "education forums" held in each region of the state. Terry Peterson, who is now executive director of the Joint Business-Education Subcommittee of the South Carolina Education Improvement Act, estimates that "13,000 people participated in discussion groups and offered advice on the directions of the reform package."

South Carolina business leaders have characterized accomplishments in the state schools over the past five years as "a quantum leap." Terry Peterson lists the following accomplishments:

1. South Carolina led the nation in the grade given by teachers to educational reform during the past five years in a study conducted by the Carnegie Foundation for the Advancement of Teaching.
2. The number of students meeting minimum basic skill standards has increased substantially.
3. SAT scores improved to the extent that South Carolina led the nation in points gained over the past five years.
4. Student attendance improved since 1983 so that South Carolina ranked among the top six states in attendance in each of the past four years.
5. Advance Placement enrollment (high school courses for college credit) has increased by more than 350 percent, and more students taking the courses are passing the national exams.
6. The percentages of high school graduates going to college and passing freshmen course work have increased to their highest levels in recent history.

7. Overall job placement rates for graduates of vocational programs and in fields related to their vocational training have
improved.
8. Overall teacher, parent, and public satisfaction with the
South Carolina Education Improvement Act continues to be
very high.
9. The improved attitude toward public schools manifests itself
further in a shift of almost 6,000 students from private to
public schools.

South Carolinians have learned that the seed for improvement
and the continuing interest necessary to maintain and expand
state initiatives can come from partnerships in education. One of
the seven major divisions of the EIA is captioned "creating more
effective partnerships among the schools, parents, community and
business." As Terry Peterson has observed: "Business-education
partnerships have played and are playing an increasingly important role in these reform initiatives and are one key ingredient in
South Carolina's success in beating the odds." Volunteers and
partners in education have become committed to the cause of better education. The number of business-education partnerships in
the state has grown from 800 in 1983 to approximately 6,000 in
1989.

Incredibly, the unusual momentum that led to the passage of
EIA has continued to the present day. "Target 2000" focuses on
"dropout prevention, early childhood development, flexibility
and innovation at the school site, higher-order thinking and basic
skills, arts education, expanded partnerships, broadening accountability measures, recruitment of minority students into
teaching, and parent education on family literacy." These new and
expanded initiatives are being paid for by additional funding of almost $10 million, with $5 million more added to the original EIA
fund. The leadership in this latest continuing movement for reform has been supplied by a different kind of education governor—who couldn't afford to go to college right after he graduated
from high school, but whose respect for education is confirmed by
his own persistent efforts to continue his schooling when others in
his situation might not have found the time.

Ten Education Governors

John Ashcroft (R-Missouri)

By providing tutors for some lagging first graders, Missouri has dramatically cut the number of children repeating that grade.

Terry Branstad (R-Iowa)

Branstad is building the first two-way video network so teachers can reach students statewide.

Carroll Campbell (R-South Carolina)

His partnership with business to improve literacy and job training is the nation's most extensive.

Bill Clinton (D-Arkansas)

One of America's most articulate reform advocates, he has pioneered new approaches to early childhood development.

Garrey Carruthers (R-New Mexico)

A former economics professor who will give New Mexicans an annual report card on the state's 88 districts.

Booth Gardner (D-Washington)

Gardner was one of the first to take a hard look at what students will need to know in the twenty-first century.

Madeleine Kunin (D-Vermont)

Instead of relying on standardized tests, Vermont is pioneering the use of a portfolio of student work to assess math and writing skills.

Ray Mabus (D-Mississippi)

To ensure that children start school ready to learn, the state screens three-year-olds. Those who need help get it.

Rudy Perpich (D-Minnesota)

Parents can choose among schools statewide, and high school students can take courses in state colleges.

Tommy Thompson (R-Wisconsin)

Wisconsin is experimenting with choice and with cutting welfare for parents whose children are truants.

Fortune, Special Issue, Spring 1990.

Is Money
the Answer?

Public education is invariably discussed in terms of money. Most people tend to assume improvement is taking place if per-pupil spending is up. John Chubb of the Brookings Institute, an outspoken leader of the "choice" movement, is also one of the nation's leading debunkers of the "spending equals excellence" philosophy. Chubb maintains that the United States spends more money on education than Japan, and that Sweden, which leads all nations on educational expenditures per pupil, comes in last among major countries in math and science achievement. Still, as we have seen, state systems have been overturned on the basis of inequitable funding. Sometimes the disparity is immense, as appears in the accompanying excerpt from Jonathan Kozol's *Savage Inequalities.* At the very least, effective spending must occur within the appropriate format.

This chapter presents examples of effective and ineffective spending: times when private funds have been spent sensibly; a citizens' commission whose work yielded billions of additional public dollars because a strong case was made for responsible expenditure; and a tragic case of millions of dollars being poured down the rat hole of an erroneous educational premise.

If Money Doesn't Matter, Why Does Jonathan Kozol Find "Savage Inequalities"?

Camden, New Jersey, is the fourth poorest American city of more than 50,000 people. Its children have the highest rate of poverty in the United States. Its entire property wealth of $250 million is less than the value of one casino in Atlantic City. What is life like for children in this city? I spent several days there in the spring of 1990. Because it has no hotel, I stayed in Cherry Hill, a beautiful suburban area of handsome stores and costly homes. The five-minute drive to Camden was a journey between different worlds.

Pyne Point Junior High School is a two-story building, yellow brick, its windows covered with metal grates, the flag on its flagpole motionless above a lawn with no grass; its 650 children are 98 percent black or Latino. Children come to school with rotting teeth, leaning on their elbows in discomfort as they sit in class. Many kids have chronic, untreated illnesses. The first day I was there, a child with diabetes had a blood-sugar level close to coma and another was shot twice in the chest.

A number of teachers don't have books for even half their students. The typing teacher shows me her students' typewriters, which, she says, "should have been thrown out 10 years ago." In a basic math skills class, an eighth-grader can't add five and two. In another class, brownish clumps of plaster dot the ceiling where there once were sound-absorbing tiles. A science class uses workbooks in a lab without lab equipment.

The playing field next to the school is bleak and bare. There are no goal posts and no sports equipment. Beyond the field is an illegal dump where contractors from the suburbs dump trash. A suburban medical lab recently deposited a load of waste including hypodermic needles. Children then set fire to it. There have been several recent fires, but the fire alarm hasn't worked in 20 years....

Defendants in a recent lawsuit brought by parents in New Jersey's poorest districts claimed that differences like these should be honored as the consequence of "local choice." But that "choice" is determined by lack of other choices. East Orange children cannot choose lacrosse or soccer or modern dance in fields or in dance studios they do not have; nor can they keep clean in showers their schools cannot afford. Little children in East Orange do not choose to wait 15 minutes for a chance to hold a jump rope. In suburban Millburn, per-pupil spending is about $1,500 more than in East Orange, where the tax rate is three times as high.

The high school dropout rate in Jersey City, 52 percent, translates to failure for 2,500 children every four years. The rate in Princeton, under 6 percent, translates to only 40. Behind the good statistics of the richest districts lies the triumph of a few. Behind the sad statistics of the poorest cities lies the misery of many....

Raymond Abbott, the Camden boy who was lead plaintiff in the case, is today a 19-year-old high school dropout with seventh-grade reading skills. A learning-disabled student who spent eight years in Camden public schools, his problems were never diagnosed, and he was mechanically passed on each year. On the day the court decision came down, Abbott, now a cocaine addict, heard of his belated victory from a Camden County Jail cell.

Jonathan Kozol, education activist, former teacher, and author of *Death at an Early Age* and other books, is author of *Savage Inequalities: Children in America's Schools* (New York: Crown). Condensed, with the author's permission, from *Teachers Magazine,* 3 (October 1991), 36–45, this excerpt from *Savage Inequalities* appeared in *The Education Digest* (March 1992) and has been condensed further for this book. ©1991, Jonathan Kozol.

Richard Riordan and Richard Dowling
Writing to Read in Mississippi

In the autumn of 1991 Sabre Razeyeh began kindergarten at the Boyd School in Jackson, Mississippi. Unlike many of the young black Mississippians who preceded her, Sabre found IBM computer terminals in her classroom on the first day of school. These terminals are part of a new statewide public school program based on the premise that Sabre and other kindergarteners arrive at school knowing many more words than they can write or read. The Mississippi experiment is part of IBM's Writing to Read program, developed by Dr. John Henry Martin, a veteran educator.

The program teaches children 42 phonemes (letter-sound combinations) as a starting point in the process of learning to read and write. With one third of its adult population functionally illiterate, Mississippi desperately needed a new approach to literacy. It got one thanks in large part to the leadership role played by two strong-willed and generous mentors.

Richard Riordan is a successful California lawyer-investor who now devotes a portion of his time to philanthropy. Richard O'R. Dowling is a wealthy New York entrepreneur. Together they offered to put up $7 million to implement the five-year Writing to Read program if the state would put up $6 million. The state agreed.

Both Riordan and Dowling have long been interested in education; currently they are university board members, financial contributors, and parents. Riordan had given the same IBM system to school districts in the past, and it was he who was first approached by an IBM executive with the notion of implementing Writing to Read throughout an entire state. After enlisting his friend Dowling, Riordan and IBM convinced Mississippi to go forward with the plan—no mean feat. As with virtually every educational initiative, the program has its advocates and its critics.

Not every educator believes that phonics—or computers, for that matter—present the best way to teach the fundamental skills of reading and writing. Upon learning of the program, for example, LeRoy Finkel, coordinator of instructional technology in California's San Mateo County Office of Education, commented, "It's too bad the teachers in Mississippi weren't given a choice." Dr. M. D. Roblyer, an expert on computer-based teaching, observed, "If they're expecting miracles in Mississippi, they're going to have to try harder." On the other hand, Mississippi Governor Ray Mabus has given the program his strong personal endorsement, although he and the state superintendent of education both note that Writing to Read must be part of a broader educational plan.

Based on experiences in other states, the program's chances of success in Mississippi were high. In Riordan's home state of California, test scores for the 1984 California Assessment Program in one city had been below the expected levels. But in 1985 Writing To Read was installed in the city schools, and the third graders who were involved in the program scored higher on that year's test than third graders with similar demographics in surrounding districts. In Juniata, Pennsylvania, kindergarten students scored in the 44th percentile on the Stanford Achievement Test before taking the program and in the 71st percentile after using Writing to Read in the first grade. After the program was instituted in Norfolk, Virginia, the number of students needing to repeat first grade decreased 50 percent.

Writing to Read involves more than computer terminals. The children use headsets and hear a taped voice pronounce the words they have typed. Among other components of the overall system is a "listening library" in which students can hear tape recordings of books. Tactile materials are part of the mix, and some of the instruction comes in the form of games. Of course, everything occurs under the guidance of teachers trained in the system.

Conventional spelling is not addressed until after the child has progressed through the program. IBM literature gives the following example of an early composition: "When I was little and had no teeth I Wanted dads inglish muffen.bUt he wold not let me have it.So I sat on it.My dad was disopointed." At the Boyd School, Sabre Razeyeh began one of her earliest efforts in a more traditional manner, based on the fairy tales she had heard at home: "Wuns epone tim...."

Paul M. Ostergard
Banking on Education

Paul Ostergard, who for years ran General Electric's substantial and effective foundation, now oversees Citibank's philanthropy as vice president and director of corporate contributions and civic responsibility. One of the more knowledgeable and creative veterans in the field, Ostergard frankly admits that he does not have all the answers and that money is not an automatic cure-all. The bank gives education a high priority, with half its contributions channeled there. Even so, Ostergard reports, "Ten years of support for K–12 school improvement convinced us long ago that getting out corporate checkbooks is not the answer. Private funds are valuable if they're flexible and can be put to work quickly to underwrite good ideas from teachers and school staffs. They can also fund structural improvements, such as Citibank's $7.5-million grant to further school-based management in 30 schools and our $3 million to Ted Sizer to help create smarter classrooms."

By supporting educational initiatives in both the practical and theoretical realms, Citibank is able to effect change in today's schools while supporting research that might improve tomorrow's teaching efforts even more. The goal of "Banking on Education," Citibank's $20-million, decade-long commitment to improving the quality of education for kids in kindergarten through twelfth grade, is to see every child in a Citibank-funded program graduate from high school prepared for higher education or employment.

Citibank also provides funding for programs that "promote stability and quality of life in our communities." Based on a belief that the arts and culture are vital aspects of a healthy community, Citibank donates to programs that promote excellence while they increase participation and access. In Houston, for example, Arts Partners (initiated and still supported by Citibank) unites 14 arts institutions and 13 schools to coordinate field trips, in-school performances, and arts instruction.

In the words of Citibank Chairman John S. Reed, "Fulfilling our corporate responsibility to society is not only morally and ethically appropriate; it is, in the long run, good business practice." But at Citibank the commitment doesn't end with the signing of a check. Often Citibank volunteers become active participants in the organizations that receive the company's support. "To leverage dollars for success," advises Ostergard, "companies can also contribute ideas and caring. In our case, we see Citibank mentors, tutors, school board members, and volunteers as our most important asset committed to improving education."

Trading Commodities to Finance a New Charity Fund

A little bit of charity is creeping into the rough-and-tumble commodity pits.

A top U.S. futures trader, Paul Tudor Jones, and one of the most successful sponsors of leveraged buy-outs in the mid-1980s, Raymond Chambers, are teaming up to form a $125-million commodity fund that plans to hand over most of its profit to social programs picked by Chambers and a group of advisers. Their main goal is to encourage children from disadvantaged backgrounds to stay in school and pick up business skills.

Capital for the new fund, known as the One-to-One Charitable Fund Inc., will come from foundations, other institutional investors, and wealthy individuals. It will be managed by Jones and three other veteran commodities traders, who have been among the top performers in their field.

The notion of trying to further social justice by trading in cutthroat markets such as soybeans or stock-index futures strikes some as odd. As veteran Chicago commodity trader Mark Ritchie observed in his autobiography: "There is a stunning lack of sportsmanship in the way this game is played.... I got the feeling I was being trained as a socially sanctioned bookie."

Sponsors of the fund, however, say they are totally serious about their new charitable mission. "The problems in our inner cities are so severe," says Chambers. "This isn't a silver bullet that will solve everything, but it's an opportunity to help people feel connected to the mainstream."

So far, major investors have tentatively committed about half the $125-million target, and fund executives hope to have fully raised the money by June of 1992, at which time it will start operations.

As spelled out in its offering circular, the One-to-One Fund would try to line up volunteers nationwide to serve as mentors for students from disadvantaged backgrounds. Students periodically would get small cash awards—drawn from the fund's commodities trading profits—if they stayed in school, avoided drugs and crime, and picked up business skills.

At age 23, or perhaps earlier, students who completed the program would each get a $10,000 grant designed to help them start their own business. While program sponsors say it is too early to tell how many students might ultimately benefit, they indicate that if the futures-trading operation does well, it could support several thousand students....

Helping channel money to various mentoring programs will be Chambers and a panel of experts led by Leroy Keith, president of Morehouse College, and Sybille Mobley, business school dean at Florida A&M University. Organizers of the One-to-One Fund say they plan to work mostly with existing mentoring programs, such as Big Brothers/Big Sisters of America, but may help develop some new programs, too.

Chambers is best known on Wall Street as a founding partner of Wesray Capital Corp., the leveraged buy-out boutique that earned big riches from its acquisitions of Gibson Greetings Corp. and the Avis car-rental business in the 1980s. Since 1987, though, Chambers has withdrawn from active work at Wesray and spends most of his time on social programs in the Newark, New Jersey, area.

Excerpted from George Andrews and Stanley W. Angrist, "A New Charity Fund Puts Its Bets in Cutthroat Commodity Pits," *The Wall Street Journal,* April 6, 1992, C 9–10.

===

Joe Flom
The Capital Task Force

Joe Flom's brilliant career as a lawyer and the prime force behind Skadden, Arps, Slate, Meagher, & Flom, one of the nation's most successful and largest law firms is not relevant here. What is relevant, however, is Flom's role as a mentor to New York City's school children. His contributions are immense. When I asked him where he found the time for his many activities in support of schools, he said, "You don't find it. You have to make it."

Like Eugene Lang, Flom has sponsored an I Have a Dream (IHAD) class, and his students can often be seen walking through the halls of Skadden, Arps, where many of them have internships or summer jobs. Flom works closely with these young people, has guaranteed each of them college tuition if they qualify, and has retained a fine staff to work with him and with the class. But Flom's greatest contribution to the public schools, although virtually unheralded, comes not from his IHAD sponsorship but from his leadership in enabling the city to build billions of dollars worth of new schools in the decade to come.

In 1987 the president of the New York City Board of Education and the chancellor of the city's public school system appointed a 12-member Task Force on Capital Financing and Construction. Joe Flom and Dr. Robert L. Polk, executive director of the Council of Churches of the City of New York (whom you met earlier in this book through his work at Riverside Church), were designated chairpersons of the group, also called the Capital Task Force. As a member, I had a front-row seat for a remarkable lesson in the art of government.

Any problem in the New York City school system is a big one. There are more students in the city's public schools—one million—than there are citizens in most of America's large cities. There are 62,000 teachers. More to the point of the task force, there are just over 1,000 school buildings, covering about 103 million square feet. Half of the school buildings are more than 45 years old, and some are nearly 100 years old. Only the federal government has a greater real property management responsibility; no other city or state agency comes close.

One of the first acts of the Capital Task Force was to conduct a study of the schools. It confirmed the worst fears of task force members. At more than 400 schools children could not find adequate seating. More than 600 buildings required some type of major repair work or component replacement. At many schools students did not have access to drinking fountains, bathrooms, or playgrounds.

The system absorbs building and maintenance money like a sponge. At the time the task force was appointed, the board of education received about $40 million each year for direct maintenance costs and approximately $200 million for capital projects. But years of deferred maintenance and inadequate capital funding resulted in a backlog of maintenance and capital needs measured in billions. The vast sums expended annually on the city's school buildings were at best a band-aid applied to a hemorrhaging wound. Every year the physical plant deteriorated further as enormous waste resulted from inadequate processes and a maze of unnecessary regulations enforced by entrenched special interests.

The Capital Task Force soon concluded that it had two jobs: one, to develop a way to finance and build schools in the most efficient manner; and two, to establish a system to maintain buildings in the best condition and to provide for their optimal use. The city had earned the grade of F in both areas.

It was not difficult to locate the authority at the core of the problem: the board's Division of School Buildings (DSB) was responsible for design, construction, and operation and maintenance. The Capital Task Force learned that it took eight to ten years to build a school in New York. Although DSB was in charge of the process, it actually had little or no control over the different stages of approval once the decision had been made to proceed. The process is worth examining in some detail because it reveals just how difficult reform can be—reformers often learn the hard way that a good idea is not enough—and it shows the immense challenge that confronted Flom and his colleagues.

The staff of the Capital Task Force divided the decade-lōng procedure involved in school construction into three stages: the first involved defining the need, projecting the scope of the project, and selecting the site. This stage entailed independent approvals by the community school board, the Office of Management and Budget, the City Planning Commission, the community school superintendent, and the Uniform Land Use and Review Procedure (which itself involves public hearings and separate approvals by state and city environmental agencies). This first step, which also required Board of Estimate approval on at least four distinct occasions, generally took four years.

The second stage included selecting the architect, choosing the preliminary and final designs, and accepting construction bids; it took from two to three years. In addition to approval by many of the same agencies required in stage one, this second stage also required approval by the City Art Commission, the Landmarks Preservation Commission, and the Board of Standards and Appeals. This step also involved the infamous Wicks Law, which required the city to bid out separately four prime contracts (electrical, plumbing, HVAC, and general contracting). Probably a reform in some bygone era, the law as currently enforced required the lowest bidder to get the contract, even if the contractor had performed poorly on a previous job, which virtually guaranteed inordinate delays. The Wicks Law proved to be one of the Capital Task Force's most difficult hurdles.

The final stage, construction, also took two to three years. Approval by the city's Buildings Department was required here, as was approval by the Mayor's Office of Construction and the Board of Estimate.

In a system in which each school took a decade to build, a comprehensive plan for citywide construction was virtually impossible. In addition, the inability to maintain, renovate, or use the buildings properly once constructed—the second area of DSB's responsibility—dampened any zeal that might otherwise have existed to expedite construction.

At first glance, the repair process appeared almost efficient in comparison with the construction maze: only five levels of approval were necessary before a decision could be made. But the paucity of funds, lack of skilled personnel, and the tight grip of the Custodians Union on procedures for maintenance and school management soon confirmed to the Capital Task Force that DSB was equally counterproductive while wearing its second hat—repair and renovation.

Until 1988 New York City's school custodians were responsible for the cleaning, heating, and minor repair of school buildings. Through a chief custodian, they reported to a bureau within DSB. They were paid through an "indirect" system in which they were given an "allowance" with which to carry out their duties. With these funds they paid staff and purchased the supplies they deemed necessary. Whatever was left from this annual allowance at the end of the year the custodians kept for themselves. (Buffalo is the only other city in New York state with this system.)

The custodians also controlled the times when the building could stay open outside of school hours and charged fees for the time they permitted the buildings to be used before or after school. In the 1960s the Stichman Commission, looking into corruption in government, found that custodians in large high schools were making incomes of well over $100,000 per year. That commission proposed statutory reform, but the powerful Custodian Local 891 was able to bring about the defeat of the legislation.

The Capital Task Force found that the custodians had a relatively free hand in how they used their allowances and other fees.

Because their contract with the board was classified as a "require-ments contract," many items, such as graffiti removal or keeping the school open from 3 to 6 p.m., were separately negotiated for additional fees. Most custodians refused to make minor repairs, claiming that these were not covered by the contract. They hired nonunion labor and were not required to clean the schools every day. Remarkably, the supervisors who were supposed to check on the custodians' performance were members of the same union as the custodians themselves. In spite of obvious flaws in the system—which were subjected to public review every few years when the cus-todians renewed their contract with the board—the system en-dured. It seemed impossible to rout the custodians from their entrenched position.

Enter Joe Flom. The Capital Task Force submitted a draft report at the end of 1987 and held hearings at various school sites in early 1988. Curative legislation developed by task force staff was submit-ted to the state assembly and passed in the summer of 1988 but was defeated in the senate. The state AFL-CIO opposed any revision of the Wicks Law. At Flom's suggestion, United Federation of Teach-ers President Sandy Feldman entered the fray and persuaded the leadership of the AFL-CIO to agree to a five-year suspension of the Wicks Law. Changes were made in the legislation, negotiations en-sued with legislative leaders, and a statute creating the New York City School Construction Authority (SCA) passed in December 1988. The Custodians Union, subjected perhaps to greater scru-tiny than ever before, was willing to make some concessions in their pending collective bargaining agreement.

Plant managers and supervisors—the people who managed and evaluated the custodians—were no longer allowed to be members of the custodians' union. Although the allowance system contin-ued, largely because staggering sums would otherwise have been necessary to fund long-vested pensions, custodian's salaries were brought more in line. The schools stayed open from 3 to 6 without additional fees. All in all, genuine progress had been made.

The major change, though, was the creation of the SCA, a state agency given responsibility for the design and construction of New York City schools. A five-year plan was promulgated, contemplat-ing $4.3 billion for rebuilding and new construction. The DSB was replaced by a new Division of School Facilities (DSF), which re-ports directly to the chancellor and is responsible for school maintenance and plant operation. Although the indirect payment option for custodians was retained, a performance-based system has also been instituted.

Under the SCA and the DSF, billions of dollars are going into renovation, modification, and construction. The first new school was completed in the spring of 1992. The entire process from concept and site selection through construction and final approval now takes less than four years.

Joe Flom has moved on from bricks and mortar to a new area of concern. "We cannot ignore the kids at the top," he says. He does not want them to get lost in an educational process that is too often massive and impersonal. Accordingly, a principal target of the foundation he has established with his wife Claire is the "gifted disadvantaged."

Satellite Learning Centers

What can be done when funds for school construction are not immediately available? Florida's Dade County Public Schools (DCPS), the nation's fourth-largest school district, serves more than a quarter-million students. Faced with an ever-increasing student population, the district struggles to put a cap on the extreme overcrowding that already plagues several of its schools. In June 1987, then Dade County Public Schools Superintendent Joseph Fernandez addressed the members of the Greater Miami Chamber of Commerce. His goal was to convince companies, many of which were already operating successful on-site daycare centers, to operate public education facilities in conjunction with DCPS.

Fernandez's proposed Satellite Learning Centers (SLC) would link schools and businesses in a well-defined partnership. The SLCs would serve the children of the host company's employees in kindergarten through second grade. The company would provide classroom space, maintenance, utilities, and security. DCPS would provide the teachers, learning materials, and the curricula.

Each Satellite Learning Center would be linked with a nearby elementary school—a "host" school—the principal and a designated lead teacher from which would share administrative responsibilities.

R. Kirk Landon, CEO of American Bankers Insurance Group (ABIG), learned of Fernandez's plan and was willing to give it a try. At the time, ABIG, a company with more than 1,000 employees, was providing daycare for approximately 90 children ranging in age from six weeks to five years old. With determination and fast action, ABIG and DCPS were able to open the ABIG center's doors in the fall of 1987. That first year 24 kindergarten students took advantage of the school, the first of its kind in the nation. During each of the next two years, an additional grade level was added; the school now accommodates children in kindergarten through second grade.

Today six SLCs are being run in Dade County, including one at Miami International Airport and one at Miami Dade Community College, North Campus. Dr. Rodolfo Abella has evaluated SLCs in *Evaluation of the Satellite Learning Centers Program: February 1991.* A few of the findings are listed here.

1. An analysis indicates that students attending the SLC are performing above the county and national averages in all major content areas (i.e., math, reading, science). The findings hold true for students who have attended the SLC program since kindergarten. SLC students also have better attendance records than comparable DCPS students.

2. Parents judged the program to be a success. They were pleased with the SLC facilities and with the program's instructional activities. Parents reported that the program allowed them to spend more time with their children, increased their involvement in their children's education, saved them money, and reduced the complexity of their daily schedule. They also reported improved work production, punctuality, and attendance as a result of participating in the program.

3. Both the school system and American Bankers benefited from their participation in the program. The SLC program helped DCPS reduce overcrowding at the schools and reduced expenditures by eliminating construction costs (an estimated $1.9 million for three SLCs in operation during 1989–90) as well as security, utilities, maintenance, and transportation costs. The program also increased parental involvement in education and encouraged the professionalization of teaching. It benefited ABIG by improving worker productivity. SLC parent-employees, supervisors, and high-level management all agree that the SLC program had a positive impact on work behavior, leading to better work attendance, punctuality, and lower employee turnover. In addition, SLC parent-employees were rated as being better adjusted to their work environment and as being more satisfied with their jobs and their employer.

In Dade County, an expedient driven by a shortage of classroom space led to a program that not only provided the necessary space but yielded unforeseen benefits to both parents and children involved. Fernandez is now chancellor of the New York City Public Schools. The first Satellite Learning Center in that city opened last year; he tells me many more will follow.

Joseph Grannis
When Money Isn't the Answer

A classic example of the effect of massive spending to solve a major problem in education is New York City's $120-million four-year program (1985–89) to reduce the dropout rate. A major role in measuring the program's effectiveness was played by Professor Joseph C. Grannis of Teachers College, Columbia University.

The dropout problem is a reality throughout the country but is most pronounced in the inner-city schools, especially among students who are members of minority groups. In New York almost 30 percent of students drop out before high school graduation. (This is a conservative estimate. A major impediment to progress in this area is the difficulty in ascertaining precisely how many students begin high school, and then determining exactly what happens to them. Do they transfer to another school under another name, or do they leave the system forever? In 1988 a study published by a group of African-American, Hispanic, and Native American educators stated that the rates for minority students had reached "epidemic proportions," with 62 percent of Hispanic students, 53 percent of African-American students, and 46 percent of Native American students dropping out before graduation.)

In 1985 New York resolved to do something about this horrendous problem. Two separate prevention programs, later combined, included 150,000 participants. The four-year program was funded at $120 million ($30 million per year or $8,000 per student). This extraordinary funding was derived in part from the mayor's budget but principally from the state government. According to the *New York Times*, bills sponsored by the chairmen of the senate and assembly education committees "were written to assure that most of the money went to the most troubled urban schools, bypassing the usual formulas that critics said often shortchanged the city in favor of suburban and rural areas."

The 150,000 students in the program came from 36 high schools, 98 middle schools, and five elementary schools. Attendance and academic records indicated that these students were likely to drop out. The program emphasized methods devised to intensify attendance and provide guidance. Strategies included after-school programs, job training, counseling, and even telephoning students in the morning to get them to school.

═══ Elementary School "Dropoffs" ═══

For the past 15 or 20 years, the high school drop-out rate (high and rising) has generated justifiable outrage. In the center cities, particularly among minority youth, it is an epidemic. In New York City the rate for minority students is currently greater than 50 percent—an alarming and frightening statistic. Many who do graduate lack the basic reading, writing, and mathematical skills to gain entry-level employment. Lack of education is one of the causes of the growing "underclass," a group of people unequipped for gainful participation in our society.

High school dropout statistics monopolize public and private attention. Educators, politicians, and corporations throw up their hands and, in well-intentioned ways, spend millions for remedial training.

But the problem does not go away. It intensifies. Why? Because dropping out of high school is the last stage of a long process. Before there is a drop out, there is a dropoff. And often the dropoff is only seven or eight years old.

The elementary-age child who has not received the basic learning skills at school and the necessary reinforcement at home has, for all practical purposes, dropped off the learning tree. The child can no longer be nurtured, supported, or encouraged by the traditional educational system. He or she is being left behind, ceases to grow intellectually, and grows more and more frustrated, alienated, and lost, socially and emotionally. The child legally cannot physically drop out, but the child's mind and heart have dropped off. Dropoffs of today are the dropouts of tomorrow.

To the child unable to keep up, to achieve, or to gain satisfaction from progress, other activities—negative or positive, but usually negative—become more interesting. These may provide a quick fix for status and a quasi sense of accomplishment and self-worth. The dropoff becomes the dropout who, in turn, becomes the adult increasingly left out of society. The convoluted world of drugs, crime, and welfare dependence is seen as the route to meeting basic needs. In the center city this trilogy has become more and more deadly.

Our national attention should, in part, be redirected to the younger students, those who with proper attention will not drop off, and who will be less likely to drop out. High school is too late when the problem begins as early as second grade. Restructuring of United States education cannot only be from the top down; it must include our very young. If they don't get a good start, they will never have the opportunity to reach the top!

—Robert A. Jeffers, Pastor,
St. Augustine School of the Arts,
Bronx, New York

Five years later Professor Grannis and his colleagues at Teachers College released their five-volume study on these dropout prevention efforts. The study found that 50.7 percent of the students in the program dropped out after three years. According to the *New York Times,* "Those results were not appreciably higher than the figures for eligible students who did not participate." In short, $120 million was spent, with a gain of essentially zero.

All was not lost, however. Grannis's work at the Institute for Urban and Minority Education at Teachers College is renowned for its thoroughness. Graduate students working with him spent months in designated schools trying to get at the root of the problem. Based on the detailed data collected, Grannis made a number of recommendations, including: "Schoolwide improvements cannot be achieved by applying existing resources differently; new resources must be nurtured."

Observed Robin Willner, executive director of the city's board of education division of strategic planning, after Grannis's study was released, "The initial program focused on what was wrong with the children and did not sufficiently focus on what was wrong with the school." It is not enough to monitor the students and press them to attend school. The schools themselves must change. They must be made more interesting and relevant to the students.

One of the more poignant findings of Grannis's study is that the at-risk students in the program did not expect to fail. Although many did not know how far their parents went through school, of those who did know, more than half reported that their parents had completed high school. An interim survey of middle school students contained this finding: "A large proportion (43 percent) of the respondents thought they would finish college, an additional 22 percent anticipated attending some postsecondary school. Only 6 percent of the respondents said they did not expect to graduate from high school."

Two days after the release of the Teachers College study, Schools Chancellor Joseph Fernandez announced *Project Achieve.* The project, Fernandez said, would "encourage comprehensive and systematic change in the schools. Efforts to support students at risk will be combined with ongoing efforts to bring about school improvement." Grannis was pleased. "It's remarkable that the chancellor has assimilated our recommendations as much as he has."

The dropout problem is complex; many experts feel that it must be anticipated in the preschool years and is most effectively dealt with in elementary school, before problems become too ingrained to remedy. Teenage pregnancies, difficulty with English, and drug abuse—all substantial problems themselves—contribute significantly to the number of dropouts. The solution lies in a multifaceted approach that can deal with all aspects simultaneously. As Grannis observed in an earlier report, "The stigmatization of at-risk students in a small scale approach is not wise; better to employ many diverse strategies for many different kinds of students."

MENTOR:
A Precedent

Law firms are notoriously conservative institutions. If you want a firm to undertake a project—unless it is one suggested by a major client or that promises a large retainer paid in advance—you are asked two questions: "What did we do last year?" and "What are the other firms doing?" If you can't provide the right response to one of these questions, it becomes very tough sledding to make something new happen. Oddly enough, this is even more so in the pro bono field because lawyers' traditional work is to represent indigent clients, and the idea of a pro bono activity that does not fall directly within a firm's traditional confines is a further compelling reason to do nothing.

Of course, MENTOR—the program I helped create to expose at-risk kids to the law as a profession—failed all of these tests. In short, MENTOR represented something lawyers abhor: a case without ready precedent.

By most measures MENTOR has been a successful program. Since its founding in 1983 MENTOR has grown in two directions: horizontally into a program involving 40 law firms in New York City, some 550 schools, and about 30,000 students in 20 states and two Canadian provinces; and vertically to include a separate high school for law and justice and a one-to-one mentoring program for senior lawyers. It has also led to similar programs involving other professions and vocations.

None of this expansion, however, happened without problems. So now I present this program, warts and all, to you as a case study demonstrating some of the problems and opportunities you might face in establishing a new program. For me, this example provides the added advantage of not having to turn a spotlight on someone else's mistakes.

In 1982 officials in the social studies department of the New York City Board of Education contacted a number of leading lawyers. At a luncheon meeting held in midtown Manhattan, lawyers were told that many high school students were interested in law as a possible career, and many others were fascinated by the subject simply because of what they had seen on television or read in the newspapers. The officials suggested that this might be fertile ground for a program to interest young people in staying in school. I was not at the meeting; but as I later heard it, many of the assembled lawyers made favorable comments. Yet, in spite of follow-up calls from the officials to the lawyers, nothing happened. No program was developed.

I did not know about this false start. But I had reviewed a successful school program involving doctors and a successful Explorer Scout program involving dentists. From this experience I saw that young New York City students were "turned on" by being involved, if only as observers, in the work of professionals. So I felt strongly that a program in the law would work.

Lawyers have often taken students to court or on a one-day tour of their offices, but I was not aware of any precedent for a sustained relationship between law firms and public schools (certainly not in New York). I plunged ahead anyway. Fortunately, I was senior enough in my own firm simply to start the program and inform my partners and associates by memo that it had begun and that they were welcome to participate. Since Joe Flom and Bob Fiske were in a similar position, and Fiske was president of the Federal Bar Council (and I was a vice president), we made MENTOR a project of the council and involved two other amenable firms as well. Five firms, we reasoned, made a respectable "pilot."

Through the New York Alliance I had excellent access to the schools. The Board of Education was excited about MENTOR, and Charlotte Frank (executive director for curriculum and instruction of the New York City Board of Education), Elliot Salow (director of social studies), and Dr. Lloyd Bromberg (Salow's assistant) all pitched in to select the schools. We picked one in each borough of the city and parceled them out among the firms.

The school with which my firm was paired was Curtis High School in Staten Island. When I arrived at the school, the principal showed me around. As we went through the school, he gave me a long list of areas in which money was needed. When we got back to his office, I told him that our program was not one that would be expected to generate funds. We wanted to show students what the practice of law was like and what the courts were like. I hoped that would be of some help to him. Another point that I had to make at the outset, this time to the teacher, was that our program was not a job or internship program. Law firms typically don't have that many jobs for high school students. (As the relationship developed between our firm and the school, we did hire some students, and some of the other firms in the MENTOR program arranged for scholarships for some students in their schools. But money and jobs were never a major aspect of the program.)

The content of the program was worked out in discussions among the firms and with the board. We decided on four basic events: a visit to the school, to explain the program, introduce the lawyers, and answer any questions students might have about the law; a visit to the firm; and visits to the state and federal courts (one emphasizing criminal law and the other civil law).

Over time, however, the program has developed into an almost continuous relationship throughout the school year. The lawyers work with the students on a moot court competition, coach the school's team for the state bar's mock trial program, visit the classroom to discuss interesting points of law, and set up Law Day presentations at the school. After each event outside the school, we have the students back to the firm for a sandwich lunch around the conference table. This casual meal during which the lawyers and students get to know each other is, in my view, one of the most valuable parts of the program, with its friendly exchange of ideas.

The kids are genuinely interested in the law. Although they are somewhat awestruck by the surroundings at first, once the students get to know us better, the prevailing thought becomes: "These people may be good, but I can do it, too."

After the experience of the first year, we felt strongly that the program worked. At that point the information with which we could evaluate the program was entirely anecdotal. When, for example, one of the law firms inadvertently scheduled a visit to bankruptcy court in the middle of the school's spring vacation, the kids came anyway and enjoyed the session even though bankruptcy court, frankly, is not our most exciting tribunal. At one high school, an angry group of parents protested on parents' night that their kids were not in the program. The students' classmates had enjoyed it, and their kids wanted to be included. (Regrettably, we have never had enough openings to accommodate student demand.)

The teachers pointed out case after case in which students who had not been interested in school and who had abysmal attendance records turned around after they had entered MENTOR. From the beginning, however, we wanted a more objective confirmation of whether the program was working. We received a detailed report from the Board of Education's evaluation unit in each of the program's first two years. The evaluation on the five-firm pilot program contained the following observation: "Students' perceptions of things they learned in MENTOR correspond quite closely to many of the program's goals as stated in the MENTOR Handbook. The program has been successful in meeting these goals. The effect on some students' behavior attributed to MENTOR suggests that the program may be fulfilling an additional goal of teaching students to recognize the impact of the law on their daily lives. While all five pairs accomplished the program's objectives, the school where the fewest students were college-bound (less than 40 percent) showed the most pronounced effect on the way students behaved in school. These students gave responses such as 'I respect my teachers more' and 'I watch everything more carefully now; I respect school rules.'"

The board's evaluation during the program's second year was again positive, with the following assessment: "All participating school-firm pairs believed overwhelmingly that the program's goals were achieved. Seventy-two percent of the students interviewed said that MENTOR had altered their attitudes toward the law. Some said MENTOR increased their desire to become attorneys. Others said that the program helped them to realize the complexity of the legal system in the United States and that law really was more fair than they had initially believed.... Interestingly, two out of the five students interviewed from the Manhattan school [where fewer than 25 percent of the students will attend a four-year college] believed that they had become more law-abiding as a result of MENTOR."

At the end of the first year, the list of schools that wanted to get into the program far exceeded the number of firms immediately available. Since five major firms had been in the pilot, we now had a precedent, and more than 20 firms participated in the second year.

My office, more particularly my secretary Judy Breck and I, supplied the central administration of the program. Judy had been a schoolteacher and a copywriter before joining our law firm; and these skills, in addition to a significant natural talent for administration, helped the program move smoothly and expand. I wrote a short handbook detailing MENTOR's components and telling newcomers how to go about setting up the program. (One section I thought particularly valuable was entitled "The Importance of Lunch.") Since then Judy Breck has expanded this small volume, which is complete with examples that should encourage further enlistment in the program.

We had some false starts, however. When someone at the Board of Education suggested that the lawyers act as counsel to students who wanted to present petitions or complaints to other students who served as part of the board's longstanding program the "Model City Council," it sounded like a good idea. We found, however, that Wall Street lawyers did not know much about the New York City Council. As a result, that part of the program fell flat on its face.

When half a dozen of our lawyers worked with Dr. Bromberg at the Board of Education to prepare a year-long day-to-day curriculum for MENTOR, that, too, turned out not to be a success. Teachers were used to the curriculum that they had developed over the years and felt far more comfortable fitting MENTOR into that. They did borrow parts of the MENTOR curriculum as the years went on, but the time spent developing it turned out not to have been productive.

One misjudgment we made early on was to assume that only large firms would be able to participate in the program. We were wrong. One of the local bar associations acted as the conduit for the participation of smaller firms. We later found in the national program that small firms could easily participate on their own.

The MENTOR program required very little funding. The firms understood that they would have to pay their own expenses, but this involved nothing more than providing sandwich lunches in the course of the year, together with some funds for duplicating documents and other minor disbursements. Even the amount of attorney time required was not that much; only a few lawyers were needed to take the students to court and on tours through the firm, and no "billable time" was involved in the lunches (young attorneys seem as predisposed as anyone to a free meal). It was only when the program had grown larger that we found it necessary to hire a full-time administrator, funded by the Federal Bar Council's foundation and the Aaron Diamond Foundation. And the Board of Education gave us office space.

The National Program

After MENTOR was up and running in New York City, I was asked to speak to various organizations interested in law-related education programs. One such group was the National Institute for Citizen Education in the Law (NICEL) in Washington, D.C. Ed O'Brien, who with Jason Newman established NICEL (originally known as "The Street Law Institute") a number of years ago, helped train some of our lawyers on how to act in the classroom. I then went down to Washington and helped Ed recruit firms for MENTOR, and the program was established with a dozen firms in Washington. Another MENTOR lawyer traveled to San Francisco on a similar mission. As a result of these trips and others, MENTOR sprang up in a number of locations throughout the country, generally assisted by our New York MENTOR handbook.

Three years ago, I was able to convince Jo Rosner—a former schoolteacher turned lawyer who ran an extremely successful MENTOR program in the state of Washington—to administer a national MENTOR program. This program publishes teaching materials, recruits law firms elsewhere in the country (generally through state bar associations), and otherwise helps to expand MENTOR to other locations. On a very tight budget—and the generosity of the Washington State Bar Association, which gave Rosner office space and secretarial and staff assistance—we raised $135,000, which was used to finance the program in its pilot phase over three years. National MENTOR is now growing at a rapid pace.

Starting a School

In September 1987 New York City Mayor Edward I. Koch and Board of Education President Robert F. Wagner Jr. asked me to serve as cochair, with Police Commissioner Ben Ward, of a commission investigating the establishment of a theme high school in which law and justice would be central. The commission was composed of four MENTOR lawyers, judges, public officials, teachers, administrators, and union leaders. Soon thereafter the Board of Education designated the Martin Luther King Jr. High School as the home for the new Institute for Law and Justice. The commission hired a staff director and an in-house coordinator, and funding was provided by the city. We set ourselves the tough goal of establishing a high school by the following fall and made it happen.

The commission divided itself into task forces assigned to various broad subject areas. During the summer teams of teachers fashioned curriculum for specific courses, largely based on task force input and focused on the central theme of law and justice. Consequently, a forensic science course, developed with the assistance of the faculty of John Jay College of Criminal Justice, is used to teach principles of math and science. Case writing is a component of broader instruction on writing skills. Reading lists suggest legal theme books like *To Kill a Mockingbird, Anatomy of a Murder,* and *Twelve Angry Men.* Although detective fiction is a staple for tenth-grade readers, by their senior year the students have moved on to *Crime and Punishment.*

The guiding principle underlying the commission's deliberations was the idea that a thematic law and justice curriculum, combined with developmental experiences exploring law and justice issues outside the classroom, would have a significant educational benefit for the students in the institute. While the commission expected and hoped that some students in the institute would ultimately undertake careers in the law, its primary objective was to design a curricular and extracurricular program that would challenge students to think, learn, and discover their potential as individuals.

The law and justice theme presents a rich array of issues that will challenge the institute's students—questions regarding the nature of community and the terms of the social contract; the role and obligations of government in designing and enforcing society's laws; the place of the family as a social unit; the rights of individuals and the responsibilities of citizenship; the rationale and purpose of civil disobedience; the distinctions between civil, economic, and social justice.

From the outset it was understood that the commission's guiding principle would not only be implemented in the curriculum of the school but would be aided by a major extracurricular effort. Commission members also agreed at the outset that the theme would not simply be "criminal justice," but that justice would have a much broader meaning, specifically including the teachings of Dr. Martin Luther King Jr.

As with two other "houses" at Martin Luther King High School, the Institute of Law and Justice is a school-within-a-school. It is located in a self-contained space, with shared access to the school's centralized facilities and services. This approach to school redesign utilizes small, separate instructional units that have demonstrated a positive impact on the self-esteem of low-achieving students.

From the beginning it was decided that the student body at the Institute for Law and Justice would not be an elite group, culled from applicants throughout the city on the basis of superior achievements or test scores. Instead, a representative group of students was selected by using the education options admissions formula, which allows for a screened, heterogeneous student enrollment determined by such criteria as reading level, attendance patterns, geographical distribution, and career interest.

All entering students are tested for competence in basic skills, as well as interest and aptitude. As anticipated, 50 percent of the incoming ninth-grade class require remedial assistance. The overwhelming majority of the students come from poor sections of the city, and the student body is largely African American and Hispanic.

Significant student and parent interest has developed in the institute. Even before it was actually up and running, some 850 parents of potential students attended an Orientation Day, and a Parents Association has been formed. After the institute had been open for one semester, some 2,500 students applied for the 250 openings. Since then, over 3,000 students have applied for the incoming class of 200 each year. Student and faculty morale are high. The first class graduated in the spring of 1992, with 95 percent of the students having applied to college and many having been accepted in Ivy League and other outstanding schools.

The "True Mentors"

A mentoring component at the institute was planned from the outset. At the beginning, the mentors were supplied largely from city departments and our law firm. The mentor-to-student ratio was programmed at 1:5. Part of the remediation component was to be a tutoring program with student volunteers from NYU, Fordham Law School, John Jay College, and other colleges and universities. After three years the Senior Lawyers Committee of the Association of the Bar of the City of New York established a one-to-one mentor program, and it is worth reviewing here to understand exactly what can come out of such a program.

Victor Futter, who had retired as Associate Counsel and Secretary of Allied Chemical Corporation and was now a partner in a New Jersey law firm, brought the one-to-one program to the attention of the committee. Its chairman, Al Driver, was familiar with the MENTOR because he had been general counsel of J.C. Penney Company, and Penney's legal department had participated in MENTOR. This relationship began as an experiment to see whether a corporate law department could function as well in the program as a law firm. It did.

The committee sponsored two meetings to elicit further interest from association members. As a result, 83 lawyers—some retired but many actively practicing—enlisted in the program and agreed to spend two sessions a month and at least an hour each time with their students. The mentors were given individual instruction on what they could expect from these relationships, and they agreed to stay with their students for up to three years, until they graduated from high school. Some of the mentors are now broadening the experience to include activities outside of the school, such as office visits, a museum trip, or a Knicks game.

Some mentors discovered that their students had unexpectedly narrow backgrounds that could be readily expanded. One 17-year-old from the South Bronx had never heard of Park Avenue, for example, and had never ridden in an elevator. On the other hand, mentor horizons expanded as well: a 30-year-old lawyer who had an infant daughter was surprised to find that her 15-year-old mentee did, too. "She is a mother who needs to be mothered," the lawyer said. But the mentor was impressed by her student's courage in the face of adversity: "She will be a star. She really will."

Every MENTOR lawyer has seen youngsters turned around by the experience. But as in most of the partnership programs, one of the true benefits of MENTOR is the fact that it has motivated the lawyers to participate further in the public schools. Many of the

MENTOR lawyers have joined other programs because they are now familiar with the problems of public schools and they are encouraged by the results that can be achieved by individuals who care.

How You Can
Make a Difference

When private citizens talk about public schools, their language often runs to military terms. *A Nation at Risk,* for example, observed that we would consider it "an act of war" if a foreign power had imposed this (mediocre) school system on us. Proctor & Gamble's chairman John Pepper, restless with our failure to cure education's woes, asked: "I wonder if we are talking about this issue the way the U.S. sat down to talk about what to do after Pearl Harbor? Do we have the same degree of intensity, the same degree of absolute determination that there is no way we are going to fail?" And both former Secretary of Education William Bennett and American Federation of Teachers President Albert Shanker—two men not noted for frequent agreement—have, as noted, said that what the schools need is not minor change but a "revolution."

One thing is certain: we cannot achieve fundamental change in our schools unless thousands of private citizens become involved. Not just interested, or aware of the problems, or concerned about the inadequate skills of our workers or the failings of our students—but involved. Without this massive participation by private citizens, entrenched interests will prevail. Nor can we wait for a grand master plan or even a consensus on what reforms are most effective. While we are waiting, the system will continue to erode, and another generation of children will be lost.

Throughout this book I've tried to draw lessons from successful partnership and reform movements. To move most effectively, you must know what works. You must also understand the forces that have both contained these successes and prolonged the existence of a system that too often does not work.

In 1990 the president and the nation's governors agreed to a series of proposals entitled The National Education Goals, which represent an informed consensus of what must be achieved to alter the downward spiral of education in America. Throughout this book you have seen private citizens working with the public schools to attain remarkable results that move us closer to meeting one or more of the goals.

You have read about communities in Arkansas in which HIPPY has brought children to school ready to learn (Goal 1). In Cincinnati mentors working with at-risk students have brought the dropout rate to 1 percent, far less than the prevailing norm among other students in the same community (Goal 2). In New Haven Dr. James Comer designed a school system in which students who once were viewed as hopeless now move in synch with or ahead of their peers (Goal 3). In Houston Carol Lowery, working with the LEGO-Logo program, is showing elementary school students that math, logic, computer applications, and other elements of engineering can be used in fascinating ways to solve real problems (Goal 4). In Mississippi, where one third of the adult community cannot read, children entering kindergarten are working with IBM computers and finding that they can Write to Read; they will break the chain of generational illiteracy (Goal 5). And finally, you have read in these pages of many schools, some located in tough inner-city areas, that are now free from drugs and violence (Goal 6).

Granted, these achievements do not mean that we are already "first in the world in math and science" or that "every adult American will be literate." But there is significant evidence that the downward spiral can be reversed and that real progress can be made toward the national goals and genuine educational achievement.

Below I try to set out the lessons learned in the various programs that have made a difference. These lessons are set out in a step-by-step format you can follow to improve and change your own programs or schools. At the book's conclusion, you will also be provided with a list of resources, including literature, organizations, and numbers to call for help or for advice.

All this may seem pretty clear-cut. So clear-cut, in fact, that you might be wondering whether you're really needed. If you are unsure, remember that except for programs such as those mentioned in these pages, there has been little change in the lamentable condition of our schools since 1983 when the alarm bell sounded in *A Nation at Risk*. Many things stand in the way of educational improvement: lack of funds; entrenched interests opposed to change; bureaucracy; poverty; drugs; violence. Your path may also be blocked by well-meaning individuals and groups that insist they have the one true solution. Or you may find two (or more) groups at odds in your community that will insist on getting THEIR program passed even if it means stalemate ensues and nothing gets done.

This is why you must get involved. I believe there are paths through these minefields. Others have found them; you will too. But before you can begin, you must have some sense of the elements of the great education debate—nationally and locally—that engulfs those who want to work in our schools.

The Great Education Debate: National

AMERICA 2000. In April 1991 President Bush and Secretary of Education Lamar Alexander introduced the administration's plan to achieve the National Education Goals. It was called "AMERICA 2000: An Education Strategy." The plan offered a four-part strategy, described as "four giant trains ... big enough for everyone to find a place on board." The Department of Education published a 62-page booklet detailing its specific components, which included comprehensive strategies for raising private funds to establish new kinds of schools (this can be done through the New American Schools Development Corporation, an entity created just for this purpose) and for establishing a program of national achievement tests. The testing—together with another pillar of the AMERICA 2000 program, vouchers for "choice"—has been the most widely criticized element of the program.

In recent years "choice"—a strategy that would make available to parents a wide range of alternatives within the public school system—has gained great popularity. But the Bush administration's version of choice goes one step further than was encompassed by the original concept: it encourages public funding to finance attendance at private schools.

Advocates of the AMERICA 2000 choice proposal say that it goes no further than the GI Bill, which enabled veterans to choose which institutions (including church-sponsored colleges and universities) they would attend with federal financial support. The proposal's opponents say that it would breech the constitutional barrier between church and state by providing funding to attend parochial schools and would also have the effect of making impoverished schools even worse as they are abandoned by those who choose to go elsewhere.

Early in 1992 Americans had an opportunity to witness The Great Education Debate on the floor of the United States Senate, as President Bush sought to move forward AMERICA 2000 and Democrats offered an alternative program. The principal sponsor of the Democrat's alternative bill was Senator Edward M. Kennedy, Democrat of Massachusetts. At the beginning of the debate, he said that "if President Bush wants to be the Education President, he has to do more than talk about it."

The "choice" amendment was offered by Republican Senator Orrin G. Hatch of Utah and would have provided subsidies to poor families choosing to send their children to private schools. Senator Hatch pleaded that "education is a key factor in lifting individuals from poverty." Senator Howard Metzenbaum, Democrat of Ohio, however, contended that the Hatch amendment would violate the constitutional separation of church and state, and countered by saying that "once we pass this, the door is open to further and further aid to private schools and is the first step to the abandonment of our public school system." Senator Kennedy characterized the Hatch amendment as "the preparatory school relief act." When the Democrats' bill was finally passed, it did include some elements of AMERICA 2000, but private schools were excluded.

The National Education Goals set out by the Democrats in the final bill reflect the six goals promulgated in Charlottesville at the Education Summit, but with variations that are worth noting. The *New York Times* described them as follows: "The education bill lays out national education goals to be met by the year 2000. Among them are the inclusion of all eligible preschoolers in the Head Start program, more Federal money for updating teacher training in mathematics and science and a sweeping extension of adult literacy programs. The bill also establishes a council of political leaders and education experts to develop a national academic report card to measure educational progress and shortcomings across the country."

The bill passed by a vote of 92 to 6, with 37 Republicans joining 55 Democrats in support of the measure. The bill as passed provides for $850 million in grants to states to be distributed among local schools that have proposed improvement plans. States may withhold a portion of the money for statewide efforts to create model schools and to finance programs to train teachers. At least three quarters of the money would be devoted to the most needy schools.

But the Great Education Debate is by no means concluded. One part of AMERICA 2000—The New American Schools Development Corporation, which relies on private funding—remains intact, as do the various initiatives (e.g., AMERICA 2000 communities) that require largely state or local action. The Democrats in the House passed a bill that does provide money for private schools in states "where local law permits it." Only two states, Vermont and Wisconsin, qualify, but Senate Democrats have already been strongly critical of the House version, contending that it flies in the face of traditional boundaries between church and state.

The Great Education Debate: Local

Locally, in your city or town, the great education debate has both administrative and substantive aspects. Administratively, the dominant issue is whether the schools will be run from a central agency or whether each district, or even each school, will be responsible for its own administration. The trend seems to be away from central administration. Still, old methods die hard. SBM and SDM—school-based management and shared decision-making—are the bywords of reform and restructuring. Their stated objective is to move administration away from central headquarters. While this situation is often a maze of political intrigue, you can find a way through it if you develop the right approach and attitude from the outset. Be warned, however, that there is "turf" here, and as you proceed you will undoubtedly be stepping on someone's toes.

Substantively, there are a number of strongly held views, as well. There is the traditional content-skills battle. Those in the first camp complain that "our students know nothing," generally pointing to Hirsch or Bloom or Ravitch and Finn to show that high school students today know very little, at least compared to people who are able to read these shocking reports in the newspapers. On the other hand, there are those who point out that in today's society, individuals will have to learn many new jobs in a lifetime even if they stay with same company, and that the main burden of the schools should be to teach students how to learn and think. Choice, merit pay for teachers, testing, and accountability are also key substantive issues. All of this is overlaid with strongly held views on multiculturalism and whether tests and curricula are fair to minorities.

The partnership field presents its own local issues: Should you support the present system or insist on restructuring and reform? Perhaps the important point now is that each of these issues has been dealt with in a reasonable way someplace and that there are models for you to follow to avoid paralysis.

Lessons Learned

The earlier parts of this book have been organized to take you through examples of mentors working as individuals and through a number of organizations, some created by individuals and some of long standing in the community, that support schools. The book then turned to reform efforts, proceeding from individual schools through cities and states. There was a reason for this organization. In my view, if you want to make a difference in the public schools, you must begin as soon as possible. This will generally mean in your individual capacity as a volunteer or working with an organization with which you are familiar.

Unlike proponents of some of the better known initiatives now abroad in our country, I do not believe that educational reform can be imposed from the top down. There must be "widespread public commitment" to the creation of better schools. This is the phrase that educational historian Lawrence Cremin used to describe the background on which the public school movement in this country was achieved. It is just as necessary now as it was 150 years ago when Horace Mann and others initiated the free school movement. There are too many people out there, for generous impulses or selfish reasons, who want to perpetuate the present system. They will not be moved by lofty slogans or even by well-articulated programs written by education experts and delivered by corporate executives who then leave the scene. Both in the last century and in recent decades, the public schools have been improved only when private citizens have taken the time and the interest to become involved. For this reason, and in this context, I offer the following suggestions for those about to get involved:

Start Now. Most of the partners you have read about in this book started in some individual capacity, as a parent, mentor, or volunteer. Some had the advantage of heading a corporation or civic organization when they began, but most started with few, if any, resources. In many cases, as their interests grew, these volunteers broadened the scope of their work. We've seen how an individual can progress from one phase to another. But even if you never go beyond helping out in a school or acting as a "true mentor," or whatever your individual role happens to be, you can be assured that you will make a difference.

Working as an individual in the schools, you will be bringing something of value to the present system. Perhaps you will be bringing only the willingness to listen to a student who will be paired with you in a one-to-one mentor relationship. Here, in your role as an adult possessing both time and patience, you will most likely bring a new ingredient to the life of a student who presently may have no one to turn to. The "true mentors" who work in the Law and Justice Institute described in the previous chapter are constantly surprised at the impact they have on their mentees. Sometimes they don't realize it and have to be informed by the teacher. At the very least, these relationships tend to keep students in school as many mentors in this book have testified.

There is another extremely important reason to start now. As you become involved, you will learn more about the system, which, in turn, will open up entire new visions of what you might do. Max Miller found that the vocational training was meager in the Memphis school system and established his program with AutoZone. He then found that Memphis was not alone in this need and the program went national. In Kentucky and South Carolina there were active partnership movements before comprehensive reform and restructuring, and these programs grew even larger and more widespread after reform.

Start Small. The British participants in the Fifth National Symposium on Partnerships in Education made this general observation on partnerships: "The highly successful focus, as in Britain, is on local needs and issues.... Another lesson, repeated by almost every presenter, was the importance of starting small." In my view, the lesson is as true with reform and restructuring of schools as it is with partnerships. The successful "choice" program in District 4 started small, with three alternative schools in 1974. Some schools grew, but to no more than 450 students; many to no more than 50 students. Because educational reforms and cognitive theories are often not as profound or absolute as their proponents contend, starting small also ensures that failures will be contained. Successes, once proved in the laboratory of the small school, can move to other areas.

N.Y.C. to Create Small, Theme-Oriented High Schools

The New York City school system is moving on several fronts to create at least 15 small, theme-oriented high schools to provide more supportive environments for students and to expand their choices among the city's high schools.

While the typical New York high school serves 2,000 to 3,000 students, Chancellor Joseph A. Fernandez has announced plans to create 10 new high schools in the next two years that would enroll between 500 and 700 students each.

"The very size and general curricular focus of many of our older high schools tend to create an impersonal setting for youngsters in desperate need of a more personalized, caring environment," Mr. Fernandez noted in a memorandum to the city board of education explaining his initiative.

In addition to the 10 schools envisioned under Mr. Fernandez's plan, the district and the Fund for New York City Public Education are developing requests for proposals to create five smaller schools.

These schools, which would enroll no more than 500 students apiece, must include grades nine through twelve, but also could include earlier, consecutive grades. The "New Visions Schools Project" is being supported by a three-year, $676,250 grant from the Aaron Diamond Foundation.

While the proposals will invite "all interested parties"—including universities, community organizations, principals, and teachers—to submit ideas for new schools, the proposals must be jointly designed by one of the city's 32 community school districts and the central Division of High Schools.

The Metropolitan Corporate Academy, the first of the 10 proposed schools, opened in February 1992. Housed in a former office building in Brooklyn, the curriculum is designed to help students enter the corporate sector. Goldman, Sachs & Company contributed not only furniture and computer equipment, but also extended a commitment to assist the students in their search for employment.

Five additional schools are scheduled to open in the fall of 1992.

—Ann Bradley

Education Week, April 1, 1992.

Evaluation. At various points in this book, I have inserted longitudinal studies that confirm the lifetime effect that certain programs such as Head Start can have on participants. Lifetime studies are rare, but most large-scale programs are able to obtain evaluations from school boards or from independent agencies in the business of evaluating programs. Book It!, for example, was evaluated by a team from the University of Rhode Island. A detailed objective study often proves useful in raising funds and in retaining those parts of a program that work and eliminating those that do not.

At this point, however, there is no need to be so elaborate. Evaluators of most programs never go beyond what is generally referred to as "anecdotal data." It is often disparaged. As you enter the world of schools, you will find yourself at the center of the debate on the need for testing and accountability. By playing a role in a school, you can become a more informed participant (as a voter or as a member of the school community) in this discussion. As you begin your work, however, and a second grader who has not been able to read starts reading aloud to you, or a high school senior is able to go to college because of a scholarship you helped organize, you will know that you are making a difference.

Winston Churchill and Standardized Tests

One of the more controversial components of the AMERICA 2000 program is the proposed establishment of national achievement tests. Proponents urge that there must be some guideposts to determine whether the schools are doing their job. Critics point to the difficulty in truly ascertaining student achievement, particularly if standardized tests such as the multiple choice variety often used in the college admission process are used. One example out of history is described below.

At age 12 Winston Churchill applied to Harrow, a prestigious boy's academy. The entrance examination contained only a few questions on arithmetic and no grammar, no French, no geography or history. "I should have liked to be asked to say what I knew," Churchill later wrote. "They always tried to ask me what I did not know. When I would have willingly displayed my knowledge, they sought to expose my ignorance. This sort of treatment had only one result: I did not do well on examinations." In the custom of the time, this British public school (similar to a U.S. private school) examination involved primarily translation from the Latin and Greek. "I found I was unable to answer a single question on the Latin paper," Churchill recalled. "I wrote my name at the top of the page. I wrote down the number of the question, 1. After much reflection, I put a bracket round it thus (1). But thereafter I could not think of anything connected with it that was either relevant or true."

In this case failure to perform well on the standardized test was deemed less important than Churchill's status as the grandson of the Duke of Marlborough and the son of Lord Randolph Churchill. Winston Churchill was accepted at Harrow. But for five years he remained at the bottom of his class. "We were considered such dunces," Churchill wrote in his memoirs, "that we could only learn English.... I learned it thoroughly. Thus I got into my bones the essential structure of the ordinary British sentence—which is a noble thing. And when, in after years, my school fellows who had won prizes and distinction for writing such beautiful Latin poetry and pithy Greek epigrams had to come down again to common English to earn their living or make their way, I did not feel myself at any disadvantage."

Accountability. When Admiral James Watkins discovered that 35 percent of the San Diego boot camp dropouts could not read at the sixth-grade level, he was surprised. When he learned that 97 percent of those reading at less than a sixth-grade level held high school diplomas, he was "appalled." A diploma is no longer a certification that its bearer has received an education. There must be some kind of assessment so that we can measure the performance of schools, teachers, and students. The exact nature of this assessment is at the heart of both the national and local great education debates.

But reform cannot wait until there is a consensus on measurement devices. Although Ted Sizer's methods are probably at the other end of the spectrum from the cramming for multiple choice tests that often takes the place of education in today's schools, students in Essential Schools have done well on "standardized tests." Presumably a variety of forms of tests will come to supplement or replace the current examinations and assessments as we learn more about how children learn.

Of course, this is another reason for a series of simultaneous "small" efforts in mentoring, volunteering, and redesign. We cannot afford to wait for a massive agreement on a single method or even a broad consensus before beginning. There are too many superb models to choose from now—models that have worked, that are demonstrably better than what is most often in place. If schools and programs are smaller, they can be more readily assessed, and responsibility for performance can be more directly ascribed. This proliferation of schools and formats is undoubtedly not as neat as a series of programs being implemented according to a master plan. But as Ted Sizer points out, "The changes will be messy. Democracy is messy."

Make Time. When you look back at the mentors described in this book, you will see that many of them are exceptionally busy people. Betty Flood puts in a full day at the office before she assumes direction of her youth center. Jeffrey Graham's adopt-a-school program does not lessen his commitment to enforce the law in Cobb County. Kay Whitmore and Jim Renier run major corporations. If you are not sure about your own schedule and do not want to take on something that you may have to drop for lack of time, start small. Senior lawyers who are working one-to-one with students at Martin Luther King, Jr. High School in the new phase of the New York MENTOR program commit to spend two one-hour sessions per month with the students. With travel time, these lawyers spend, perhaps, four hours a month on the program, yet they know they are making a difference. When you begin, ask the school or the organization with which you will be working how much time is required, and tailor your schedule accordingly. Unless private citizens such as yourself make time, the schools will not change.

Beginning Is Easy. The advice of the retired Virginia schoolteacher cited earlier is pretty good here: "Walk into the principal's office of any school that is near where you live or work. Someone will show you what you can do that will make a difference." Your school district may have a person in charge of volunteer programs.

Other resources, which you have already read about, are the many civic and business organizations available to help you find your proper role. Some organizations work independently of the schools. They give you the choice whether to work in your neighborhood or within the schools. One such organization is the Explorer Scouts, which provides a large, extremely well-designed program to interest young people in various careers. Here you would serve as a role model, as Lyn Henderson does in the medical field, and show interested youngsters what you do.

Your Role Is Support and Reform. We are involved in a war. The enemies are poverty, bureaucracy, lack of personnel, and lack of funds. Even the most optimistic supporters of AMERICA 2000 concede that it will take 1.5 years to "adopt a strategy" and take the other three basic steps beginning the work of reform. We cannot stand aside and let students who are mired in bad schools or are without family or community support simply drop out in the meantime.

This thought is important enough to repeat still again: The supporting and reforming roles are not incompatible or mutually exclusive. In South Carolina, for example, an extensive statewide reform movement has involved a simultaneous growth of partnerships: there were 800 partnerships in 1983, the year before the Educational Improvement Act was passed, and there were 6,000 in 1989, the year of the Target 2000 legislation. And even after the Rochester Experiment was well-launched and largely implemented, Kodak chief executive Kay Whitmore still encouraged 2,500 of his company's employees to enter the schools to work with local teachers of math and science. Properly employed, partnerships encourage reform and support a newly restructured system as it begins its work.

There is a spirit of reform abroad in the land. We would be fools not to make use of it. AMERICA 2000 has enlisted a significant number of communities; and many governors, mayors, school chancellors, and administrators have proposed significant changes of their own. Since Memphis became the first AMERICA 2000 city in July of 1991, thousands of additional communities and states have committed to join the four-point program, which is slightly less demanding than originally conceived. New York City has announced a plan to establish a series of newly designed schools, including more along the line of Ted Sizer's Essential

Schools. Chicago has announced a citywide plan for reform. Duluth has retained a private company to run its schools while it searches for a new superintendent. And you have read in these pages about the dramatic changes that have taken place in Rochester and Boston, in South Carolina, Kentucky and Texas, and in many other communities.

But there can be false starts. New York city's ill-fated four-year multimillion dollar dropout initiative, Rochester's attempt to add expanded counseling duties to teachers who could not handle the increased burden, Boston's unfulfilled expectation that if business met its goals, the schools would ipso facto meet theirs, all stand as warnings that every program does not automatically proceed according to plan, especially if these plans are imposed from the top down. In each of these instances, however, repairs were instituted that, with persistent community support, seem to be effective corrections.

Even where dramatic goals have been announced and task forces have been appointed, a full-court press is needed. As a number of educators have pointed out, if we accept the idea that there is no single best way to learn, a series of efforts and a diversity of schools hold out the greatest promise. Start now.

If you are teaching public school students, as is Bill Kellogg; or if you are working as a mentor in the schools, as is Ken Oya; or if your organization has adopted a school, such as Jeffrey Graham and the Cobb County Sheriff's Office; or if you have a program to teach values at all of the schools of the city, such as Sanford McDonnell, you must get involved in the process of reform. With autonomy and diversity at the local level, working closely with inspired teachers and administrators who will often welcome increased community support, you will be able to achieve a meaningful transformation of the public schools.

Be warned, however, that you may find yourself in the midst of your particular local version of the great education debate. If you've been involved in the schools, you will probably know who the players are in your community. Former Secretary of Education William Bennett finds opposition to reform embodied in what he refers to as "the education establishment, which includes the unions and other 'professional' educational organizations." Bennett believes that the education establishment has opposed "every common-sense reform measure." He believes that they see reform as "a direct and open challenge to their monopoly control of American education." Still, I have seen Sandy Feldman, the head of the New York City teachers union, move to resolve the conflict that paralyzed school building reform, and in Rochester teachers union president Adam Urbanski was one of the leaders of the reform movement.

Look closely at your local situation. Certainly there are well-organized elements in every community that seek to maintain the status quo. You've read about the Custodians Union that for a time was able to thwart Joe Flom's well-orchestrated crusade to reform the financing of new school construction. Community inertia had permitted the custodians to get a stranglehold on the public schools and to determine when they would be open or closed and the extent to which they would be cleaned and renovated. Their motivation was clear. They had a very good deal going, a monopoly that enured greatly to their economic benefit. And they had enough political clout to maintain this monopoly until Flom and Chancellor Joseph Fernandez were able to marshall community attention and soften their grip. Often, selfish economic considerations will motivate a well-organized interest to frustrate reform. But just as often, people who have been doing the same job for years may sincerely believe that their way of doing things is the best way, even if it is not. The greatest danger is often posed, as Supreme Court Justice Louis Brandeis once suggested, "by men of zeal, well meaning but without understanding."

As these battles are fought in your community, you will find, once again, the great advantage in starting small. On the issue of publicly funded choice, for example, it might be advisable to establish a pilot program in one small school district, in a state where such a program would be permitted by law. Such a pilot could, on the one hand, establish a precedent for federal constitutional litigation and could also set a model to determine whether neighborhood schools must inevitably deteriorate under tax-supported choice. In the area of preschool enrichment and education, if the children in your neighborhood or in a particularly troubled inner city neighborhood are not receiving help by way of Head Start or a similar local program, you and other concerned citizens can contact The National Council of Jewish Women about developing a HIPPY program for these children. If you start small, as many Arkansas communities did, you will find the financial and personnel commitments achievable.

The Golden Rule, Indianapolis Style

Like many cities, Indianapolis has struggled over the issue of choice: (a) whether to offer choice, and (b) whether to extend it to private as well as public schools. In August 1991 executives of Golden Rule Insurance Co. decided to make choice a reality in Indianapolis, with or without the support of the school board. The company offered $1.2 million in vouchers to assist low-income families in covering the cost of school tuition. The vouchers, worth up to $800 apiece, covered half of the student's tuition to one of Indianapolis's private or parochial elementary or middle schools. The vouchers were in such high demand that Golden Rule's funding ran out. Eli Lilly & Co. picked up the baton and committed to provide $75,000 in vouchers over the next three years.

Clearly the Indianapolis school board had been handed a challenge. In Indiana the state distributes funding to schools on a per-pupil basis. It is estimated that the wave of Golden Rule students fleeing to private schools depleted funding for the public schools by as much as $1.6 million. In short, the business community had forced the school board's hand. In February 1992 the Indianapolis school board approved a choice plan for the public schools.

—Hilary Stout

From "Business Funds Programs in Indianapolis Letting Poor Children Flee Public Schools," *The Wall Street Journal,* February 27, 1992.

Virtually all of the successful new schools you have read about started small. James Comer began with two schools in New Haven, and now there are hundreds of "Comer Method" schools throughout the country. The Coalition of Essential Schools, which now numbers over 200 schools, began when a few bold educators like Debbie Meier in New York had read Ted Sizer's book *Horace's Compromise* and were able within their own systems to start or continue their small schools based on the Sizer principles. Marva Collins's classical Chicago school has been replicated elsewhere. Whether Joe Kellman's corporate school will also be replicated will depend on its performance. But all of these schools started small.

Special Training. The extent and type of training will depend on what you choose to do. MENTOR senior lawyers go through a one-hour training session before they go into the field as mentors. Most programs also provide an orientation on what to expect at the public schools; you may find they are very different from what they were when you attended school. If you will be teaching, tutoring, or participating in a program that requires a special skill, you should expect to be interviewed. The program's organizers will want to ensure that you have the requisite skills and may help you replenish a source of knowledge you might not have tapped in some time—a graduate engineer may not recall just what it was that he or she learned in high school physics. In most instances, however, nothing more will be required than your knowledge of your job or avocation or other things that you are doing at this point in your life. You will find that many students hunger for what you already know.

Liability. A great lesson you can pass on to your students is that they can make mistakes and still survive and enjoy life. Too many of them withdraw rather than risk failure. As a lawyer, I can, regrettably, assure you that if you make a mistake in your work as a volunteer there may well be somebody out there who could bring a legal action. Federal legislation to give greater protection to volunteers is pending, but almost every state has such legislation on its books now. Gregg Petersmeyer of the White House's Office of National Service is trying to gain federal legislation to expand this program. At the back of this book you will learn how to obtain a pamphlet entitled "Answers to Volunteers' Liability and Insurance Questions," which has been prepared by the National Council of Non-Profit Associations. For now, please be assured by this brief excerpt from the booklet: "The first thing to know is that the threat of lawsuits need not keep you from volunteering. Lawsuits against volunteers are rare and actual liability even less common. Moreover, insurance ordinarily can take care of your legal defense and pay a claim on your behalf so that personal possessions and savings will not be at risk."

Spreading the Word. You've just read about a number of successful programs and will learn in the appendix of this book how to obtain information about other programs. In a similar vein, your work will become known if it is producing results. At events such as the National Symposium, you can share this information with others. You may find that your program's success spawns a problem of a different type: How can you be sure that the quality of your program will be maintained in someone else's hands. When your program is being duplicated, you may want to develop guidelines or refer your new participants to guidelines established by organizations in the field (such as the National Association of Partners in Education). There are no absolute guarantees, but I find that when organizations have to submit even a brief oral report on what they're doing, they work to ensure that their efforts have been productive and up to standard. If the program is not working, its sponsors will find it very difficult to maintain.

Enlist Now! Education is broader than the schools. The most influential educators are probably parents. What they do, or do not do, plays a crucial role in the lives of their children. Various forces in the community, for good or bad, play a major role in the education of a child. In this book the focus has been on the public schools. It is an area we can do something about. As you have seen, you can make a difference if you work in the schools. Bill Millikin of Cities in Schools (the outfit that designed Rich's Academy) concluded long ago that the schools were not only a primary source of education, but also a point of delivery where other valuable social services and counselling could be centered to address social problems. I believe that you can touch more problem areas working in the public schools than in any other single institution.

Enlist now. As you review the various ways to help which have been pursued by other people, you will see that many of them started with a program they felt was manageable in terms of their time and then found that they were able to go on to other things. You will find that once you begin, as you learn about the schools and the results that can be achieved, you will probably want to broaden your activities. You have the time. Start small if you like. But start now. You are needed.

Resources

The appendixes that follow provide information that will help you decide what you want to do and how to do it most effectively. You will find that significant resources are available in all the areas discussed in this book.

Appendix A: Help Is Available
How to obtain funding
Colleges and universities as resources
Organizations that can help
New professionals

Appendix B: Bibliography
Key periodicals in the education community
Articles, pamphlets, and books

Appendix C: More About the Mentors

Appendix D: The National Education Goals and Objectives

Acknowledgments

Index

Appendix A:
Help Is Available

How to Obtain Funding

If you want to expand your work, and perhaps start a program of your own, you may need money, although, as you have seen, many successful mentors have started on a shoestring. Fortunately there is ample literature in the field, and information is generally furnished without charge by experienced organizations, so you do not have to reinvent the wheel. Guides such as the *Foundation Directory* will provide useful data about potential sources of money, and there are experienced grant-writers.

Occasionally you will find that public funds are available (but don't hold your breath). AMERICA 2000, the New American Schools Corporation, and similar state and local programs will be supplying funds principally for demonstration projects. Remember that funding requirements diminish with the number of volunteers you can enlist and the resources you can bring in without charge. If you have an evaluation which shows that your program is effective, raising money may be easier. You may be surprised to find that your employer would like to contribute some financing.

Be realistic, but refuse to be daunted if you want to begin a program. Virtually everyone who has begun a successful partnership program was told at the outset, by some informed and experienced individual, that the program was impossible.

The fourteenth edition of the *Foundation Directory* was published in 1992 ($150) and is generally available in your local library or in a nearby university library. It is also available from:

The Foundation Center
79 Fifth Avenue

New York, NY 10003
(212) 620-4230; (800) 424-9836

See also:

Flanagan, Joan. *The Grass Roots Book: How to Raise Money in Your Community.* Chicago: Contemporary Books, 1982.

Shannon, James P., Editor. *The Corporate Contributions Handbook: Devoting Private Money to Public Needs,* a publication of the Council on Foundations. San Francisco: Jossey-Bass, 1991.

Colleges and Universities as Resources

As you have seen, collaborations with colleges and universities can be effective resources in improving the public schools. The initial enrichment programs of Claire Flom's New York Alliance for the Public Schools came from a coalition of five graduate schools of education. Similarly, the commission that established the Insitute for Law and Justice drew on university resources in developing its initial plan. The Boston Compact, Rochester Experiment, Book It!, and the New York City Dropout Prevention Program also benefited from university or college collaboration.

Because I am most familiar with the resources available at Columbia University's Teachers College (where I serve as chairman of the board), I am going to review the programs offered there in some detail. (As I do this, and despite checking this list, I know that I will miss a number of major projects and will hear about it. Still, even a partial list should be useful.) Most likely you can find these or similar assets in your community when you begin to build a program or redesign a school.

Several programs seek to increase the number of qualified minority educators and administrators, e.g., the Peace Corps Fellows Program, a joint effort of Teachers College, the U.S. Peace Corps, and the New York City Board of Education that trains returning Peace Corps volunteers for teaching careers by placing them in needy New York City public schools. Almost all of the program's graduates are currently still teaching, and most stay in the New York City school system. The Minority Leadership Fellows is a five-year program that prepares African-American and Hispanic men and women for careers in secondary school administration. It was created to combat the shortage of minorities in school leadership positions, as was the college's Teachers Opportunity Corps.

The college has developed several programs aimed at increasing the number of teachers in subjects in which there are shortages, such as mathematics, science, bilingual education, special education, and English as a second language. The Teachers College Writing Project is aimed at improving the teaching of reading and writing in nearly 500 public schools throughout New York City. Classroom, Inc., a collaborative effort of Teachers College, Morgan Stanley & Co., the Mariposa and Andrew W. Mellon foundations, and the New York City Board of Education, under the leadership of college trustee Lewis Bernard, uses computer programs to teach inner-city youth about the business world and prepare them for future employment. The Teachers College Literacy Center has developed and operates intergenerational literacy programs, preparing parents in poverty to help their children learn to read.

Because a clear correlation has been found between healthy diets and children's performance in schools, the college has created several programs in nutrition and health care. For instance, the Healthy Heart Project monitors the diet and cardiac status of residents of Washington Heights, a predominantly African-American and Latino neighborhood. The Nutrition Education Resources Project, attempts to instill in preschool students from Harlem sound nutritional habits.

Teachers College is renowned for its research capabilities. You have already read about the dropout studies prepared by Professor Joseph Grannis of the college's Institute for Urban and Minority Education. More recently, Professor Robert L. Crain and others published a striking report on the effectiveness of New York City's career magnet schools. The National Center for Restructuring Education, Schools and Teaching, directed by Dr. Linda Darling-Hammond and Dr. Ann Lieberman, is in the forefront of the movement to restructure education along more productive lines and is currently developing and monitoring a restructuring pilot in eight public schools.

Teachers College also has partnerships with several New York City public schools, such as the Colgate-Wadleigh model and the Professional Development Schools, under Professor Francis Bolin and others, which focus on teacher training and are coordinated by Dr. Ed Quinn.

Among the college's many publications, *The Teachers College Record,* published since 1900, is perhaps the best known. Recent articles focusing on urban education included: "What Makes Ghetto Schools Succeed or Fail?" and "Toward Effective University-Public School Partnerships: An Analysis of Contemporary Models."

For more information concerning the programs of Teachers College, Columbia University, please contact:

Office of External Affairs, Box 306
Teachers College, Columbia University
New York, NY 10027
(212) 678-3755

Available assets will depend largely on the colleges and universities located near you and the public schools you hope to serve. You will find further leads in the bibliography and organization sections of this appendix; specific information on useful models may also be obtained from:

Dean Richard M. Bossone
University Dean for Instructional Research
University/Urban Schools National Task Force
c/o The Graduate School and University Center
The City University of New York
33 West 42nd Street
New York, NY 10036
(212) 642-2962

Dr. Robert Sperber
Boston Higher Education Partnership
c/o Boston University
Boston, MA

Organizations That Can Help

A number of organizations both can help you in your decision about what kind of work you want to do with the schools and later can assist in what you are doing. The National Association of Partners in Education (NAPE) was established specifically to assist in this field and has recently promulgated guidelines for partnerships. The National Symposium of Partnerships in Education is organized so that you can review its comprehensive annual program in advance and decide which sessions to attend based on your particular needs. The National Chamber of Commerce offers a variety of programs for member organizations. The Conference Board holds national and regional meetings as does the Business

Roundtable. The National Council on Educating Black Children has focused on the area of its particular concern and has produced useful surveys of activities in the field.

The Department of Education has an office of Partnerships in Education that has produced a number of useful pamphlets, most prominently a series called "What Works." More recently the department has been engaged in promoting AMERICA 2000; despite the political debate that engulfs the president's program, many cities are becoming AMERICA 2000 communities, and a number of privately funded model schools will undoubtedly be established. Points of Light Foundation, inspired by President Bush, is a private foundation with bipartisan congressional backing and some federal funding. It is intended to channel volunteers into appropriate activities (including education). Finally, United Way, in addition to conducting broad-based fund-raising and distributing grants, now participates in proactive programs where its experts structure projects and develop coalitions to see them through.

The list that follows may appear much too long, but after a quick perusal you can select the few organizations that touch on your particular areas of concern. Fortunately, in almost every instance the name of the organization describes its mission.

American Bar Association
Youth Education for Citizenship
541 North Fairbanks Court
Chicago, IL 60611
(312) 988-5735

American Council on Drug
   Education
5820 Hubbard Drive
Rockville, MD 20852
(301) 984-5700

American Federation of Teachers
Educational Issues Department
555 New Jersey Avenue NW
Washington, DC 20001
(202) 879-4400

American Institute of Nutrition
9650 Rockville Pike
Bethesda, MD 20814
(301) 530-7050

American Reading Council
45 John Street, Suite 811
New York, NY 10038
(212) 619-6044

Big Brothers/Big Sisters of America
230 North 13th Street
Philadelphia, PA 19107
(215) 567-7000

Boys and Girls Clubs of America
771 First Avenue
New York, NY 10017
(212) 351-5900

Business Roundtable
200 Park Avenue, Suite 2222
New York, NY 10166
(212) 682-6370

Washington Office:
1615 L Street NW, Suite 600
Washington, DC 20036
(202) 872-1260

Center for Educational Innovation
52 Vanderbilt Avenue
New York, NY 10017
(212) 599-7000

Chamber of Commerce of the
    United States
Education Division
1615 H Street NW
Washington, DC 20062
(202) 659-6000

Children's Defense Fund
122 C Street NW
Washington, DC 20005
(202) 628-8787

Committee for Economic
    Development
477 Madison Avenue
New York, NY 10022
(212) 688-2063
and
1700 K Street
Washington, DC 20006
(202) 296-5860

Conference Board
845 Third Avenue
New York, NY 10022-6601
(212) 759-0900

Council for Aid to Education
51 Madison Avenue, Suite 2200
New York, NY 10010
(212) 689-2400

Council of Chief State School
    Officers
400 North Capitol Street
Washington, DC 20001
(202) 393-8159

Council on Foundations
1828 L Street NW
Washington, DC 20036
(202) 466-6512

Education Commission of the States
707 17th Street, Suite 2700
Denver, CO 80202-3427
(202) 299-3611

Educational Testing Service
Rosedale Road
Princeton, NJ 08541
(609) 921-9000

The Fresh Air Fund
1040 Avenue of the Americas
New York, NY 10018
(212) 221-0900

William T. Grant Foundation
Commission on Work, Family and
    Citizenship
1001 Connecticut Avenue NW,
    Suite 301
Washington, DC 20036
(202) 775-9731

Joining Forces
400 North Capital Street, Suite 379
Washington, DC 20001
(202) 393-8159

Junior Achievement, Inc.
45 East Clubhouse Drive
Colorado Springs, CO 80906
(719) 540-8000

Literacy Volunteers of America. Inc.
5795 Widewaters Parkway
Syracuse, NY 13214
(315) 445-8000

Math/Science Network
Preservation Park
678 13th Street, Suite 100
Oakland, CA 94612

Narcotics Education, Inc.
6830 Laurel Street NW
Washington, DC 20012
(202) 722-6740; (800) 548-8700

National Alliance of Business
Center for Excellence in Education
1201 New York Avenue NW
Washington, DC 20005
(202) 289-2925

National Assessment of Educational
  Progress
CN 6710
Princeton, NJ 08541
(609) 734-1624

National Association for
  Industry-Education Cooperation
235 Hendricks Boulevard
Buffalo, NY 14266
(716) 834-7047

National Association of Partners in
  Education, Inc.
209 Madison Street, Suite 401
Alexandria, VA 22314
(703) 836-4880

National Association of Private
  Industry Councils
1015 15th Street NW, Suite 601
Washingtion, DC 20005
(202) 289-2950

National Association of Secondary
  School Principals
1904 Association Drive
Reston, VA 22091
(703) 860-0200

National Association of State Boards
  of Education
1012 Cameron Street
Alexandria, VA 22314
(703) 684-4000

National Center for Education and
  the Economy
39 State Street, Suite 500
Rochester, NY 14614

National Committee for Prevention
  of Child Abuse
332 South Michigan Avenue,
  Suite 950
Chicago, IL 60604
(312) 663-3520

National Council of Urban
  Education
c/o NEA
1201 16th Street NW
Washington, DC 20036
(202) 822-7161

National Council on Educating
  Black Children
P.O. Box 71021
Chevy Chase, MD 20813
(301) 680-8804

National Council on Measurement
  in Education
1230 17th Street NW
Washington, DC 20036
(202) 223-9138

National Dropout Prevention
  Center at Clemson University
393 College Avenue
Clemson, SC 29634
(803) 656-2599

National Education Association
Instruction and Professional
  Development
1201 16th Street NW
Washington, DC 20036
(202) 822-7015

National Governors' Association
444 North Capitol Street, Suite 250
Washington, DC 20001
(202) 624-5300

National League of Cities
1301 Pennsylvania Avenue NW
Washington, DC 20004
(202) 626-3030

National School Boards Association
1608 Duke Street
Alexandria, VA 22180
(703) 838-6722

National Science Foundation
1800 G Street NW
Washington, DC 20550
(202) 357-9498

New American Schools
    Development Corporation
100 Walnut Boulevard, Suite 2710
Arlington, VA 22209
(703) 908-9500

One-To-One
2550 M Street, NW, Suite 500
Washington, DC 20037
(202) 862-0121

Points of Light Foundation
736 Jackson Place
Washington, DC 20503
(202) 408-5162

Reading Is Fundamental, Inc.
Smithsonian Institution
600 Maryland Avenue SW, Suite 500
Washington, DC 20560
(202) 287-3220

Society for Nutrition Education
1736 Franklin Street, Suite 900
Oakland, CA 94612
(415) 444-7133

Triangle Coalition for Science and
    Technology
5112 Berwyn Road
College Park, MD 20740
(301) 220-0872

United Way of America
701 North Fairfax Street
Alexandria, VA 22314-2045
(703) 836-7100

University/Urban Schools National
    Task Force
c/o The Graduate School and
    University Center
The City University of New York
33 West 42nd Street
New York NY 10036
(212) 642-2962

New Professionals

As the partnership movement has grown, so has a new profession with individuals schooled and experienced in the work of partnerships. Consultants are available to corporations and associations that need expert counselling. Only a few of the new professionals are mentioned below because the list of skilled people in the field is extensive. Probably the best way to obtain the name of a partnership expert in the field or geographic area in which you are interested is to contact the National Association of Partners in Education (please see the list of organizations for the address and phone number).

Kathy August
Education Consultant/Grant Writer
387 9th Street
Brooklyn, NY 11215
(718) 449-5293

Wayne Carlson
Los Angeles Unified School District
Partners and Adopt-A-School
450 North Grand Avenue, H237
Los Angeles, CA 90012
(213) 626-6439

Jann Coles
Colgate-Palmolive Co.
300 Park Avenue
New York, NY 10022
(212) 310-2000

Bill Milliken
Cities In Schools
1023 15th Street NW, Suite 600
Washington, DC 20005
(202) 861-0203

Susan Otterbourg, Ed.D.
Delman Educational
    Communications
7 Kira Lane
Englewood, NJ 07631
(201) 567-5397

Janet Reingold
Reingold & Associates
3001 McKinley Street NW
Washington, DC 20015
(202) 686-8600

Diana Rigden
Council for Aid to Education
Director of Precollege Programs
51 Madison Avenue, Suite 2200
New York, NY 10010
(212) 689-2400

Barbara Russell
Director
Division of Adopt-A-School
Room 261
2597 Avery Avenue
Memphis, TN 38112
(901) 325-5622

Dr. Al Sterling
Director, Chicago Adopt-A-School
1819 Pershing Road
Chicago, IL 60609
(312) 890-8346

Dr. Wayne Walker
Executive Director
St. Louis Regional Education
    Partnerships
5585 Pershing, Suite 150
St. Louis, MO 63112
(314) 361-3900

Appendix B:
Bibliography

Key Periodicals in the
Education Community

A Different September: The Newsletter of Public School Reform.
A Different September Foundation is a not-for-profit organization supporting the cause of education reform. This free newsletter is published six times each year and can be ordered from A Different September Foundation, 19 Deerfield Street, 3rd Floor, Boston, MA 02215. (617) 353-9526.

American Educator
The professional journal of the American Federation of Teachers, this quarterly publication is available to nonmembers for $8 per year. Contact the American Federation of Teachers, AFL-CIO, 555 New Jersey Avenue, Washington, DC 20001-2079. (201) 879-4420.

American Teacher
This bimonthly newspaper costs $10 per year and can be ordered from the American Federation of Teachers, AFL-CIO, 555 New Jersey Avenue, NW, Washington, DC 20001-2079. (202) 879-4400.

The Chronicle of Higher Education
This weekly newspaper costs $67.50 per year and can be ordered from P.O. Box 1955, Marion, OH 43305. (800) 347-6969. Editorial and business offices are located at 1255 23rd Street NW, Washington, DC 20037. (202) 466-1000.

The Education Digest
This digest of articles from education publications is issued monthly, September through May, for $30 annually. Contact Prakken Publications, Inc., 416 Longshore Drive, P.O. Box 8623, Ann Arbor, MI 48107. (313) 769-1211.

Education Today: Helping Parents Make a Difference
This newsletter is published 15 times each year for $15. Contact the Educational Publishing Group, Inc., 376 Boylston Street, Boston, MA 02116. (617) 424-1361; (800) 927-6006.

Education Week
This newspaper is published 40 times each year for $59.94. Contact Editorial Projects in Education, Inc., 4301 Connecticut Avenue NW, Suite 250, Washington, DC 20008. (202) 364-4114.

From the Center
The bimonthly newsletter of the National Center for Neighborhood Enterprise (NCNE), which is a nonprofit, nonpartisan organization founded in 1981 to assist low-income Americans with solving their communities' problems. Contact the National Center for Neighborhood Enterprise, 1367 Connecticut Avenue NW, Washington, DC 20036.

Partnerships in Education Journal
The journal is published monthly for $37.50. Contact InfoMedia Inc., 2907 Country River Drive, Parrish, FL 34219. (813) 776-2535.

Partners in Education: The National Newsletter for Education Partnerships and School Volunteer Programs
This newsletter is published monthly, with the exception of July and August; the nonmember price is $100 per year. Contact the National Association of Partners in Education, Inc., 209 Madison Street, Suite 401, Alexandria, VA 22314.

Articles, Pamphlets, and Books

A whole body of literature has grown up about the partnership movement, a fairly comprehensive list of which follows. While there is no charge for some of these, payment is required for others.

Several of the books have extensive bibliographies that should be consulted, as should the following for further information. *Fortune* magazine has published useful special issues on education (and partnerships in particular) and holds periodic "summits" of business leaders on the support and reform of the schools. Often, your local or citywide school district will have a guide to opportunities. An excellent example is *Are You Involved?* (Office of External Affairs, NYC Public Schools). The problem is not so much finding a book or pamphlet in this field as in selecting the most helpful materials in a veritable sea of publications.

Adams, Don, ed. *Partnerships That Work.* Largo, FL: InfoMedia Inc., 1989.

American Association of Higher Education. *National Directory of School-College Partnerships: Current Models and Practices.* 1987. (Database available.)

American Association of School Administrators, Council of Great City Schools, and National School Boards Association. *The Maintenance Gap: Deferred Repair and Renovation in the Nation's Elementary and Secondary Schools.* January 1983.

Asante, Molefi Kete. *The Afrocentric Idea.* Philadelphia: Temple University Press, 1988.

Atkin, J. Myron, and Ann Atkin. *Improving Science Education Through Local Alliances.* New York: Network Publications, 1989.

Bensman, David. *Quality Education in the Inner City: The Story of the Central Park East Schools.* New York: Kramer Communications, 1987. For a copy of this report, send a check or money order for $2.50 to: Central Park East School, 1573 Madison Avenue, New York, NY 10029.

Berryman, Sue E. *Breaking Out of the Circle: Rethinking Our Assumptions about Education and the Economy.* Occasional Paper 2. New York: National Center on Education and Employment, Teachers College, Columbia University, July 1987.

Berryman, Sue E. *Education and the Economy: What Should We Teach? When? How? To Whom?* Occasional Paper 4. New York: National Center on Education and Employment, Teachers College, Columbia University, April 1988.

Blair, Louis H., et al. *The Urban Institute and National Association for Partners in Education. Guidelines for School-Business Partnerships in Science and Mathematics.* Washington, DC: Urban Institute Press, 1990.

Boyer, Ernest L. *School Reform: A National Strategy.* Washington, DC: The Business Roundtable, 1989.

Breck, Judy, ed. *The New York City MENTOR Handbook.* c/o Martin Luther King High School, 122 Amsterdam Avenue, New York, NY: 1991. (Provides guidelines for participating schools and law firms and well as an explanation of the program for potential participants.)

The Business Roundtable. *A Blueprint for Business on Restructuring Education.* New York: 1989.

The Business Roundtable. *Essential Components of a Successful Education System: The Business Roundtable Education Public Policy Agenda.* New York: 1990.

The Business Roundtable. *The Business Roundtable Participation Guide: A Primer for Business on Education.* New York: 1990.

Children's Defense Fund. *Children 1990: A Report Card, Briefing, and Action Primer.* Washington, DC: January 1990.

Chion-Kenney, Linda. "A Report from the Field: The Coalition of Essential Schools," *American Educator,* Winter 1987.

Chubb, John E., and Terry M. Moe. *Politics, Markets and America's Schools.* Washington, DC: Brookings Institution, 1990.

Cohen, Michael. *Restructuring the Education System: Agenda for the '90s.* Washington, DC: National Governors' Association, 1989.

Comer, James. *Maggie's American Dream: The Life and Times of a Black Family.* New York: New American Library, 1988.

Comer, James. *School Power: Implications of an Intervention Project.* New York: Free Press, 1980

Committee for Economic Development. *Business and the Schools: A Guide to Effective Programs.* 1989.

Committee for Economic Development. *Children in Need: Investment Strategies for the Educationally Disadvantaged.* 1987.

Committee for Economic Development. *Investing in Our Children: Business and the Public Schools.* 1985.

Committee for Economic Development. *The Unfinished Agenda: A New Vision for Child Development and Education.* 1991. (A Statement by the Research and Policy Committee.)

Council for Aid to Education. *Business and the Schools: A Guide to Effective Programs.* New York: 1989.

Darling-Hammond, Linda, and Carol Ascher. *Creating Accountability in Big City School Systems.* New York: NCREST Publications and ERIC Clearinghouse on Urban Education, 1991.

Dewey, John. *Human Nature and Conduct.* New York: Random House, 1992.

Education Commission of the States. *The Next Wave: A Synopsis of Recent Education Reform Reports.* February 1987.

Education Writers Association. *Wolves at the Schoolhouse Door: An Investigation of the Condition of Public School Buildings.* Washington, DC: 1989.

Finn, Chester E., Jr. *We Must Take Charge: Our Schools and Our Future.* New York: Free Press, 1991.

Firestone, William A., et al. *The Progress of Reform: An Appraisal of State Education Initiatives.* New Brunswick, NJ: Center for Policy Research in Education, October 1989.

Fiske, Edward B. *Smart Schools, Smart Kids: Why Do Some Schools Work?* New York: Simon and Schuster, 1991.

William T. Grant Foundation Commission on Work, Family, and Citizenship. *The Forgotten Half: Non-College Youth in America.* Washington, DC: January 1988.

Gross, Theodore L. *Partners in Education: How Colleges Can Work with Schools to Improve Teaching and Learning.* San Francisco, CA: Jossey-Bass, 1988.

Heritage Foundation. *Can Business Save Education? Strategies for the 1990s.* Washington, DC: 1989.

Hirsch, E.D., Jr. *Cultural Literacy: What Every American Needs to Know.* New York: Random House, 1987.

Hodgkinson, Herold, L. *All One System: Demographics of Education; Kindergarten Through Graduate School.* Washington, DC: Institute for Educational Leadership, 1985. (Outlines demographic changes in the U.S. population for the year 2000 and describes the education consequences.)

Honeyman, David S., R. Craig Wood, David C. Thompson, and G. Kent Stewart, "The Fiscal Support of School Facilities in Rural and Small Schools," *Journal of Education Finance,* 227–39. Winter 1988.

Johnston, William B. and Arnold E. Packer. *Workforce 2000: Work and Workers for the 21st Century.* Indianapolis, IN: Hudson Institute, Herman Kahn Center, June 1987.

Kane, Pearl, ed. *Independent Schools, Independent Thinkers.* San Francisco: Jossey-Bass, 1992.

Kaplan, George. *Who Runs Our Schools? The Changing Face of Educational Leadership.* Institute for Educational Leadership, 1989.

Kearns, David, and Denis Doyle. *Winning The Brain Race: A Bold Plan To Make Our Schools Competitive.* San Francisco: Institute for Contemporary Studies, 1988.

Kolderie, T. "Education That Works: The Right Role for Business." *Harvard Business Review,* 56–62, Sept./Oct. 1987. (Argues that business should be helping to see that the schools get opportunities and incentives to innovate on their own.)

Kozol, Jonathan. *Savage Inequalities: Children in America's Schools.* New York: Crown, 1991.

Levine, Marsha, and Roberta Trachtman, eds. *American Business and the Public Schools: Case Studies of Corporate Involvement in Public Education.* Committee for Economic Development. New York: Teachers College Press, Teachers College, Columbia University, 1988.

Lieberman, Ann, Linda Darling-Hammond, and David Zuckerman. *Early Lessons in Restructuring Schools.* New York: NCREST Publications, 1991.

Lund, Leonard. *Beyond Business/Education Partnerships: The Business Experience.* Research Report 918. New York: The Conference Board, 1988.

Lund, Leonard. *Corporate Mentoring in U.S. Schools: The Outstretched Hand.* Research Report 1007, New York: The Conference Board, 1992.

Mann, Dale. *All That Glitters: Public School/Private Sector Interaction in Twenty-Three U.S. Cities.* New York: Exxon Education Foundation, September 1984.

Marburger, Carl L. *One School at A Time: School Based Management, a Process for Change.* Columbia, MD: The National Committee for Citizens in Education, 1989.

Martin, R.L. *Business and Education: Partners for the Future.* Washington, DC: U.S. Chamber of Commerce, 1985.

Mayberry, Claude A. *Parents Make a Difference.* Silver Spring, Maryland: CAM Publishing Group, 1990.

National Alliance of Business. *A Blueprint for Business on Restructuring Education.* Washington, DC: 1989.

National Alliance of Business. *Business Strategies that Work: A Planning Guide for Education Restructuring.* Washington, DC: 1990.

National Alliance of Business. *Corporate Action Agenda: The Business of Improving Public Education.* Washington, DC: undated.

National Alliance of Business. *Shaping Tomorrow's Workforce: A Leadership Agenda for the 90's.* Washington, DC: 1990.

National Alliance of Business. *Who Will Do The Work? A Business Guide for Preparing Tomorrow's Workforce.* Washington, DC: 1989.

National Association of Partners in Education. *Practical Guide to Creating and Managing School/Community Partnerships.* Washington, DC: undated.

National Center for Education and the Economy. *A Nation Prepared: Teachers for the 21st Century.* The Report of the Task Force on Teaching as a Profession. May 1986.

National Education Association. *Early Childhood Education and the Public Schools.* Washington, DC: 1990.

National Governors' Association. *From Rhetoric to Action: State Progress in Restructuring the Education System.* 1991.

National Science Foundation. *Educating America for the 21st Century: A Plan of Action for Improving Mathematics, Science, and Technology Education.* September 1983.

Oakes, Jeannie. *Keeping Track: How Schools Structure Inequality.* New Haven: Yale University Press, 1985.

One-to-One Partnership, Inc. *Guide to Workplace Mentoring Programs.* Washington, DC: 1992.

Otterbourg, Susan D. *School Partnerships Handbook: How to Set Up and Administer Programs with Business, Government, and Your Community.* Englewood Cliffs, NJ: Prentice-Hall, 1989.

Otterbourg, Susan D., *How to Monitor and Evaluate Partnerships in Education: Measuring Their Success.* Largo, FL: InfoMedia Inc., 1989.

Peterson, Terry. *Sustained Business Involvement in State School Reform: The South Carolina Story.* Occasional Paper 11. Washington, DC: Institute for Educational Leadership and the Edna McConnell Clark Foundation, August 1989.

Ravitch, Diane, ed. *The American Reader: Words That Moved a Nation.* New York: Harper Collins, 1991.

Ravitch, Diane, and Chester E. Finn, Jr. *What Do Our 17-Year-Olds Know? A Report on the First National Assessment of History and Literature.* New York: Harper & Row, 1987.

Reingold, Janet. *The Fourth R: Workforce Readiness. A Guide to Business Education Partnerships.* Washington, DC: National Alliance of Business, 1987.

Reingold, J. R., and Associates. *Current Federal Policies and Programs for Youth.* Washington, DC: William T. Grant Foundation Commission on Work, Family, and Citizenship, revised 1989.

Rigden, Diana W. *Business and the Schools: A Guide to Effective Programs.* New York: Council for Aid to Education, 1992.

Rigden, Diana W. *Business/School Partnerships: A Path to Effective School Restructuring.* New York: Council for Aid to Education, 1991.

Schlesinger, Arthur M., Jr. *The Disuniting of America: Reflections on a Multicultural Society.* New York: Morrow, 1991.

Shelton, Cynthia. *The Doable Dozen: A Checklist of Practical Ideas for School-Business Partnerships.* National Community Education Association, 1987.

Sizer, Theodore R. *Horace's Compromise: The Dilemma of the American High School.* Boston: Houghton Mifflin, 1984.

Sizer, Theodore R. *Theodore R. Horace's School: Redesigning the American High School.* Boston: Houghton Mifflin, 1992.

Timpane, P. Michael, and Laurie Miller McNeil. *Business Impact on Education and Child Development Reform.* New York: Committee for Economic Development, 1991.

Triangle Coalition for Science and Technology Education. *A Guide for Building an Alliance for Science, Mathematics, and Technology Education.* September 1991.

U.S. Department of Education, National Commission of Excellence in Education. *A Nation at Risk: The Imperative for Educational Reform.* Washington, DC: 1983.

U.S. Department of Education, Office of Educational Research and Improvement. *Making Sense of School Budgets.* Washington, DC: August 1989.

U.S. Department of Labor. Office of Public Affairs, Employment and Training U.S. Department of Labor: Commission on Workforce Quality and Labor Market Efficiency. *Investing in People: A Strategy to Address America's Workforce Crisis.* Washington, DC: 1989.

Wise, Arthur E., and Tamar Gendler, "Rich Schools, Poor Schools: The Persistence of Unequal Education," *The College Board Review.* No. 151, 12–17, 36–37. Spring 1989.

Appendix C:
More About the Mentors

You can obtain more information about the mentors in this book and their programs from the contacts listed below, who remain active in organizations that can supply information. In some cases a fee may be charged.

The Best-Known Mentor

Eugene M. Lang
"I Have A Dream" Foundation
330 Seventh Avenue
New York, NY 10001
(212) 736-1730

Working from the Inside

Betty Flood: The Rec Center
PSE&G
P.O. Box 570
Newark, NJ 07101-0570
(201) 430-7000

Bill Kellogg: An Old-Fashioned Teacher
General Packaging Products
1700 South Canal
Chicago, IL 60616

Ann Hennessy
School Liaison
Portage Park Elementary School
5330 Berteau
Chicago, IL 60641
(312) 534-3576

Geoffrey Laff: A Daringly Educational Marvel of Science
DEMOS
School Volunteers for New Haven
54 Meadow Street
New Haven, CT 06519
(203) 787-6950

Carol Lowery: LEGO/Logo
Spring Branch Independent School District
955 Campbell Road
Houston, TX 77024
(713) 464-1511

The 1940 IBM Lab (videotape)
Jacoby/Storm Productions, Inc.
22 Cresent Road
Westport, CT 06880

Nancy Lieberman and Mary Foster: Learning Through Art
Learning Through Art
1071 Fifth Avenue
New York, NY 10128
(212) 360-3651 or (212) 360-3510

Tom Pilecki: The Power of Music
St. Augustine School of the Arts
1176 Franklin Avenue
Bronx, NY 10456
(212) 542-3633

Hillary Clinton and Miriam Westheimer
HIPPY
National Council for Jewish Women
53 West 23rd Street
New York, NY 10010
(212) 645-4048

Ypsilanti Longitudinal Studies
High/Scope Educational Research Foundation
600 North River Street
Ypsilanti, MI 48198
(313) 485-2000

Ernie Lorch: A Full Court Press
Riverside Church
490 Riverside Drive
New York, NY 10027
(212) 222-5900

Lyn Henderson, R.N.: A Medical Explorer
Clovis High Plains Hospital
P.O. Box 1688
Clovis, NM 88101
(505) 769-2141

Walter Lochbaum: A Retired Volunteer
American Association of Retired Persons
1909 K Street NW
Washington, DC 20049
(202) 434-2277

Jim Watkins: The Navy and the Public Schools
U.S. Department of Energy
Office of the Secretary
Washington, DC 20585
(202) 586-5534

Adopt-A-School Is Alive and Well

Barbara Russell: Godmother of Adopt-A-School
Director
Division of Adopt-A-School
Room 261
2597 Avery Avenue
Memphis, TN 38112
(901) 325-5622

Jeffrey Graham: The Sheriff's Office and the Public School
Cobb County Sheriff's Office
Public Safety Building
185 Washington Avenue
Marietta, GA 30090-9650
(404) 499-4600

Ken Oya: A True Mentor
Project ASPIRE
Woodward High School
7001 Reading Road
Cincinnati, OH 45237

Wayne Carlson: Directing a Large City
Los Angeles Unified School District
Partners and Adopt-A-School Program
450 North Grand Avenue, H237
Los Angeles, CA 90012
(213) 626-6439

Max Miller: A Vocation for Teaching
Federal Express
3035 Directors Row, Bldg. 7
Memphis, TN 38131
(901) 369-3600

AutoZone, Inc.
Corporate Manager, Partners in Education
3030 Poplar Avenue
Dept. 8029, Box 2198
Memphis, TN 38101

Start Your Own Organization

Milton Heimlich and Victor Bergenn: FACTS
FACTS
Dr. Edward Powers
1171 65th Street, Room 310
Brooklyn, NY 11219
(718) 256-7235

Claire Flom: An Alliance for the Public Schools
New York Alliance for the Public Schools
32 Washington Place, 5th Floor
New York, NY 10003
(212) 998-6770

Eunice Ellis and Arthur Gunther: Book It!
Book It! Reading Incentive Program
Pizza Hut, Inc.
P.O. Box 2999
Wichita, KS 67201
(316) 687-8401

Regina Snowden: Partners for Disabled Youth
Partners for Disabled Youth
c/o Office of Handicapped Affairs
One Ashburton Place, Room 1305
Boston, MA 02108
(617) 727-7440 Voice and TDD (800) 322-2020

Judith Berry Griffin: As Solid as ABC
A Better Chance
419 Boylston Street
Boston, MA 02116
(617) 421-0950

Gary Simons
Prep for Prep
163 West 91st Street
New York, NY 10024
(212) 769-4310

Dr. Virginia Leibner: Homework Hotline
Homework Hotline
Ted Tunison
NEA
St. Louis, MO
(314) 652-0721

Sanford McDonnell: A Valued Program
Linda McKay, Coordinator
Personal Responsibility Education Program (PREP)
THE NETWORK
6800 Wydown Boulevard
St. Louis, MO 63105
(314) 727-3686

Wendy Kopp: Teach for America
Teach For America
1221 Avenue of the Americas, 33rd Floor
New York, NY 10020
(212) 974-2456

Barbara Bush: Leadership and Literacy
Barbara Bush Foundation for Family Literacy
1002 Wisconsin Avenue NW
Washington, DC 20007
(202) 338-2006

Celebrities as Mentors

Marjorie Vincent
Miss America Organization
P.O. Box 119
Atlantic City, NJ 08404
(609) 345-7571

Bill Cosby
P.O. Box 808
Greenfield, MA 01301

Arturo Barrios
c/o Elite Racing
2431 Morena Boulevard
Suite 2H
San Diego, CA 92110
(619) 275-5440

Arnold Schwarzenegger
President's Council on Physical Fitness & Sports
450 Fifth Street NW, Suite 7103
Washington, DC 20001
(202) 272-3421

Mentors or Merchants?

Chris Whittle: The Whittle Companies
Whittle Communications
505 Market Street
Knoxville, TN 37902
(615) 595-5300

Ann Moore: Sports Illustrated For Kids
Beth Mooney, Education Manager
Sports Illustrated For Kids
1271 Avenue of the Americas
New York, NY 10020
(212) 522-1212

Creating a New School

Marva Collins: Chicago' Westside Preparatory School
Westside Preparatory School
4146 West Chicago Avenue
Chicago, IL 60651
(312) 227-5995

Joseph Kellman: Chicago's Corporate/Community School
Corporate/Community Schools of America, Inc.
Project Headquarters
407 South Dearborn, Suite 1725
Chicago, IL 60605
(312) 427-0468

Leo Jackson: Atlanta's Rich's Central
Rich's Central
1080 Euclid Avenue
Atlanta, GA 30307
(404) 330-4161

Exodus
96 Pine Street NE
Atlanta, GA 30308
(404) 873-3979

Cities in Schools
1023 15th Street NW, Suite 600
Washington, DC 20005
(202) 861-0203

Jim Renier: Minneapolis's New Vistas School
New Vistas High School
Honeywell, Inc.
P.O. Box 524
Minneapolis, MN 55440-0524
(612) 870-5200

Ted Sizer: The Coalition of Essential Schools
Coalition of Essential Schools
Brown University
Box 1969
Providence, RI 02912

The Center for Collaborative Education
Deborah Meier, President
Heather Lewis, Executive Director
1573 Madison Avenue, Room 201
New York, NY 10029
(212) 348-7821

Sy Fliegel
Center for Educational Innovation
52 Vanderbilt Avenue
New York, NY 10017
(212) 599-7000

James Comer: The Comer Method
Yale Child Study Center
33 Cedar
P.O. Box 3333
New Haven, CT 06510

Reform! Reform!

David Kearns: Winning the Brain Race
Office of the Deputy Secretary
U.S. Department of Education
400 Maryland Avenue SW
Washington, DC 20202-0500

Diane Ravitch: What Every 17-Year-Old Should Know
Office of the Assistant Secretary
U.S. Department of Education
555 New Jersey Avenue NW
Washington, DC 20208

Sam Ginn Joseph Alibrandi: The California Business Roundtable
California Business Roundtable
P.O. Box 7643
San Francisco, CA 94120-7643
(415) 794-5721

Joseph Alibrandi
Excellence Through Choice in Education League (EXCEL)
2250 East Imperial Highway
Suite 220
El Segundo, CA 90245
(310) 416-9601

Transforming a City

Ken Rossano: The Boston Compact
Boston Plan for Excellence in the Public
    Schools Foundation, Inc.
60 State Street, 6th Floor
Boston, MA 02109
(617) 723-7489

Massachusetts Higher Education Assistance
    Corporation Youth Programs
Department
330 Stuart Street, Suite 500
Boston, MA 02116
(617) 426-0681, ext. 237

Kay Whitmore: The Rochester Experiment
Eastman Kodak Co.
343 State Street
Rochester, NY 14650
(716) 724-4000

· Transforming a State

Ross Perot: Texas
The Perot Group
1700 Lakeside Drive
12377 Merit Drive
Dallas, TX 75251

Jack Moreland: Kentucky
Dayton Schools
999 Vine Street
Dayton, KY 41074
(606) 491-6565

Governor Carroll Campbell: South Carolina
P.O. Box 11369
Columbia, SC 29211
(803) 734-9818

Is Money the Answer?

Richard Riordan and Richard Dowling
Writing to Read
c/o Bob Edwards
IBM
80 State Street
Albany, NY 12207

Paul M. Ostergard: Banking on Education
Director of Corporate Contributions
Citibank, N.A.
850 Third Avenue
13th Floor
New York, NY 10043

Joe Flom: The Capital Task Force
Skadden Arps Slate Meagher & Flom
919 Third Avenue
New York, NY 10022
(212) 735-3000

Joseph Grannis: When Money Isn't the Answer
c/o Teacher's College
Columbia University
525 120th Street
New York, NY 10027

MENTOR: A Precedent

The New York City MENTOR Program
Debra Lesser, Executive Director
The Justice Resource Center
Martin Luther King Jr. High School
122 Amsterdam Avenue, Room 504A
New York, NY 10023

The National MENTOR Program
Jo Rosner, Director
c/o Washington State Bar Association
500 Westin Bldg.
2001 6th Avenue
Alexandria, VA 22314
(703) 836-4880

How You Can Make a Difference

The Great Education Debate
U.S. Department of Education, *AMERICA 2000: An Education Strategy.*
Washington, DC: 1991. For information, call 1-800-USA-LEARN.

Secretary Lamar Alexander
Office of the Secretary
U.S. Department of Education
400 Maryland Avenue SW
Suite 4181
Washington, DC 20202
(202) 401-3000

*Voices from the Field: 30 Expert Opinions on "America 2000," the Bush
Administration Strategy to "Reinvent" America's Schools.* Washington, DC: The
William T. Grant Foundation Commission on Work, Family and
Citizenship and Institute for Educational Leadership, 1991.

Lessons Learned
Nonprofits' Risk Management and Insurance Institute and the
Continental Corporation Foundation. *Answers to Volunteers' Liability and
Insurance Questions.* 1991. For a free copy, send a stamped, self-addressed
business envelope to:

Nonprofits' Risk Management and Insurance Institute
1731 Connecticut Avenue NW, Suite 200
Washington, DC 20009
(202) 462-8190

Appendix D:
The National Education Goals and Objectives

The National Education Goals were adopted unanimously by the president and the nation's governors at the Education Summit held at Charlottesville, Virginia, in 1989. This statement of goals and objectives appears in a Department of Education pamphlet entitled *AMERICA 2000: An Education Strategy* (1991, 35–37).

Readiness for School

Goal 1: By the year 2000, all children in America will start school ready to learn.

Objectives:

- All disadvantaged and disabled children will have access to high-quality and developmentally appropriate preschool programs that help prepare children for school.

- Every parent in America will be a child's first teacher and devote time each day to helping his or her preschool child learn; parents will have access to the training and support they need.

- Children will receive the nutrition and health care needed to arrive at school with healthy minds and bodies, and the number of low birthweight babies will be significantly reduced through enhanced prenatal health systems.

High School Completion

Goal 2: By the year 2000, the high school graduation rate will increase to at least 90 percent.

Objectives:

- The nation must dramatically reduce its dropout rate, and 75 percent of those students who do drop out will successfully complete a high school degree or its equivalent.

- The gap in high school graduation rates between American students from minority backgrounds and their nonminority counterparts will be eliminated.

Student Achievement and Citizenship

Goal 3: By the year 2000, American students will leave grades four, eight, and twelve having demonstrated competency in challenging subject matter including English, mathematics, science, history, and geography; and every school in America will ensure that all students learn to use their minds well, so they may be prepared for responsible citizenship, further learning, and productive employment in our modern economy.

Objectives:

- The academic performance of elementary and secondary students will increase significantly in every quartile, and the distribution of minority students in each level will more closely reflect the student population as a whole.

- The percentage of students who demonstrate the ability to reason, solve problems, apply knowledge, and write and communicate effectively will increase substantially.

- All students will be involved in activities that promote and demonstrate good citizenship, community service, and personal responsibility.

- The percentage of students who are competent in more than one language will substantially increase.

- All students will be knowledgeable about the diverse cultural heritage of this nation and the world community.

Science and Mathematics

Goal 4: By the year 2000, U.S. students will be first in the world in science and mathematics achievement.

Objectives:

- Math and science education will be strengthened throughout the system, especially in the early grades.

- The number of teachers with a substantive background in mathematics and science will increase by 50 percent.

- The number of United States undergraduate and graduate students, especially women and minorities, who complete degrees in mathematics, science, and engineering will increase significantly.

Adult Literacy and Lifelong Learning

Goal 5: By the year 2000, every adult American will be literate and will possess the knowledge and skills necessary to compete in a global economy and exercise the rights and responsibilities of citizenship.

Objectives:

- Every major American business will be involved in strengthening the connection between education and work.

- All workers will have the opportunity to acquire the knowledge and skills, from basic to highly intellectual, needed to adapt to emerging new technologies, work methods, and markets through public and private educational, vocational, technical, workplace, or other programs.

- The number of quality programs, including those at libraries, that are designed to serve more effectively the needs of the growing number of part-time and mid-career students will increase substantially.

- The proportion of college graduates who demonstrate an advanced ability to think critically, communicate effectively, and solve problems will increase substantially.

Safe, Disciplined, and Drug-Free Schools

Goal 6: By the year 2000, every school in America will be free of drugs and violence and will offer a disciplined environment conducive to learning.

Objectives:

- Every school will implement a firm and fair policy on use, possession, and distribution of drugs and alcohol.

- Parents, businesses, and community organizations will work together to ensure that the schools are a safe haven for all children.

- Every school district will develop a comprehensive K–12 drug and alcohol prevention education program. Drug and alcohol curriculum should be taught as an integral part of health education. In addition, community-based teams should be organized to provide students and teachers with needed support.

Acknowledgments

Over a year ago, when I told my daughter Heather that I was writing a book on citizen involvement to improve the public schools but was having trouble whipping the materials I had accumulated into readable shape, she introduced me to Marian Salzman. Since then, Marian has become my agent, has introduced me to my publisher, and has played a major role in making this book a reality. I write in the early mornings before I begin my normal workday, on weekends, and on vacations. Without the help of Marian and her talented colleague Christy Lane, I could not have managed my extensive files, conducted all of the interviews that have become an integral part of this book, or polished the many drafts into a readable whole. While I will express the usual caveat that this book is my own and that I alone am responsible for everything that I have written, I have also profited from the many conferences in which we have brainstormed the book. Heather also offered many useful comments as the work progressed, as did my daughter Paige and my wife Lois. My son Logan provided valuable insights. Dr. Susan Otterbourg was very helpful in the development of the resource section of the book, and Editorial Director Jim Gish of Peterson's Guides, my publisher, provided the right combination of carrot and stick as I winnowed the material into final form. Finally, I would like to thank all of those who have worked with me in the partnership movement and particularly the partners and associates in my law firm, most of whom have their own pro bono activities but who have joined me in MENTOR and have encouraged me in this work over the years.

Index

The appendixes to this book contain many references to the programs and people listed below. Be sure to check relevant chapters, subjects, and names throughout them.